# SHAKTI
# WOMAN

▼▼▼▼▼▼▼▼▼▼▼▼

*Also by Vicki Noble*

Circle One: A Woman's Beginning Guide to Self-Health
and Sexuality (with Elizabeth Campbell)

Motherpeace Tarot Cards (with Karen Vogel)

Motherpeace: A Way to the Goddess Through Myth,
Art and Tarot

The Motherpeace Tarot Playbook (with Jonathan
Tenney)

# SHAKTI WOMAN

*Feeling Our Fire, Healing Our World*

▲

*The New Female Shamanism*

VICKI NOBLE

HarperSanFrancisco
*A Division of* HarperCollins*Publishers*

Text design by Irene Imfeld

FIRST EDITION

**Library of Congress Cataloging-in-Publication Data**

Noble, Vicki.
    Shakti woman : feeling our fire, healing our world : the new female shamanism / Vicki Noble. — 1st ed.
        p.      cm.
    Includes bibliographical references and index.
    ISBN 0-06-250667-6 (alk. paper)
    1. Women—Religious life. 2. Shamanism. 3. Feminism—Religious aspects. 4. Spiritual healing. 5. Goddess religion. 6. Women—
—Psychology.      I. Title.
BL625.7.N63   1991
291.1'78344—dc20
                                                                89–45959
                                                                     CIP

91  92  93  94  95  RRD(H)  10  9  8  7  6  5  4  3  2  1

# Dedication

This book, like all my work, is dedicated to the Dark Goddess, who has been rejected and demonized by patriarchal culture and lies dormant in all women. Her awakening is the source of energy and healing power, for us as individuals and for the planet. This work is intentionally devoted to that cause. May She arise in us and bring peace on earth again.

# CONTENTS

# Acknowledgments

Thanks to everyone who has helped me with the *Shakti Woman* work, especially my students, who have tested these theories and put these practices into action in my classes, and the apprentices and teachers whom I've trained to take the work seriously in their lives. Thanks to Khara Whitney-Marsh, my faithful assistant, who administered my school, screens all my phone calls, and thoroughly supports me when I shut the door to my writing room. Thanks to Reba Rose and JoAnn Peirce, who have listened so carefully, asked all the right questions, grown with me over the years, and who have begun to take the work out into the world.

Thanks to my husband, Jonathan Tenney, who has forced me to become more powerful than I believed I could be. Even the original dream I had about this book came out of one of our core arguments demanding transmutation. Our relationship—a dharmic one, with a sacred commitment to deep, personal transformation—has tempered and shaped me over the years. Like crystals that grow through each other, we have become aligned with each other's growth. More than once, the ax blade of the Black Dakini has dropped, and we have lost our heads, but our deep bond remains unsevered.

I am grateful for the technical assistance I received on this book. Thanks to Jennifer Roberts, who originally made sketches for my magazine, *Snake Power: A Journal of Contemporary Female Shamanism,* and who has allowed me to use them here as well. Thanks to photographic friends Irene Young, Craig Comstock, Catherine Allport, Robert Ansell, and Helen Nestor for generously sharing their work. And deep gratitude to Laurelin Remington-Wolf, who remained undaunted by my whimsical assignment of some twenty-odd drawings in a short time. Her artwork has brought figures of the Goddess to life in a way that could happen only through personal faith and primal contact with female source energy. Thanks to Margaret Pavel, Anne Herbert, and Karen Vogel for giving my manuscript a careful and thoughtful reading, providing creative feedback at the right moment in time and to Kate Kaufman for coming up with the ingenious subtitle.

A little more than a year ago I was still stubbornly resisting the urgings of all my friends to use a computer for my writing. I maintained that the computer was the body of the colonizing beast that had taken over the planet! When I decided to publish my magazine, it was as if I died and was reborn. Without a single doubt (and through a great deal of personal debt), I bought a MAC II and a laser printer, then I used them to write this book. I would be remiss if I did not also thank my beautiful machine for such good work.

Thanks, too, to Clayton Carlson at Harper San Francisco, who said, *"Yes, what a good idea, let's do it,"* when I first told him about *Shakti Woman.* And I appreciated Jan Johnson's intelligent eye and thoughtful approach to my work, until her departure from Harper. Now I thank my new editor and ally, Barbara Moulton, for her seriousness and appreciation of my work and for her helpful suggestions along the way. I'm very happy with the cover design, and give many, many thanks to artist Mayumi Oda for allowing me to share her version of the Black Dakini with my readers.

Finally, I thank the universe for my life and for the experiences I have had that allowed me to write this. I believe that any experience that comes through me can also come through others, and from this standpoint I teach and write about sacred things that cannot be fully expressed. May the Goddess be active in your life, as She is in mine, and may we renew our ability to embody Her energies at this time of planetary crisis. Blessed be.

VICKI NOBLE
WINTER SOLSTICE, 1990

# SHAKTI WOMAN

▼▼▼▼▼▼▼▼▼▼▼▼

# Introduction

FOR THE FIRST THREE YEARS OF
my marriage, I fought repeatedly with my psychologist husband over his frequently voiced (and very loving) concept of
the Feminine. The Feminine to Jonathan was related to the
planet Neptune and the elusive watery element and seemed
from my perspective to be weak, insubstantial, and conve-
niently not really there. The Jungian view of the "anima" as
vacuous and seductive, alluring yet forever unattainable, was
offensive to my feminist consciousness and, in the final analysis, threatening to my personal sense of self. "If that is the
Feminine," I would scream at Jonathan, "then what am I?!"

I felt personally negated and betrayed by the
apparent ambiguity of my partner's choosing me as his wife
while he seemed to view some other type of female expression
as the Feminine. In reading more about the life of the cultural
hero-mentor Carl Jung, I learned that Jung himself had a
wife whom he loved and lived with and a mistress who
embodied the "spiritual anima" he described so elaborately in
his work. I became more furious and intolerant with my husband, more volatile and irrational in our supposedly intellectual discussions of this matter.

Finally one night I dreamed the title and
structure of *Shakti Woman*. It was to be a book for women,
and in it I would communicate a certain truth about the Feminine that was in direct opposition to the Jungian concept of

1

the anima. The Feminine, in my version, was fiery and substantial, taking up real space with her real expression of self, and demanding to be encountered rather than imagined.

This healing dream freed me from the futile arguments that had so baffled my gentle husband and left me shaking with unresolved anger, hurt, and frustration. It redirected me in a clear and unmistakable way onto my own path of choosing to honor my own authority and to encourage other women to do the same. My need for Jonathan's approval lessened in the face of the compelling suggestion from my own unconscious that I communicate the truth of my experience to the world rather than argue with him about it in our tiny arena of the couple.

It is more or less this shift in focus that I am suggesting to the women who study with me and the women who read this book. We have been deeply conditioned to relate in a primary way to men and to make a primary alliance with one man who will father our children and provide for our physical needs. This myth, of course, goes unfulfilled for most of us these days, with the structure of the nuclear family basically falling apart and marriage itself being seriously called into question.

Still, on the deeper, structural level, women do feel secondary and tend to grant men authority to speak about things that matter in our lives. We might be reactive and angry with them, but still somehow we allow them to define us. Most psychologists and psychiatrists are men, most ministers and almost all priests are men, doctors are predominantly male, as are lawyers and judges, writers and intellectuals. Almost all popular theory comes from the minds of men and into the mass psyche via the television, movies, and news media, which are controlled by men. Even after twenty years of active feminism in our country, U.S. women have almost no idea how actually to take back the authority that has been systematically stolen from us and projected onto men who, in every situation, are assumed to be the experts.

The most obvious example of how far we have strayed from our organic roots as a female community is the birthing practices of our present-day culture. Women have actually come to believe that we don't know how to have babies. We fear it, dread it, look to the "experts" to help us do it right. We go to sterile, unloving environments away from home and family in order to lie down with our feet propped up and have a technician remove the babies from our bodies. We have become convinced that if we do this any other way, we will endanger the children we are bringing into the world—that we will do the ultimate disservice and be ultimately irresponsible to our offspring. So we mutely accept the advice of the Almighty Doctor and his white-coated staff, and, consequently, we endure an extremely high "complication rate" in our birthing. We come to the hospital to be "safe"; we take drugs that will "help" us to do it better; we follow the rules and have our sacred parts shaved and cut, so that we won't "tear" and won't contaminate our child.

Where is the animal in us? What has become of our instinctual nature? How do we think babies got born all these millennia before we invented hospitals and men took over the practice of birthing? It is as if we have amnesia; we simply don't remember.

All over the world there are images of dismembered Goddesses—in India, in Sumer, in Mexico. These dismembered females represent the rupture away from a Goddess-centered world to the "dominator" world we live in today.[1] As a shamanic metaphor, these images show the death or disintegration that precedes any rebirth into new form. Historically the images represent the basic shattering of the peaceful world that preceded the war-torn world we have created in the last five thousand years. The act of dismemberment is always attributed to a male god who replaced the Goddess in each culture. In India it was Indra who killed the Goddess and scattered her parts all over the countryside; these became shrines where she is still—to this day—worshiped. In Babylon the hero Gilgamesh killed the Dark Goddess Tiamat and scattered her parts to create a new world. In Mexico the war god Huitzilipotli killed his sister, the Moon Goddess Coyolxauhqui, and threw her body from the top of the mountain in broken pieces to demonstrate his victory over her (fig. 1).

The Feminine is fragmented, shattered, and scattered about the earth. Women have been isolated from one another, and within ourselves we have felt no center of authority. We experience our collective annihilation repeatedly, psychically and physically, as a woman is raped every thirteen seconds in North America, as our children are abused and molested and shamed every day. The incredible loss of nine million

▲ *Fig. 1   Coyolxauhqui, the Aztec Moon Goddess, dis-*
*membered. A stone sculpted with her image was*
*unearthed in 1977 in Mexico City next to the zócalo, or*
*central square, where the government buildings and*
*cathedral are located. Her unexpected presence led to the*
*discovery of the ruins of Tenochtitlán, ancient capital of*
*the Aztecs. The unearthing of this stone signals a return*
*of the Goddess and the rebirth that follows dismember-*
*ment. The current chaotic disintegration of life as we*
*have known it may represent a death-and-rebirth pro-*
*cess integral to shamanic initiation. Women, as cells in*
*the female body of the earth, might imagine our own*
*psychic dismemberment process as leading to eventual*
*rebirth and renewal, represented by Coyolxauhqui's*
*snakes. Drawing by Ellen Fishburn.*

"witches" (women healers) during the Burning Times in
Europe—those four centuries erased from our history books
that preceded the Age of "Enlightenment"—has contributed
to our collective and individual amnesia. If we were to
remember, would they once again kill us in large numbers?
(Mary Daly would say that they already do kill or maim us in
large numbers, through the modern practices of gynecology.[2])

The work of seizing back what has been taken from
within us by centuries of female repression and early, often
brutal childhood conditioning is a long, laborious process,
requiring faith and vigilance and the willingness to learn by
trial and error. It is our female-animal instincts that have been

denied and suppressed then replaced by false, externally imposed rules and ideas about ourselves and the world. We have lost the instinctive knowing that belonged to us by biological birthright in the millennia that preceded the development of patriarchal culture and male dominance. It is not a question of returning to the past but one of reawakening the instinctual senses and the empowerment needed to act on what our bodies know to be true.

For years feminists fought with men and the male establishment, the same way I fought with my husband over his sense of the Feminine. No matter what I said, he never knew what I was talking about. No matter how upset I got, he could not consider the possibility that my viewpoint might be valid and conceivably "more true" than his own. I have come to believe that this is generally the way it is with men and society at large. It is, I believe, pointless and hurtful for women to involve ourselves in these endlessly unsatisfying and disruptive "dialogues with the boys." Neither is it necessary, in my mind, to separate from men, eliminate them, or create a world community made up only of women.

What does seem necessary is for each of us women to pull her focus back inside herself and to begin actively and intelligently to create the world we want. This may sound abstract, simple, and impossible at the same moment, since it seems so easy to focus on oneself and so impossible to change the world. But neither is true. For a woman actually to repossess herself and to center there is a monumental task, taking years of difficult, painstaking work. This is the work I am calling female shamanism, a gradual mastery of oneself, and a healing or recovery from the chronic dis-ease of our time. Once a woman has done the work of re-membering herself, she is much more able to change the world effectively.

For any one of us to experience this crisis of ingrained dependency, and the urge to overcome it in favor of our own self-empowerment, is to awaken to healing. This shamanic healing crisis is frequently accompanied by illness, depression, or injury that causes us to face death as a real possibility and therefore to encounter life as a potential choice. When many thousands of women are having this critical awakening at the same time, we can assume this is a shamanic awakening of global proportions.

All over the United States women are in recovery. We are seeing private therapists and joining groups to talk about our pain and helplessness about incest, rape, pregnancy, loving too much, overeating, being abused by our husbands, the addictions to the various substances our culture offers for the dulling of pain and awareness, and the escape into denial that has characterized our lives. It is time we name this recovery movement and see it in the broadest sense possible, so that we include all the women who are choosing to get well. Women are choosing to heal ourselves from the world illness of Patriarchy. We have no choice—we are having a collective near-death experience, and the blinding light of it is showing us how to transform our lives.

The Western medical model has exerted such strong pressure on all of us that to imagine healing the body without drugs, surgery, or the intervention of the doctor seems impossible. But the body has its own mechanisms for healing; it knows what it needs. Animals in the woods who get sick know instinctually which plants they need to be close to or ingest. Humans are also instinctual animals, but we in the West have come a long way from our roots. The body can't heal itself if the human being is continually pouring poisons into it. If our way is to avoid, escape, and deny what our bodies are telling us and to ingest drugs, chemicals, liquors, refined sugar, and other processed foods, then the instinctual responses are dulled and start to become obsolete.

The same is true for the earth. Our continuous poisoning of her body with pollution, underground nuclear testing, burying of nuclear wastes, mining of uranium, drilling for oil, and cutting down virgin forests gives her no opportunity to heal peacefully and in her own organic way. The healing process becomes catastrophic—like the body going through a purification process in which there is fever, vomiting, convulsions, diarrhea, and boils. There is a movement from within her body that we (as cells) can't help but feel. This movement from within is the same as the healing power that releases in any of our bodies when there is illness or too much poison. There is a need to throw off the poisons, and there is energy released from within that carries with it the power to heal—to regenerate tissue, to grow new cells, to re-create. First destruction, then creation—this is the way of the Goddess, the Shakti. The fire burns through the old structures, eradicating them, transmuting their energies to a higher vibrational level. Then the creative energy released from the destruction allows for the cure of whatever ails the body — cancer, arteriosclerosis, the common cold.

And so here we are, at a point in the earth's cycle of growth where we have become both a nuisance to her and a catalyst for catastrophic change. In the massive healing crisis of the present time, we humans have made ourselves expendable, and like any other species, we may become extinct. I doubt very much that the earth will be destroyed; we, however, may or may not survive this crisis. In the process of healing and throwing off the illness that has brought her down, the earth's movements may be too much for us tiny cells in her body who have stopped relating to her as Source.

Shakti women are human females who are feeling the call of the Dark Goddess — the deep, serious will-to-live arousing from within the body of the planet. This demanding energy of the Death Goddess — she who would destroy the old forms in order to make way for the new — is pushing through us for healing and the realignment with Nature that needs to happen at this time. Why women? It may have to do with the biological imperative of the instinctual, hormonal cycles that irrevocably link us to the earth, the moon, and the constant changing tug of the magnetic tides. The Goddess of Fate spins our destinies; she works on us through the influence of the lunar cycle, to which we respond in our bodies without knowing why. Our monthly menstrual cycles represent the way in which we are held here, part and parcel of the earth's process. Men seem more able to escape this fate, imagining themselves apart from the obligations of mortality and separate from the limitations of the body. They invent religions that glorify transcendence and practice detachment from earthly desires and human needs.

What is of special interest to women in shamanic process is our biological inclination to respond to organic cycles. Because of what has been felt as our "bondage" to the hormonal cycle we experience every month, combined with our conditioning to surrender to our "lot in life," a woman comes more easily to the act of being a vessel for the healing powers. Internally we die every month. We may not have consciously related to our menstruation as a shamanic death and rebirth each month, but our bodies know it as such. Each time the

uterus sheds its lining, as a snake sheds its skin, we are literally released from the past—from what might have been—
and set free into the future. We are physically cleansed and
emotionally replenished. The hormones shift their emphasis
from birth to death and new life again.

High progesterone means aggressive dreams and a
bitchy mood—the premenstrual syndrome of being for oneself, rather than for others. Then the estrogen comes in, and
our energy returns like a new moon cycle beginning. We
begin again to reach out, starting new projects, initiating new
contacts. It is a changing of form and function. A female shaman becomes more and more like a snake, shedding her old
forms as soon as they become established. We can become
very practiced at letting go of the old, even before the new
has made itself consciously known, trusting the cyclic return
that always comes.

Since women are assumed to be intuitive, we have a
head start in this particular way of moving. The problem we
face as a group is that we have also been trained not to act.
We can know things, that is, be intuitive; but we are not really
encouraged to act from this knowledge. For example, we
don't usually learn to express ourselves clearly if to do so
would conflict with our environment. We are taught not to
act aggressively on our own behalf, even when we are being
victimized. So the work for contemporary shaman women is
to learn to move, to act, to do what our inner voices tell us we
need to do, even if it seems socially inappropriate.

Learning to act from our bellies—our instinctual
movement centers—lets us respond on behalf of ourselves
and our children. This response-ability strengthens us, making us women of power, medicine women, shamans. We
become integrated, knowing and acting from the same place,
no longer knowing one thing and doing another. In general,
female shamanic work is geared to helping women make a
stand for ourselves and on behalf of our planet, and to feel
grounded, connected, solid. We need to contact our substance, our depth, and our ability to act powerfully in the
world, so that we can face whatever comes in front of us. It
isn't just a matter of being politically active, taking up causes,
going to the streets, or joining movements. We also need to
be able to be truly present and respond appropriately to all
situations in which we find ourselves.

*Shakti Woman* is a book about female authority and the healing of the planet. It is a user's guide to shamanic healing and empowerment through the process of getting in touch with the deep Feminine and the Dark Goddess. I write it in response to what I perceive as a survival thrust on the part of our planet—a radical shift from within the body of the earth herself that is volcanic, immediate, and uncompromising. I invite all Shakti women to join me in this global response to the crisis facing sentient life at this time. May we awaken and join forces for good.

# The Female Blood Roots of Shamanism

FEMALE SHAMANISM IS BASED IN the blood cycle. Western women have forgotten the spiritual significance of the menstrual cycle and need to reconnect in order to empower ourselves. The blood mysteries of birthing and menstruation are the core of female shamanism.

The Mapuche women shamans who live in Chile at the very southern tip of the Southern Hemisphere still practice their ancient lunar rites of healing. The Mapuche woman shaman climbs up on a seven-tiered "tree" and beats her *kultrun,* or drum, which she has carved herself from a tree and filled with special crystals and stones, including the amazing *piedra de la cruz.* She has covered the drum with leather she tanned herself and has painted the cover with special red menstrual symbols. The symbols form an equal-armed cross (like the one naturally formed in the stone), and at the end of each directional pointer she has painted a crescent moon, representing the lunar menstrual cycle that is the basis of her cosmology (fig. 2). The Mapuche people say that they have been living in that spot and practicing this form of healing for twenty-five thousand years.[1]

There are many characteristics of shamanic healing that apply equally to men and women, without regard to their biological differences. All over the world there are shamans of both sexes, drumming, chanting, and healing, although in many places the tribal shamans are predominantly one sex or the other. For instance, the Huichol tribe in Mexico specializes in shamanic healing and shamanic art. For

**11**

▲ *Fig. 2  A Mapuche shaman woman
(machi) with her drum (kultrun) standing on
her seven-tiered sacred tree, where she goes
into trance and does her shamanizing. The
symbols on her drum represent Mapuche cosmology and focus especially on the lunar menstrual cycle of the female, as well as the phase
relationship between the sun and moon. Drawing by Mariela Cortés of Chile.*

the most part the men are the healers and ceremonialists (the
"shamans" and priests) and the women are the artists. (But
even that has diversity, and in recent years they have developed the art form of yarn painting, which is done mainly by
men.) Huichol men and women have always worked together
on their parallel paths of art and healing, husbands and wives
often serving their apprenticeships during the same period of
years, making different offerings to the various deities who
represent the paths of art and healing. Together, each one is
striving to reach what is called completion, and they help each
other work toward this goal.[2]

In Chile, by contrast, the Mapuche shamans are women, as they are in Korea, and as they once were in China and Japan and India. Yet shamanism in general has been defined as if it were a male form, often connected to and concerned with power, rather than focusing on healing. Our Western approach to shamanism has been to focus on the exotic elements, elements of drama, sorcery, and the like rather than learning about the deep, transformational aspects of the healing art. This makes sense, since we don't understand transformation the way we understand power. Western observers rarely notice that shamanism has anything to do with the Feminine, and yet all shamans — no matter what part of the world they are from — always work in the realm of the Feminine. They either pray to the Mother of the Animals, the Mother of All Things, the Dark Mother, Grandmother Growth, the Death Goddess, or some other manifestation of the Divine Feminine in her dark, magical, healing power. In order to perform shamanic vocational tasks, the shaman must in the long run commune with the Goddess and enter into her realm.

Geoffrey Ashe, a British scholar who researched shamanism, has written that originally shamans were women, the most ancient form of the word itself meaning "female shaman." He says the Paleolithic community broke into different tribes with different dialects, and at that time the word *shaman* took on a male connotation in the Tungus dialect, from which the current usage is derived.[3] Ashe links ancient female shamanism to the Great Bear constellation and to the Goddess Artemis and places it in the Paleolithic period. The images that come to us from the Paleolithic caves — pregnant women dancing with animals, some headless, some with bird heads or masks, bear fetishes that contain menstrual calendar notches — correspond to the signs of ritual and ceremony that accompany all the cave sites. Ashe is very clear about one thing that especially interests me: He says that ancient shamanism was not an individual phenomenon but something that was practiced by the female group. And the power of the female group is biologically rooted in menstruation and the blood mysteries of birth.

Women once bled together with the moon, as many Western women do in dormitories even today. But imagine the power of an entire community of women bleeding together each new or full moon. In order actually to begin to feel what this might mean, other than simply a synchronous group experience, we have to contemplate the nature of menstrual blood. In our present-day Western culture, menstrual blood is taboo. We are expected not to pay any particular attention to it, other than hiding it, shielding ourselves from its flow, and shielding others from any experience of it. When we bleed, we try to go about our business as if nothing out of the ordinary is happening. Since men have made it clear that they find us difficult at "that time of the month," we also try to perform our usual tasks without any undue expression of anger or emotion that might arise from our hormonal state. This is a tremendous pressure and undoubtedly contributes significantly to what our society calls PMS (premenstrual syndrome). In addition to these stresses, our modern refined and chemically laced food is nonnutritious and harmful to our natural biological cycle, making us more prone to the aches and pains of PMS.[4]

In truth, menstruation is a time that is absolutely *taboo* in the most ancient sense of the word, which means "sacred." It is explicitly nonordinary and requires that we be set apart from the ordinary tasks at hand. It is, for humans, the major magical event of the lunar month, corresponding to the waxing and waning cycle of the moon and the ebb and flow of the oceanic tides. It is the precise way in which the human animal is linked to the above and the below — the upper world and the underworld of shamanic reality. Monica Sjöö and Barbara Mor present the idea that human menstruation provided the "mechanism of female evolution," because it is the central way that human sexuality differs from our primate sisters, who are locked into an estrus cycle. Primates bleed when they are fertile and ready to be approached sexually by their ape partners; human females bleed when they are not fertile, and they are fertile at another time during the cycle.[5] This frees sexuality from procreation for humans, a freedom that has been formalized in the Tantric systems. And the composition of the blood itself makes it the most extraordinary and magical substance that exists on the planet, according to Western magical science. Professor Lawrence Durdin-Robertson, an Irish scholar of Goddess lore, reminds us that the first blood at the altar was menstrual blood, the free flow of the priestess giving back to the Earth Mother.[6] Even in modern times,

Tibetan lamas use the power of menstrual blood in their rituals to the Goddess Tara, and they consider that the first blood of a young girl is the most potent healing medicine for the whole community.[7]

Menstrual blood, according to Durdin-Robertson, is vibrationally potent and required by the earth as a "sacrifice" that takes no life. The contemporary biodynamic agricultural movement, inspired by Rudolf Steiner, makes use of various formulas and remedies that use the vibrations of the "etheric" and the "astral" planes to grow abundant, healthy food even under adverse conditions. Food grown under these magical circumstances is measurably happier and more nutritious than other food, especially our modern foods grown with chemical fertilizers and pesticides.[8] Menstrual blood is fertilizer par excellence, as contemporary feminist women have learned by using it on our house plants with great success. Today's Huichol shamans similarly pour bull's blood over the maturing corn plants in a special ceremony meant to bless the crop and bring fertility and abundance to the community. They used to use deer's blood, before the deer became too few in number. Before that, when women were in control of early agriculture (which the Mayan *Popul Vuh* says they invented[9]), they no doubt contributed their own menstrual blood to the growing plants, as both fertilizer and vibrational enhancer. Remember that early women invented agriculture and all the rituals that went along with it. This makes the folklore from Britain and Europe about women running naked through the corn furrows more sensible, as it does the tales of men and women making love in the freshly sown fields. The healthy vibrations from the blood, and the yogic sexual practices that accompanied the bleeding time, were useful in the growing of food for the community. No wonder the Venus of Laussel holds in her hand a horn of plenty carved with thirteen notches in honor of the menstrual cycle.

The Venus of Laussel, our earliest sculpture in relief, was carved in stone over the entrance to a cave of the same name in France and painted with red ocher (fig. 3). She holds in her right hand a crescent horn with thirteen notches carved on it; her left hand points to her pregnant belly. It is as if she is giving a lesson in sex education, showing all who enter the ritual cavern exactly what is to be celebrated there. Researchers into ancient cultures share a strange bias — even feminists:

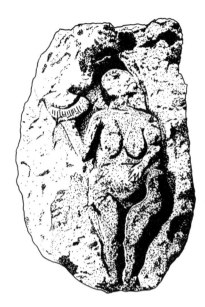

▲ *Fig. 3   Venus of Laussel, possibly the earliest relief sculpture on the planet, hung over the entrance to a sacred cave sanctuary in the south of France, which was used during the Paleolithic for ritual. Besides this pregnant Goddess-woman showing us her swollen magical belly and her thirteen lunar menstrual cycles, inside the cave are images of a male-female Tantric couple, birthing images, and a male consort figure. The crescent horn refers to the wild animals that belonged to the Goddess, and the transformation that their shedding represented, in addition to its new-moon shape. She was originally painted all over with red ocher, the pigment used to symbolize menstrual blood among primitive peoples. Drawing by Laurelin Remington-Wolf.*

They almost unanimously believe that ancient people did not understand the male role in reproduction. They cite "primitive" people who say that women are fertilized by a wind spirit or other magical force and assume that the people lack scientific understanding. Yet in this cave alone there are images of the Great (Pregnant) Mother, her consort — a divine male figure in relation to her — and a picture of male-female yogic copulation that is almost identical to an Indian temple sculpture from about twenty-five thousand years later (see figs. 4A, 4B, and 5)!

Durdin-Robertson says that in order for ritual and magic to be correctly and effectively practiced, blood is required, and that menstrual blood is the only blood that is obtained in an ethical way. All blood affects the ethers and can be used magically, but menstrual blood is stronger than all the rest and at the same time comes free of charge.[10] The ancient women were involved in a complex recycling process that included ritual ceremonies around the release of their monthly menses. Red ocher was used to paint seemingly everything of sacred importance — the statues, the cave paintings, the relief sculptures, the bones buried in the ancient graves. And tribal people today still say that red ocher is a stand-in for menstrual blood — the magical water of life.

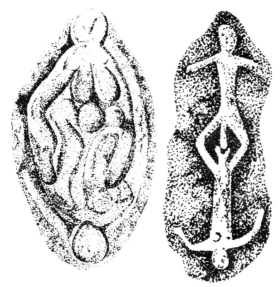

▲ *Fig. 4A & 4B
A love-making
couple from
inside the cavern
of Laussel (as
much as twenty-
five thousand
years old), and a
remarkably simi-
lar image from
old Australian
rock art (date
unknown).
Sketches by
Laurelin
Remington-Wolf.*

The very earliest artifacts are menstrual calendar bones, notched with correct lunar cycles, tabulating pregnancy and menstruation, probably used by early midwife-shamans (figs. 6A, 6B, and 6C). Before scientific investigation, researchers assumed these bones were ornamental or at best "staffs of commandment" used by the males in charge. But after the microscopic research of Alexander Marshack, we now know that the marks on the bones are exact lunar tallies, and they fall within what he calls a complex storied tradition involving at the center a female creatrix figure and all of her characteristic symbols (see figs. 7A and 7B). Marshack says that this tradition falls within a larger system of complex mathematics and science. This information makes obsolete the traditional view of "prehistory," since, as Marshack points out, the development of such a complicated system of understanding would have needed to happen over many centuries, even millennia.[11] Marija Gimbutas, in *The Language of the Goddess*, explains the structure of the early cultures and their language, as inscribed on the figurines of the cultures that she describes so carefully. Gimbutas, whose interdisciplinary approach includes, in addition to scientific archaeology, a profound grasp of mythology, folklore, and linguistics, describes a whole cosmology of the Goddess as universal matrix, with her various forms and attributes of snake, bird, bear, flower, and so on. It becomes possible to imagine

17

▲ *Fig. 5    This relief sculpture shows the same theme as that from the much older rock art of Laussel and Australia, only this image was carved on a temple in India in the Late Middle Ages and falls within the stated context of Tantra (the sexual practices of ancient and contemporary Indian Goddess worship). The similarity of the images, although widely spaced in chronological time, suggests that the earlier images were made by very ancient people practicing sexual yoga in their cave rituals, in addition to the obvious celebration of fertility. Photo reprinted by permission from Thames and Hudson, from Phillip Rawson's* **Tantra: The Indian Cult of Ecstasy.**

how early people approached life when we begin to look more carefully at their actual productivity and creative expression.[12]

Because "scientific" thinking is so linear, it has become difficult for us to understand the body-based science of our early female ancestors. What were these ancient midwife-shamans doing with those menstrual bones? What do the bones have to do with the constellation of the Great Bear? How does any of this relate to us today? To understand this science one must develop a basic understanding of astrology, using the body and the feelings as a guide. Women attempting to become healers must understand their lives in relation to the movements of the planets and stars. Mayan shamans living in the highlands of Guatemala have been asked about the meaning and significance of their ancient, sacred, divinatory calendar with its 260-day cycle. Scholars have written massive amounts of theoretical literature about this important part of the calendar, refusing to hear the simple explanation of the native people. The Indian people themselves say that the 260 days refer to the duration of a human pregnancy. Eminent scholars scoff at this simplistic, "superstitious" notion, asking, "What could divination possibly have to do with pregnancy?"[13] It takes a while for Western women to grasp the meaning and importance of astrology, but at some point, for most of us, it "takes." We suddenly realize, "Aha!

**18**

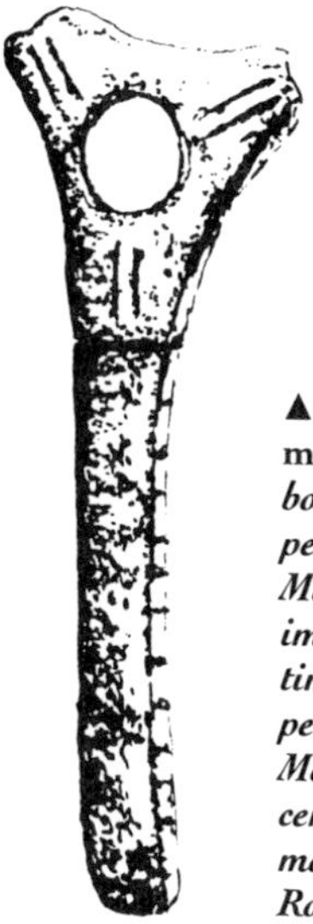

▲ *Fig. 6A    A ceremonial staff or* bâton de commandement *from the Paleolithic period, one of many calendar
bones discovered in the ancient cave sites of our European ancestors. Thanks to the works of Alexander
Marshack, we know that many of these bones and stone
implements were carved and notched precisely with lunar
timekeeping markers that noted the menstrual cycle and
periods of gestation, both human and animal. And, as
Monica Sjöö suggests, they are almost certainly the
ceremonial implements of ancient women shamans or,
more particularly, midwives. Drawing by Jennifer
Roberts.*

What happens in the sky is related to what happens on the
earth is related to what happens to me in my daily life, and I
can attune to it through my body, and it can make a difference. What a miracle. How come nobody told me this
before?"

To the uninitiated, what happens astrologically may
appear to be an abstract, conceptual science. However, the
best way to learn the meaning of the signs and planets is to
feel them with our bodies. When the moon passes through its
phases of waxing and waning, dying, and being reborn as a
new crescent, this can be felt—physically, emotionally, and
psychically. Similarly, when the moon passes through the
twelve astrological signs of the zodiac each month—from
Aries to Taurus and so on until it reaches Pisces, the last
sign—this too can be felt in the body, the emotions, as well as
the psyche. When you consider that these two cycles may also
coincide with a woman's bleeding cycle, you begin to see the
complex and interesting form of study that can go on for each
woman personally (see also chap. 4 on astrology).

And this is only the lunar cycle. There are ten planets
that we know about in the solar system. More are being discovered all the time. Each of them is having an effect on us in
every moment. These effects have particular characteristics
that astrology has cataloged, and they can be felt daily,
weekly, monthly, and yearly through the body, mind, and

**19**

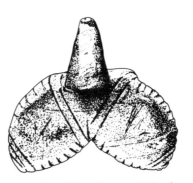

▲ *Fig. 6B & 6C   These calendar bones with emphasized breasts are clearly notched with timekeeping lines
and may have something to do with the cycle of breast-
feeding and the natural birth control practiced by tribal
people such as the Bushpeople in Africa, who space their
children by about four years, which is the duration of
nursing for each child. Drawing by Laurelin
Remington-Wolf.*

emotions. The Tantric Scriptures in India feature drawings
and teachings about the movements of the moon and planets
in relation to the particular places on a woman's body that will
naturally be charged with energy on different days during the
lunar cycle. A student of Tantra yoga learns these movements
in relation to these erogenous zones of the female body. And
a priestess of Tantra is a "power holder" who can initiate a
male student of yoga during her "red," or bleeding, time.[14]
How far back must these practices reach in terms of human,
evolutionary time? To the Venus of Laussel perhaps, or even
earlier. In a certain way, it doesn't matter whether you believe
in this or not. It works. It is ludicrous to attempt to study
ancient and tribal shamans without having at least a working
knowledge of what they were (and are). Without this we constantly underestimate them because we view their interests as
"superstitious" or "unscientific." In fact it is we who have lost
track of the arts by splitting astronomy off from the more
body-based, experiential part of it that we call astrology.

What has tended to happen with "scholarship" is that
the more "scientific" things like *bâtons de commandement* are
assumed to be male and to have been used by men for their
"shamanistic rituals" of either hunting or religion. The Goddess figures and carvings on the cave walls are considered
part of a "fertility cult" that didn't have any connection to the
"religion" of the men, or somehow supported it, in the sense

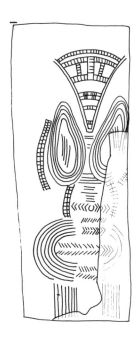

▲ *Fig. 7A   This Goddess found in Cze-
choslovakia is twenty thousand years old
and shows the early geometric markings
that Marija Gimbutas has identified as a
formative style of writing in symbols.
Alexander Marshack hypothesizes that
early people who made this figure and the
calendar bones had a sophisticated tradition of mathematics, science, and storytell-
ing rituals that centered around an
abstract female figure that we call the
Great Mother. Drawing by Laurelin
Remington-Wolf.*

▲ *Fig. 7B   This Yugoslavian figure dates
from much later in Old Europe than fig. 7A
but represents the same enduring tradition
of the Goddess and female shamanism.
Her bird mask and necklace show her to
be the sacred Bird Goddess that Marija
Gimbutas has written about, and the
designs on her dress point to weaving and
textiles in her honor. Her breasts are
emphasized and made sacred, as she is the
life-giving, transformative Goddess with
the all-seeing, visionary eye of the owl.
Drawing by Laurelin Remington-Wolf.*

**21**

that the women who danced and participated in the fertility cult must have been doing hunting magic for the men who were out killing the big game. But as Marshack and Gimbutas have shown, the female icons and religion were central to the human community of this early period—and the evidence entirely supports this thesis. Some scholars have gotten close to this kind of understanding and then have created theories insisting it was not religion at all, but "only" magic. But shamans around the world see with direct, penetrating sight and learn things through direct, tactile experience.

So what kind of a world might it have been when we were in touch through our bodies with the universal currents? What might a kinship with the animals, the moon, and the stars have felt like, as we bled and birthed with other women in the community in a sacred way? What if, like the Cherokee today, you were able to know and believe that you came from the stars? From the Pleiades, to be exact.[15] What if, like the primitive Dogon in Africa, you knew—in your body and your spirit—that the Dog Star Sirius and the Mother Goddess were one and the same? And that civilization on this planet was "seeded" from there (from her) and that you are a remnant of that original tribe on this planet?[16] You would have a sense of roots and a feeling of belonging. And what if you felt, when you began to bleed, that you were participating in a universal mystery—carrying a sacred trust, as it were—on behalf of the continuation of your species and the continuation of a sacred mystery of creation that involved the entire universe? What if bleeding made you a part of the incarnate Goddess and a part of the governing body of your society?

In a more personal way, imagine that when you bled you were able to use the psychic powers that open and become available to you at this magical time of the month. Ancient women were able to access power and vision during their periods that led to tribal decision making and the laying down of tribal law. What must their sacred sense of themselves have been under these conditions? A man coming into your psychic field would have felt honored to be in your presence because you are a woman. He would have related to you with respect and attunement, allowing himself to come into alignment with your magical tides, communing with you from your sense of internal timing and your biological imperative. If he made love with you, it would not be conquest but would happen in response to what your bodies needed. And in that process he would have been made open and transparent, experiencing a transformation for which he thanked you. How would this change your life experience? Your self-image? Your sense of who you are?

As a child you would have learned about bleeding and birthing from your mother and the elder women in the tribe, for whom you felt respect and admiration. You would not have known a "father" in the sense of a specific biological parent but would have many positive male figures in your life. One of them (your mother's brother, for instance) might take a special interest in helping to raise you in a loving way, but no man would ever think he owned you. Men in general would relate to your mother and the other women in the tribe respectfully and as equals, with the women as a group raising you and the other children together. When you desperately needed to know something, you would have gone naturally to your mother or some other nearby woman to seek the answer. Can you imagine absolutely trusting your mother to know?

Ceremonies that took place each day, week, month, or season revolved around the mothers and other women and their biological cycles of bleeding and ovulation. Pregnancy and the birthing of children took a central place in the religious observances. The whole community might sing and chant when a woman gave birth or when someone needed healing or when it was that time when all the women bled together. In the course of these religious celebrations and ceremonies that were so natural and such a normal part of life, perhaps it would be discovered that you had some particular gifts in relation to it all, and you would be recognized as a young girl and then given the benefit of the teachings and the practices that would develop your gifts into useful skills for the healing and well-being of your community.

Today in North America, the Navaho (who prefer their own name, the *Diné*) celebrate female initiation for four days when a young girl gets her period. They isolate and fuss over the girl, while she fasts and prepares cornbread for the community. The cornbread is mixed and stirred by the girl in a particularly focused ceremony, then baked in underground ovens overnight, and served by the initiate to the entire community. She doesn't eat the bread herself but simply doles it out to the others, while representing the Goddess incarnate to her people. They understand her to partake of the Goddess

23

Changing Woman and to be forever transformed through the experience of having her blood cycle.[17] Perhaps in earlier times (or even now in secret) the young girl's magical blood was included in the tribal recipe for the ceremonial blue cornbread. I draw this odd conclusion from several associations I am making from different traditions around the world. I look at the way the Tibetans appreciate the magical, healing properties of the menstrual elixir and the ways it is revered in the Tantric practices (both now and in the past). Tantrikas worshiped in *chakras* (wheels) of male and female couples, equally balanced, who while performing the sacred sexual customs also shared their magical substances from their bodies: the red menstrual blood and the white semen. So also did the Gnostic worshipers form a mixed circle to perform sexual practices and to share the holy communion of blood and semen.[18] From this early tradition comes the Christian practice of sharing the "blood" and "body" of Christ in the sacrament of Holy Communion. Durdin-Robertson tells us that the word *Charis* (the name of a Goddess) means "grace" and is derived from the word for menstrual blood, which became the root for *eucharist*.[19]

Going back much further, into early Neolithic times and the beginnings of agriculture, near a cavern in France some ten thousand "bladelets" (miniature knives) were discovered by archaeologists. At first the scholars assumed there had been a battle of some kind in which (tiny) people used these tiny blades to hurt each other. But there were no signs of warfare, and finally one of the scientists thought to do a microscopic analysis of the blades, which showed that they were covered with grass resins. They had been used to harvest wild grains in 12,000 B.C.E. Nearby, scholars found the charred remains of fire, mortars and pestles for grinding grain, and the remains of bread having been baked in the primitive ovens.[20] All this took place near ritual cave sanctuaries, just as later in Çatal Hüyük, the bread would be baked in the courtyard ovens of the ritual temples where priestesses led the sacred ceremonies (see fig. 8). Dianic witches baked moon cakes, or croissants, to share in ritual circles in celebration of the full moon, as celebrants still do across the world in China today. And later still, right up to the present, nuns (the archaic word for which is priestess) have baked the wafers used for communion in the masses celebrated in the Catholic church. Sacred women have always baked sacred bread to be

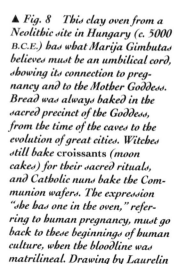

▲ *Fig. 8  This clay oven from a Neolithic site in Hungary (c. 5000 B.C.E.) has what Marija Gimbutas believes must be an umbilical cord, showing its connection to pregnancy and to the Mother Goddess. Bread was always baked in the sacred precinct of the Goddess, from the time of the caves to the evolution of great cities. Witches still bake croissants (moon cakes) for their sacred rituals, and Catholic nuns bake the Communion wafers. The expression "she has one in the oven," referring to human pregnancy, must go back to these beginnings of human culture, when the bloodline was matrilineal. Drawing by Laurelin Remington-Wolf.*

used in sacred ritual ceremonies, just as they have used menstrual blood for their magical practices. If the menstrual blood has been recognized in other times and places as having magical healing properties for the whole community, and is the main ritual of initiation for the Native American girl I described above, then why not assume that originally the first menstrual blood was included in the baking of the sacred bread that was then shared with the entire tribe in order to bring healing to all for the coming year? Only our extreme taboo toward the "wise blood" would prevent us from seeing this natural association.

In *The Great Cosmic Mother,* Monica Sjöö and Barbara Mor argue that the menstrual taboo was a "preeminently political move" on the part of men and society, "one of the most successful methods devised by men to undermine self-acceptance, self-understanding, and self-confidence in women. It acts as a constant confirmation of a negative self-image."[21] In the same way that Robert Graves points out how new religions tend to demonize the old deities that predated them, Sjöö and Mor show how "the blood ritual imitations of women's functions were turned into taboos against women's functions."[22] They, like Barbara Walker, point to the ancient menstrual cults and menstrual rites as the fundamental lineage through which the heritage of the tribe was originally passed down, as matrilineal descent. Merlin Stone, in *When*

25

*God Was a Woman*, showed that early temple priestesses owned and controlled the wealth of the tribal group, without needing class stratification or theocracy.[23] Even the Iroquois people in North America, at the time of European immigration here, were completely matrilineal, with women governing the tribe.[24]

Frédérique Marglin, in *Wives of the God-King*, describes the freedom and "auspiciousness," even in the current century, of Indian temple dancers, who were the only women in India who could own property, belonging to a "female category without its normal social ties to men."[25] Marglin shows that in India, until they were outlawed in the 1950s, the *devadasis* danced and sang daily in the temples, as well as participating in the calendrical festivals.[26] When they danced, they left drops of fluid created by their dancing ecstasy, and their dance was known as "the leavings of the shakti."[27] The sexual fluid is called *raja*, meaning also menstrual blood; the appearance of the menses in a girl is a sign that she is strong enough to bear a child, that she is "full of *raja*."[28] The *menarche* (first blood) is considered "auspicious," even though menstruating is "polluting." The word for "season" *(rutu)* is the same as one of the words for menstrual period, according to Marglin, and is closely connected to seasons in agriculture "the fertility of the earth and woman being interrelated, each being influenced by the lunar cycle."[29] A yearly festival at which the *devadasis* danced is called the Raja Samkranti and celebrated the "festival of the menses of the goddess." The earth is believed to be menstruating at that time (four days of this festival), and all women are held to be "impure" and not supposed to do any domestic work. The men prepare the food, the women "play, sing songs and swing on swings made for the occasion. The men do not plough the earth nor do they have sexual relationships with their women, who are treated as if they themselves were at their menses."[30]

In *Cult of the Goddess*, author James Preston echoes Marglin's information, discussing "the unique cluster of rites performed in villages" for Lakshmi, the Goddess of Wealth, who is "believed to be ready for bleeding," describing a strict vegetarian diet of fruit and wheat cakes, with taboos on plowing for three days. On the fourth day she is "thought to begin her bleeding, at which time the people celebrate together."[31]

It is taken for granted in India that menstruating women have access to powers of the Dark Goddess. In an essay from an anthology called *Mother Worship* edited by Preston, Pauline Kolenda states: "Anger is heat, which is associated in Hindu thought with 'feminine malevolence and divine power.'" She says anger and passion are associated with women in Hindu thought and that therefore *rajas* (passion) literally means menstrual impurity, "revealing an ancient connection between passion (including anger) and female impurity," and that "*shakti* (power as a feminine force) . . . is usually symbolized by fierceness." She quotes a male source who summarizes, "The female principle is always disturbing."[32]

Barbara Walker mentions that the "ancient world's most dreaded poison was the 'moon-dew' collected by Thessalian witches, said to be a girl's first menstrual blood shed during an eclipse of the moon."[33] Marglin speaks of the "self-born flower," a piece of cotton on which has been collected the first drop of menstrual blood from a girl in India menstruating for the first time,[34] which Barbara Walker says is "greatly prized as a healing charm."[35] Durdin-Robertson says that blood "increases vitality" and "affects the other worlds" by building forms for the spirits or "shades" dwelling there, thereby helping them "to manifest and communicate." In referring to what he calls the power of the altar, or the ancient priestess's offering of her menstrual blood, Durdin-Robertson says: "The great question, therefore, in all religions is: How can this substance be obtained? On the answer given to this depends the whole ethics of that religion." She gives it in "a natural and living way in her monthly courses."[36] Sjöö and Mor suggest that menstrual blood was "the medium of a spiritual-communal bond," which was replaced by the circumcision of male infants and the forming of a new male "covenant."[37]

Isn't it about time we begin to use our menstrual power once more, as in ancient times? The power of the menstrual blood is a core issue in returning to female self-government. Authors of *The Wise Wound* believe the human female menstrual cycle was the critical evolutionary advance that initiated human society and culture.[38] Marija Gimbutas includes in her giant book of ancient Goddess images a group of female figurines found in a vase, sitting in a circle, looking like a group of snake women sitting in council (fig. 9). The snake is linked to both menstruation and *kundalini,* and both of these are connected with the female ability to receive information

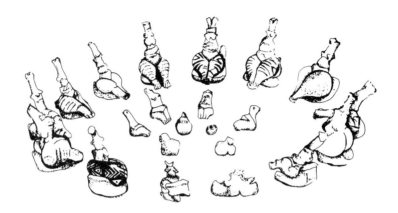

▲ *Fig. 9   These snake women sit in a circle of council,
suggesting the early grouping of women in community
rather than in the isolation we experience today. Early
women lived together with their children, and men came
and went from the matrifocal home base. Maybe these
women are bleeding together and making policy while in
that sacred state of female consciousness. Or like the
Inca "Virgins of the Sun" who lived together in a palace
in Cuzco, their lives might be dedicated to performing
religious rituals and ceremonies in the temple. These
Snake Goddesses were found grouped like this in a vase
from around 4700 B.C.E. Marija Gimbutas says it was
probably ready to be placed on an altar for the reenact-
ment of rites. Drawing by Jennifer Roberts.*

from the spirit realm and express it in the form of oracular
speech. Yoga was probably invented by women menstruating, who learned to master the tremendous energies and
forces available to them during this sacred, profound time of
the monthly cycle. Imagine group decision making taking
place at this time, for the express benefit of the whole community. Then compare that to what has happened to us in
Western culture, where for ten centuries "menstruating
women were specifically forbidden to come to church."[39]

Barbara Walker's excellent section on menstrual
blood in *The Woman's Encyclopedia of Myths and Secrets* calls it
the flower of the matrilineal clan, containing the soul of future
generations.[40] She says the Creator Goddess, who predates
the Bible, "taught women to form dolls and smear them with
menstrual blood as a conception charm," which may explain
the thousands of female figurines found all over the world,
whom scholars have insisted on calling pretty ladies and
dancing girls. The feminine form is *adamah* meaning "bloody

clay," although scholars translate it "red earth."[41] Think about Adam's rib, and "God" breathing the breath of life into creatures, and then think about the Bible's fixation on eliminating everyone who lived at the time of the writing of the Old Testament if they still worshiped "idols" in any form. And, of course, remember that our heritage includes the burning of nine million women in the Middle Ages for the crime of healing, but in a deeper sense for the crime of being women. Women who bleed. Feminist theologian Mary Daly says women are "stigmatized as *ontologically impure* and are therefore targets of hatred on this fundamental and all-pervasive level" (my italics).[42]

In a wonderful book about women's spiritual evolution as they observe it through their feminist therapy practices, Polly Young-Eisendrath and Florence Wiedemann speak about the "basic flaw" or "hidden ugliness" of all their women clients. "We have never encountered a woman in therapy who did not believe she was hiding a secret flaw that others would eventually discover."[43] Doesn't that sound like your adolescent fears of having your Kotex show through your skirt or your tampons fall out during recess or the smell of your menstruation be noticeable? How could any woman grow up in a society that hates and fears her natural, core biological function and not feel she was hiding a deep, inner flaw? The book, called *Female Authority: Empowering Women Through Psychotherapy*, chronicles a woman's passage from a negative identity as a woman that does not include a sense of inner authority through a process of confronting the "animus" inside and out and becoming a woman with her own authority. The authors don't highlight menstruation, but every single problem and characteristic they describe could as easily fall under the heading "Internalized Menstrual Taboo."

Imagine that deep down in every woman's process, there is an unconscious pull to remember the ecstasy of this ancient, sacred encounter with the forces of earth and sky coming through her body. And at the same time, she has been thoroughly socialized (through gynocidal practices) to be afraid to manifest such a longing. Is PMS so surprising under the circumstances? What would it take for us to allow the memories to surface, the fragmented images to coagulate like our monthly flow? Sylvia Perera has written a brilliant book about the female transformation process as perceived from her own counseling practice and her research into the ancient

Sumerian myth of Inanna, the shamanic Goddess whose descent is chronicled on ancient clay tablets unearthed more than fifty years ago in the Middle East and translated into English in the last decade. *Descent to the Goddess: A Way of Initiation for Women* is a guidebook for contemporary women who dare to slip below the zone of consciousness and experience the depths of female source energy. The story of Inanna making her descent into the underworld, where she must confront the Dark Goddess, die, and rot for three days, could easily be a metaphoric story of menstruation. It is our oldest mythic epic and points to even older cultures in the Middle East, such as Çatal Hüyük, where the women governed. Inanna, on hearing the call of the Dark Goddess, voluntarily descends—giving up every shred of identity in the process—in order to die and be reborn, returning to her community with power for healing. The hero, who enters the underworld in later tales, goes there with his sword raised to kill the Dark Goddess and never change.

Perera refers to the "impersonal yang energy" of Ereshkigal, the Dark Goddess, felt by contemporary women as "depression and an abysmal agony of helplessness and futility—unaccountable desire and transformative-destructive energy, unacceptable autonomy (the need for separateness and self-assertion) split off, turned in, and devouring the individual's sense of willed potency and value."[44] Inanna, says Perera, is the first to show us the way through Ereshkigal's domain, which "seems unbounded, irrational, primordial, and totally uncaring, even destructive of the individual."[45] Inanna's "openness to being acted upon is the essence of the experience of the human soul faced with the transpersonal. It is not based upon passivity, but upon active willingness to receive."[46] She talks about Inanna's sacrifice of what is above for what is below and the "exchange of libido for the purpose of renewal,"[47] all of which are familiar to women experiencing the sometimes-overwhelming monthly period, as well as the shamanic healing path. The point is transformation, or the "breaking up of the old pattern."[48] There is so much for us in the descent myth, if we can just allow the experience without outside intervention. This is true for our monthly menstrual period—no drugs, no painkillers—and our less regular depressions or more serious "breakdowns."

The healing available to contemporary women through our blood cycle is an instinctual release of what is

▲ *Fig. 10    This striking Gorgon-Medusa figure with
her tongue out like Indian Kali is in a classic birthing
posture, and like Artemis, is supported or flanked by two
animals. Medusa is our Western counterpart of the
Dark Goddess, who has healing, regenerative, and sexual powers. Like other Dark Goddesses from the transitional periods, she has been demonized and made into a
monster. Drawing by Laurelin Remington-Wolf.*

within us. Our willingness to face the dark is the key to our
own development. What we're afraid of is actually the treasure at the center of our being, the female source energy from
which we have so long been severed. The dragon that always
gets killed by the hero, the monster that lives under the ocean,
the ogress that hides in the deepest recesses of the female psyche is the liberator and savior for the Shakti woman. The
ancient Sibyls and prophetic priestesses gave oracles while
they were bleeding. Delphi means "womb." There is, naturally, suffering in these descents, which take us down into the
unconscious psyche. One of the most obvious threats is the
memory of incest or molestation that happened to so many of
us, so early. But Perera advises that "suffering is a primal
way,"[49] and suggests that we come to the Dark Goddess in a
worshipful way, sacrificing activity and simply enduring what
meets us there in the dark, after which there is the promise of
release and renewal (see fig. 10).

    One of the things that greets a woman in the dark
center when she lets herself sink down there is rage. A wom-

▲ *Fig. 11A  Medusa face: a classic one from Italy around 500 B.C.E with snakes for hair, representing the awakened kundalini power transmitting wisdom and energy in every direction. Her protruding tongue could refer back to her earlier function as a birthing Goddess in active labor or, as Robert Graves has suggested, may be a warning against intruders of the women's initiation mysteries. After all, later historians tell us that one look from Medusa could turn a man to stone. Drawing by Laurelin Remington-Wolf.*

an's "upper-world" conditioning requires a denial of anger in order to be available as caretaker and nurturer around the clock, throughout the cycle. During PMS women feel "bitchy," we are not able to go on being so self-sacrificing, squelching our instincts, quieting our actual responses. Think of wild Kali, the Indian Dark Goddess with her supposed thirst for blood, or Medusa, whose glance turned men to stone (figs. 11A and 11B). It is likely that, were we to regularly access our full menstrual power, we simply could not go on being nice girls. We might well reach a critical mass of *raja* and have to express it into our culture as revolution! It is no doubt for this reason that the menstrual taboos are carried out with such ferocity. Barry and Ann Ulanov discuss this problem in their illuminating book *The Witch and the Clown*, where they describe a modern woman's "undischarged excitement" and "unlived life." The repressed "witch" causes chronic depression and antisocial behavior in women, and even if we don't call ourselves witch, say the Ulanovs, the culture will! "The witch image depicts the force that arises when women want to create themselves and form themselves in ways other than biological reproduction" (see figs. 12A and 12B). They add, "Most of what is thought of as a witch's negative effect on her environment is really the environment infecting her."[50]

For Shakti women it is essential to reclaim all the negative epithets and make them our own, with pride. Well-known Wiccan leader Starhawk has demonstrated for a decade that we must gladly assume the title of witch in order to reclaim and resacralize our earth-based healing power. I would add to that lesbian, deviant, and all the words Mary Daly has elaborated so eloquently in her visionary book *Gyn/Ecology*. Hags, spinsters, fairies, harpies, and furies are names

▲ *Fig. 11B   This masked Medusa from
Peru has obvious snake hair yet is
always misidentified in books about
South America, referred to as the Sun
God because "he" has "rayed hair." Look
again, scholars! Her gritted teeth could
also inform us about her birthing function, since an ancient Mexican (Aztec)
counterpart Goddess gives birth wearing
the same expression. Drawing by
Laurelin Remington-Wolf.*

given to crones or women of wisdom. Daly says, "Hags live.
Women traveling into feminist time/space are creating Hag-
ocracy, the place where we govern."[51] The word *hag* comes
from the root meaning "holy woman" and "sacred grove." The
Ulanovs call up the image of a contemporary Shakti woman:
". . . the hag-woman who bursts with energy, thrusting
toward the meaning of life. She feels she must live fully before
she dies, must somehow find herself in touch with the fires of
truth or burn up trying."[52] The next time you feel irritated,
and it's close to your period, see if you can let the hag or witch
in you have some space to express herself. The Ulanovs speak
of the hag's "drive to be her own self, independent of others,
with her own purposes to effect, her own resources to pull
from, her own deep wells to draw materials from, right to the
surface."[53] Sounds like the kind of creativity available to
women who are able, for periods of time, to focus on our own
tasks — writing books, dreaming of new worlds, initiating the
means to achieve what we want for ourselves and our
children.

Menstruation is not a painful process when we allow
the natural period of time to have its own way with us. Yet by
repressing the energies of the menstrual period, we find ourselves trapped in the lack of expression such repression manifests in our lives. "The tremendous instinctual energies
amassed in the hag-unconscious find no ego-portal through
which to be realized and satisfied. All the energy crashes back
upon her in intense anguish, disappointment, and rage, so
aptly symbolized in the image of the hag gnashing her teeth
and making terrible, bitter sounds, like a wounded bear."[54]
Artemis, the she-bear, tamed and frustrated, becomes mean
and sick inside. Her shamanic power is distorted into depression or bitterness. When I had tension headaches, they

**33**

▲ *Fig. 12A This well-known Bolivian deity is alternately mis-identified as the Thunder God with his weapons in hand or (as usual) the Sun God. But notice the iconography: snake hair (Medusa), the famous serpent skirt of Coatlique in Mexico ("She of the Serpent Skirt"), and the snakes held in the hands out to the sides, like the Snake Goddess from Crete. Drawing by Laurelin Remington-Wolf.*

reached a terrible crescendo at the time of my period. Women with migraines and herpes experience their bodies going out of control during "that time of the month." Our incredible isolation from one another during the menstrual cycle (and other times) leads to a pervasive hopelessness and futility, witnessed in our surrender to the medical establishment for "curing" our "female complaints." Think of the terrible reversal that has taken place for the sacred menstrual cycle of our ancestors to have become a pathology in the eyes of modern medicine.

We can heal the isolation by coming together, experiencing our cycles as a group, creating moon lodges and quiet times. We can chant, fast, relax, dream, keep diaries, be quiet, or share with other women the sacred depths to which we dive during this magical time of the month. We can make art, letting the voice of the Goddess — the oracle — speak through us in healing words and images. Like the women in India, we can take a necessary break from the unceasing activities of modern life. If we don't have loving partners at home to "allow" us this break, we need to create female community structures that make this time of renewal possible for ourselves. Menstruation is the perfect time to perform ritual, using your menstrual blood as the potent elixir of magic and visualization. Make a protective or healing amulet for yourself, and smear it with your own holy blood. Feed your plants.

Wish for what you want in your life. Never use your blood for harm or to control anyone else; let the sorcerers have the karma of that activity. Project only what you would want to come back to you, multiplied three times. Give the blood back

▲ *Fig. 12B    The famous Snake
Goddess from the ruins of Knossos,
Crete, during the period known as
Middle Minoan (about 1600
B.C.E.). Some scholars think Crete
was matriarchal in the sense that
women might have actually ruled
rather than simply being equal to
men. Whether or not this is the
case, the images of women are all
beautiful and most of them show a
level of empowerment seldom seen
in Western women since. Drawing
by Laurelin Remington-Wolf.*

to the earth, and feel your kinship with the ancient priestesses
who invented agriculture and civilization. There is a delicacy
in this issue, due to our deep conditioning, that works against
our liberation. We must break the menstrual taboo. In that
way we can groom ourselves for becoming crones and hags,
women past the age of menstruation who are not afraid of
what people think and who are freer to do what we want than
younger women.

Mary Daly speaks movingly about the "gynocide" of
women past childbearing age. The rise of Western gynecology was built on the massacre of women healers, replaced by
male medical practitioners. Daly maintains that "the purpose
and intent of gynecology was/is not healing in a deep sense
but violent enforcement of the sexual caste system."[55] In
ancient times menopausal women were the wise grandmoth-
ers of the tribe, their wise blood stored in the body like the
wisdom stored in their psyches. In our culture women wear
out, lose their value, are treated like throwaways. The high
statistics of breast and uterine surgery are terrifying to all of
us, threatening to annihilate us as we age. When a woman
enters menopause in our culture, she is advised to take estro-
gen-replacement therapy rather than "suffer" the pathology
on its own terms. Why? So that she will escape the fate of
"hot flashes," those physical reminders that her body is somehow out of control and obviously not male. Her body

responds to hormones, and to change! As a psychic aid to women attempting to get through menopause without drugs, let me tell you what Western science has recently learned. It seems that cancer responds therapeutically to a raised body temperature; that is, cancer can be cured by raising the temperature of the body. Think about it. Hot flashes happen for a reason, besides the fact that we're toxic and need the release of heat and sweat to relieve the body. *Menopause is preparing us to be healthy old women!* It gives our body a raised temperature during the transition, which probably heals it of potential ills, such as the pervasive cancers that exist in the present moment. With all the pollutants and chemicals in the atmosphere, there are surely no guarantees for any of us, but please, sisters — Enjoy and appreciate your hot flashes. Love your menopause. Like the bleeding time, it's a kundalini experience. There has to be ecstasy in it. Tune in and let the Dark Goddess have you, and I know the outcome will be renewal.

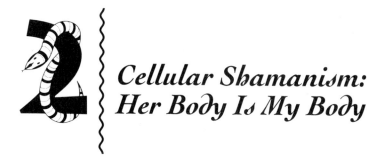

# Cellular Shamanism: Her Body Is My Body

WESTERN MEDICINE TENDS TO separate the parts of the human body into isolated units, as if they did not belong to something whole. Some malfunction of the heart or the elbow is treated as if it were a discrete segment, unaffected by the rest, with which something has gone wrong that needs to be fixed. The doctor is the professional expert who is called in to do the fixing, and he learns how to do this not through his own experience of his own body but by reading books and cutting up corpses. Then to further complicate things, Western psychology separates the mind from the body and treats them as if they also had almost no relation to each other, holding that their ideal relationship is mind over matter. Western thinking in general, supported by Western religion, describes human beings as separate and distinct from Nature and the rest of the animals on earth, with permission to dominate. Even the study of human evolution from the ape ancestor is rife with ideas about our superiority and our progressive growth away from the animal world. When we want to insult someone, we tell him he is acting like an animal; whereas, in truth, it could be the ultimate insult on this planet for someone to tell a member of any other species that she is acting like a human.

In most religious thinking the body is equated with the earth and women. Since the most ancient times on this planet, these correspondences have been apparent, and for the longest time they were a source of worship and appreciation. Woman = body = earth. The technical,

▲ *Fig. 13    This bird-headed, snake-bodied Goddess is one of many from pre-Dynastic Egypt,
before the development of kingship and slavery.
Her arms are in the upraised position known by
modern witches as "drawing down the moon," and
they look like they might as easily have held
snakes. Drawing by Laurelin Remington-Wolf.*

ancient definition of Goddess. Earth Mother. Creatrix (see
fig. 13). She who gives birth to all that lives and takes back to
herself all that ever was. She who holds us here in continual
change, constant impermanence, and shows us the magic of
generation and cyclic evolution. Matrix. Regeneratrix.
Woman, her daughter, has all the same characteristics, the
same talents. Out of her sacred body she creates or destroys,
as Nature would have it. She bleeds, grows life, harbors the
unborn, gives birth, nurtures, and feeds her young from her
own magical, erotic (i.e., living) body. She makes love, makes
energy, makes life — all in the body. From her practical relationship to her young, through the function of food sharing,
woman invented language and communication, tools, pottery,
and art.[1]

   Since a woman's body, which is so like the earth,
makes enough food for her offspring, our early ancestors
learned to trust the Mother, fashioning images of this Great
Mother with large, abundant breasts and a full, pregnant
belly. For millennia — maybe since the beginning of consciousness — the community of these women and their male
and female offspring loved, thanked, and sang praises to this
earth. Most modern archaeology dates the Venus figurines to
around 25,000 B.C.E., but recent British research points to a
date for the earliest Great Goddess figures of up to three mil-

lion years ago—the very dawn of human evolution. The earliest humans created images of the divine woman from stone, the forms of which still, amazingly, survive. The problem, according to scholar Ron Williams, is that these flint sculptures have been identified as hand axes by archaeology and are therefore completely misunderstood. Like so many other misnamed "tools" of archaeology, these objects lack the markings necessary to be something that was used in utilitarian ways (such as a chopping implement). These so-called hand axes, found in large numbers from most of the early open-camp sites, are largely locked away in museum drawers today.[2]

Traditional scholars have consistently assumed that ancient people suffered and struggled for their survival and that the quality of their life was much lower and more unpleasant than our own modern, technological one. Over and over they picture the ancients as barbaric imbeciles, grunting at each other, raping and maiming, totally uncouth and what we have unfortunately come to call primitive. But archaeological evidence shows something else entirely, and this something else is apparently quite threatening to the established paradigm, because it is rarely assimilated into modern scholarship. Even the popular feminist book and movie *Clan of the Cave Bear* presented prehistory and human evolution as a kind of Fred-and-Wilma-Flintstone idea of male authority and female submission among the tribes. Rather than this relentless view of evolution as linear and progressive, with male dominance forever the norm, we must begin to accept that ancient people were brilliant and innovative, living what we would have to call the good life if we compare it with our own global disaster. Just the fact that they appear to have existed in groups for millennia without making war is enough to suggest that we question our own culture.

Scientific people find it hard to imagine our ancestors as happy and healthy because, being so cut off from Nature and the animal in us, we actually do suffer and struggle against the elements when we are so unfortunate as to find ourselves encountering them directly. When we get lost in the woods we don't know what to do, we have no idea what to eat or not eat, and we have little access to this information from any direct sources, such as the trees, animals, and plants themselves. We can't take care of ourselves without a stock of

processed food in our backpacks and we can't navigate without compasses and maps. This makes us feel like victims who
can't survive, and we project this horrendous image onto
ancient cultures. But everything we know from living shamanic people today or from their artifacts and writing from
earlier times tells us that they are much more at home in
Nature and therefore safer. They aren't just good hunters and
gatherers, they are good listeners and intelligent communica-
tors. They coexist with the other life on the planet. They make
peace with living things, using what they find around them
and giving thanks for the miracle of this abundance. They
have access to magic and actual (physical) ways of interacting
and working with the unseen forces. Until we accept this as
absolutely real, we will never fully understand what we are
studying.

*The most basic, fundamental tool of magic is the body.*
Everything felt, seen, or experienced on other planes can be
translated through the body into the concrete, physical realm.
The body is the vessel that houses all the energies and forces
needed to do anything we might imagine, and the five senses
plus the extrasensory processes are the means of contact. We
can know things through the body more completely, more
truly than with the brain consciousness. We have the capacity
to respond just like animals, but in order to understand how
meaningful that is, we would first need to wake up to exactly
how animals are conscious. Our Judeo-Christian religious
background equates the body with mundane or banal realities. We think instinct is lower at best, and evil at worst, and
our aim is to drive it out. Failing to see the ways in which
animals are attuned to the hidden forces of Nature and the
universe, we don't realize how spiritually in touch they are.
They function from natural impulses rather than addictive
conditioned responses.

A major element in beginning shamanic work for
Western women is overcoming our addictions. In the United
States probably every single woman who is called to become
a healer is confounded in some way by her own addictions,
either physical or psychological. It is a given. Along with our
false view of reality (that everything is either physical and
visible or not real) and our ingrained sense of inferiority
because we are women (the fatal "flaw" that all women in
patriarchal culture experience at the core), we have also been
conditioned to need things that are not necessary and do not

serve our health. These addictions have been structured into our beings, like knee-jerk responses to stimuli, so that they constantly distract us from our true path and obscure our vision. We are crippled by our addictive habits, debilitated by our need for what is unhealthful, and paralyzed from acting on our own behalf and on behalf of our children. It is no wonder that women have started to enter therapy in droves, to join Twelve-Step programs in large numbers, and to form female support groups for dealing with things like incest survival and food compulsions. This trend is a mass underground recovery movement, in which women everywhere have decided to get well.

At the time of my shamanic healing crisis in 1976, my whole life changed. In the early seventies I had actively worked in the women's health movement and women's liberation, where I spoke frequently in public about the need to take back our vaginas from the medical establishment, recover our control over reproduction, and learn ways to be healthy and happy in our female bodies. I even helped start a feminist gynecological clinic in Colorado, where we did excellent birth-control counseling and sexuality and abortion work, and I coauthored the text *Circle One: A Woman's Beginning Guide to Self-Health and Sexuality.* My consciousness was raised but in a fragmented way. When my own natural healing process spontaneously emerged, I suddenly saw the bigger picture and realized, in retrospect, what a ludicrous spectacle I must have seemed on a panel at national conferences, going on about women's health with a cigarette hanging out of my mouth. This form of fragmentation extends into every aspect of our lives. Until we are faced with ourselves in a mirror that shows us more than our cultivated persona, it is difficult to begin to break the rigid structures that have conditioned us.

My break with women's health politics was sudden and complete; I simply couldn't work in that environment anymore. Holistic health had entered my mind as a new paradigm, and I knew I had to change everything.[3] I began to open psychically and to have a spiritual foundation and a connection to the universe through the force that I felt to be the Goddess. I began to perceive the physical troubles I was having in my body as only the obvious outcome of my incorrect ways of living. The headaches that had plagued me for ten years became the signposts of my bad habits, signals of how I was not taking proper care of myself. The ulcer I was developing demanded that I stop behaving in old ways, give up my anger, and try something new. When I stopped smoking cigarettes, my conditioned ways of behaving confronted me like a therapist. I had spent four years lighting cigarettes every time I was insecure or bored or didn't like what was happening to me. It was a way of comforting myself, wasting time, taking my attention off the outer situation. When I stopped smoking, I was so restless I had to act on my feelings. I had to confront people whom I had not been willing to offend and to make changes in my daily patterns that would help me become more clearly myself over the years.

It helps us to do our shamanic work in relation to other women. Support groups and ritual circles are the heart of the work, creating containers that will hold us through our willed transformations. A woman on her own, opening psychically and beginning to perceive the invisible, could feel as if she might go crazy, as many have over the years. When we "open psychically," a structural phenomenon takes place in which the energy body awakens, causing the physical body to seem "fluid" and mutable rather than solid and clearly defined. Whereas it seems that the skin is the boundary of the person in "normal" reality, when that same person opens psychically, the boundary expands. The person feels herself extending out beyond the body, taking up more space, feeling things in an extrasensory way. What we took for granted as a kind of density in the physical realm is suddenly called into question on every level. This is actually quite difficult for the ego to assimilate, and it often causes emotional problems. The person's fears rise up like specters, haunting her with "what if" and "you shouldn't" and so on. Fortunately our culture is importing a number of public demonstrations of this other reality in the form of firewalking (walking barefoot on burning coals without harm), psychic surgery (Philippine healers putting their hands inside bodies, by moving molecules aside, and removing tumors), and psychokinesis (bending forks with the will, etc.), all of which help to open the general populace to the reality of paranormal experiences.

Groups provide a form for women to join together in study, practice, and discussion of these phenomena. The circle grounds us and holds us in connection to one another and the earth. It makes the work safer and easier. The practical content of the work is aimed at basically two levels: the instincts and the intuition. The *instincts* are the "animal" part of us that can react in the body to danger or health. The *intuition* is a way of thinking or knowing that encompasses ordinary thought and intellect in something larger and more inclusive. Intuition is also body based and may come through a feeling in the physical body, a dream, or simply a complete thought that passes through the mind as information, a warning, and the like.

The major problem in dealing with these two functions, the instincts and intuition, is that they are covered over and distorted for most of us by our conditioning, which masquerades as instinctual impulses. Our culture imagines and defines our addictions as instinct, then attaches a negative value to it. We belittle and denigrate women's intuition as something spacey and inferior to pure reason. In jury selection in this country, people are asked if they can separate their feelings from their rational decisions! How incredible that we would imagine that justice could happen if a person were able to do such a thing. If a person answers, "Of course not," she is immediately removed from the pool of potential jurors. Our culture also imagines that rape is an act of instinct and murder a crime of passion. So when we then import philosophies from the East that discuss the instincts and passions as something we need to root out and kill in order for our spiritual life to blossom, the confusion is complete.

When I speak of instinctual life, I am thinking of being connected to the growth cycles of plants and animals, keeping time by the seasons, birthing and bleeding in harmony with the phases of the moon, communing with the seeds we plant and the vegetables we harvest. I am thinking of the way a man knows when the woman he loves is ovulating or menstruating or the way I know when someone is calling me on the telephone before it rings. I am not talking about the horrendous number of violent, grotesque images that have been fed to the unconscious through the ubiquitous lens of the television set or the pornography available to children at every video store or corner magazine rack or the billboard advertising that accosts the eye wherever it looks in any American city. These distortions of what is natural and human have to be removed through a process of cleansing and release that happens naturally and can also be stimulated by techniques developed for that purpose. In the simplest way of speaking, when a woman sets her mind on positive,

43

healing development, this process of cleansing and release is set in motion. To say no to negative, harmful images of women and actually to refuse to accommodate those images anymore is to bring on a process of transformation at once. The body is so relieved to regurgitate the filth it has swallowed in the conditioning process, it happily throws it off in the form of illness, skin rashes, sweating, boils, and other not-so-pleasant forms of release.

The result of this natural purging on the part of the body is a sense of refinement or transparency that concurrently awakens the psychic sight and liberates the cells to expand and take up more space. This molecular transformation is wonderful in one way, opening the being to feeling itself (maybe for the first time), creating the possibility of soul contact from the angle of the personality. The soul is directly connected to and speaks through the body. When we pollute and poison the body with chemicals and bad food, as well as negative images and distorted ideas about women (ourselves), the soul is lost to us and we are trapped, like the Hindus suggest, in the confinement of the physical bodily experience. But this is not a natural or biological condition, it is a man-made one. We don't have to be miserable in our poor bodies, looking for spiritually sanctioned ways of escape from the physical realm. We don't need to kill the instincts in order to get spiritual. What we need to let go of is the conditioning, the habit patterns that are killing us, and the patriarchal lies about reality. As these false realities are purged from our physical and psychic systems, we need to replace them with a deeper grounding in our actual instincts.

The process is one of gradually aligning more and more with the body (which is ultimately an alignment with the soul) and allowing the habitual mental process to recede into the background. The body knows what to do. The only reason it hasn't done the right thing in the past is that it is consistently overruled by the mind and poisoned by toxic chemicals. When left to its own devices, it is miraculously, lovingly correct in determining what it needs and how to go about getting it. Just as animals know what to eat as medicine from what grows wild and when to fast and where to lie down for the best "energy treatment," so also do our bodies have these instincts. We inhibit our bodies because we would feel silly and embarrassed letting them loose in natural ways, and, on a deeper level, we fear persecution. We don't birth our

▲ *Fig. 14A    Shakti Woman, an
example of "photopsychic art" by Irene
Young. The photo was taken of the
author and her snake, Bacchus, when
he was two years old.*

own babies, we don't heal our own illnesses, and we don't
process our own food. We have been convinced, in all of these
instances, that there are experts who know better than we do.
We let our loved ones die lonely deaths in hospitals hooked
up to machines, we allow our government to spend our tax
money on more and more lethal technologies while people in
our neighborhoods are homeless and hungry, and we sit in
horrific traffic jams and breathe carbon monoxide for hours,
even though we know that it (and the lead) are killing us. We
(women) smoke cigarettes in greater numbers every year in
response to an advertising campaign that doesn't value our
lives, and we give up our bodies to unnecessary surgical procedures for the removal of our female organs at the insistence
of our (male) medical professionals.

I have a boa constrictor named Bacchus (fig. 14A) —
a gift from a student of mine — who rests in his cage most of
the time. He likes being held and stroked, but when he is
alone, he rests, coiled in a deep state of trance. One day he
began to move about in his cage as if agitated. He moved
around the cage, climbing and shifting his position so much
that by the next day, when he hadn't stopped behaving in this
unusual way, we went out for food supplies for him. We
thought he surely must be starving to be so active. Finally he
was standing straight up, the full length of his almost-three-
foot body vertical, his head pressed against the wall, as if
listening. After about twenty-four hours of his ceaseless

**45**

agitation, the San Francisco Bay Area experienced a 7.1 earthquake. It was the largest earthquake any of us had ever felt, and it did significant damage. After the quake Bacchus settled down, but we had become more observant. When one day he stood up and "listened" again for several hours, we initiated a phone tree to let people know that the snake was "dancing." We were not predicting an earthquake or even really issuing a warning but simply asking people to be watchful. That night we experienced a smaller quake that made people feel grateful we had called them.

Over the years in California I had noticed that I usually got a headache for a few days before large earthquakes, and two days before the big earthquake, I woke up from an earthquake dream with a tickle and a cough in my chest. Since I had just been through somewhat of a crisis or emergency in my work, I assumed that the dream was reflecting that experience back to me metaphorically. It probably was, but it was also telling me of the approaching earthquake. In looking back, I can see that there were three signals about the quake: my dream, the sudden tickle in my chest, and the snake standing up. Over the years we in California have become a little blasé in relation to the earthquakes because we have lived through so many of them, and so many have been almost completely harmless. If you're not worried about your survival, an earthquake is pretty interesting, even exciting in its power. Next time I would pay more attention and take it more seriously if those three things manifested together. But life is never quite like that. Generally things don't happen the same way twice, and we are so overstimulated in our culture (especially in the cities) that it is difficult to know what is causing what reaction. Things often are separated by periods of time as well, and unless we keep good records, we don't even remember to connect our premonitions with the later events.

Our bodies are fully capable of registering unusual movements within the earth, but our behavior is not patterned in a way to express what we are registering. Most shamanic traditions tell of power places in the body of the earth, where emanations are released that can be felt and experienced in the body. Scientists have begun to identify links between such "power spots" and earthquake faults. Snakes have always been known to respond to the magnetic field of the earth and its erratic changes. In ancient times communities had oracular centers. In these centers priestesses of the Goddess gave oracles or prophecies to the community. Like the famous Cassandra of Troy, they were so sensitive in their bodies that they could divine the future through dreams and visions, through eating or drinking hallucinogenic substances, tuning in to the earth currents, or through the presence and intervention of the sacred snakes that lived in the oracular temples with the women. Sometimes the snakes were poisonous, and researchers have suggested that the bite of a poisonous snake, rather than being fatal, was perhaps hallucinogenic for these priestess women. It is known that if you withstand the first bite, the ones after that meet up with your immunities and are less lethal than the first.

When patriarchal peoples overran the ancient Goddess religion five thousand years ago, one of the most important things that changed had to do with these sacred oracle centers. Robert Temple's book *The Sirius Mystery* unfolds the story in detail, but I will summarize it for our purposes here. Temple's research shows that the oracular centers were placed over the globe in a precise geometric way: They were in a musical relationship to one another, like the eight notes of a musical scale. He focuses primarily on centers in ancient Egypt but says the same is true of the centers that are more familiar to Western history that existed in ancient Greece. Delos, Dodona, Delphi—these are three of the ancient centers where people made pilgrimages during the course of the year to pay homage to the Earth Mother and hear prophecies from her priestesses. The oracle center at Delos belonged originally to Artemis and later was moved to Delphi, where it eventually belonged to the god Apollo, even though the priestess was still female and still had a snake—the famous python (fig. 14B). This *Pythia,* as she was called, was able to forecast who would win which battle and so on during the transitional patriarchal times. Temple says that the people moved seasonally and cyclically around the musical scale, and, as such, around the countryside, during the course of a year in their journeys to these oracle centers. He believes as well that the centers were in immediate contact with one another through the use of passenger pigeons, which they kept and used to send messages.[4] It is very interesting, in this context, to remember that the Goddess in the Aegean was always connected to the dove and that even the ancient Mayan ruins at Uxmal include a "house of the doves."

▲ *Fig. 14B This is the Delphic
Omphalos, the "navel of the
world," the umbilicus linking the
oracular priestess at each center
with the source energy of Mother
Earth. When Patriarchy became
entrenched in the Western world,
the oracular center was pinned
permanently to one place—Delphi—where the oracle still spoke
through the "Pythia" or priestess
but on behalf of Apollo, the Sun
God, who had slain the original
python. Drawing by Laurelin
Remington-Wolf.*

Michael Dames also wrote about this seasonal, cyclic
movement of the people of the Old Religion from oracle center to oracle center in ancient Britain. In *The Silbury Treasure*
and *The Avebury Cycle*, Dames shows that ancient Britons considered the earth to be the body of the Mother, and their pro-
cessional walk from place to place honored her sacred body,
upon which they built mounds and structures of stone to represent and mark certain aspects for their religious and scientific purposes.[5] Like the ancient Egyptians and Greeks, they
processed during the course of the year, completing a circle
and, if Temple is correct, probably a musical scale as well.
This sense of the earth's body was not in any way removed
from one's personal sense of one's own body. Ancient people
weren't holding a concept in their minds, abstract and metaphorical, to which they paid repetitive religious homage.
They were physically registering and responding to signals
and messages from Nature in their sensitive physical vehicles.
Our inability to consciously feel and respond to the planetary
energies and the earth currents is not a sign of "progress" but
a sad commentary on our recent separation from life itself.
The physical body was once so integrally linked with the
physical planet that communication and response came naturally. Far from our ancestors' being barbaric or idiotic, we are
the ones who seem rather stupid to have forgotten how much
we belong to the earth.

Archaeoastronomy and geomancy show us that the
ancient structures in Britain and other places are aligned with
the "dragon currents," those currents or lines of force that run
all through the earth under the surface and can be felt and

tracked by those who are sensitive or have the proper instruments. People who study geomancy have suggested correspondences to the sciences of Chinese acupuncture and the Hindu chakra system, suggesting that perhaps the huge standing stones were placed in a certain way to mark or stimulate certain "points" or "centers" in the earth's body. There are more than forty thousand earthworks in Britain alone, likewise in the Yucatán peninsula of Mexico. Temples were later built on the mounds in Mexico, but first the mounds stood alone as temples of the ancient Goddess religion.

Temple's whole book on the oracle centers is built around the magic and mystery of this bright star Sirius, named Sothis by the Egyptians, the early name of the Goddess Isis. According to esoteric science, Sirius "seeded" this planet with civilization, agriculture, religion, and with all that early humans invented. Temple refers to the living Dogon people in Africa and their ancient written tradition of accurate information about the astronomy of this star that our scientists didn't "discover" until very recently. He explains that "modern" (meaning patriarchal) culture moved the oracle centers to one permanent location in each area (Delphi in Greece, Memphis in Egypt) at the time of the Dynasties, when invaders wanted to establish permanent royal control in the domain. Think of the story of Apollo, the Sun God, slaying the python with his sword, pinning her to the ground in his historic victory over the Goddess religion. The epoch of traveling oracle centers ended, the procession of the people from place to place throughout the agricultural cycle ceased, along with the free-moving currents of force or energy in the earth, and the oracle at Delphi or Memphis became the official or "state" oracle from that time on. It was owned and controlled by the king or pharaoh or great man in charge.[6]

The Tibetans have an interesting legend about the ancient "demoness" who lives in the earth. Like the Australian Aborigines and the Rainbow Serpent, they seem to mean by this that she both created and is the earth itself. They discuss her "free-ranging" movements from the ancient times, before she was pinned down, and her natural free movements deliberately restrained, by the building of Buddhist structures in Tibet. But unlike the Python of Apollo, the Tibetan demoness did not die; she was simply kept from moving freely by these structures. This demoness, called Srin-Mo, represents and refers to Tibet's ancient matriarchal past, the truly indigenous culture before the invasion of either the Bon or the Buddhist religions. Along with evidence that "women held a powerful place in early Tibetan society," Janet Gyatso maintains that the demoness belongs to the worldwide tradition of conquest-domination over the original chaotic feminine "stuff of which the world is fashioned." Because the demoness was not killed, she ("the religious culture or worldview that is being dominated") is very much alive and "threatens to break loose at any relaxing of vigilance or deterioration of civilization."[7]

In modern times China has invaded Tibet, toppling the ancient Buddhist structures and forcing the Tibetan lamas into exile. Could the ancient demoness be getting free again, and is she really the old earth dragon of the ancient women shamans? Synchronistically, the heretofore secret teachings of the Tibetan Black Dakini are becoming public and available even in the West, as Tibetan lamas visit the United States and other countries, giving empowerments and facilitating rituals to this Dark Goddess. One of her many important attributes—and an outcome of her rituals—is the destruction of epidemic illnesses and the eradication of fear. The Chöd ritual is specifically identified with a "sacrifice" of the physical body, just as it is, to feed the hungry demons, that they might be fulfilled and ease their destructive impact on the planet. Containing elements from the old shamanic religion of Bönpo in Tibet, as well as Buddhist elements, the Chöd is a ritual in which the practitioner offers her body up for transformation into nectar. This process is overseen by the Black Dakini, with her crescent knife for dismembering the ego and her skullcap for stirring the toxins of the practitioner into nectar. (The image of the Black Dakini on the cover of this book is a contemporary portrayal created by Japanese-American artist Mayumi Oda.) Namkhai Norbu points out that although the body is offered up as a "feast," the internal demons that will enjoy it are "all the usually latent fears, such as the fear of sickness or death, that can only be overcome when they are brought to the forefront of consciousness, but there also exist demons in the sense of negative energies that the practice enables the practitioner to magnetize and, ultimately, to master."[8] Norbu emphasizes that the body itself is not a problem but is regarded as a "precious vehicle for the attainment of realization." The problem is the ego's attachment to the body and the resultant self-protection, and that is what the Black Dakini and her Chöd practice work to cut away.

▲ *Fig. 15   These ancient figurines from Mexico (1500 B.C.E. from Tlaltilco) provide a splendid example of sacred women or priestesses in their shaman garb. The leggings may be a garment of some fabric, but I wonder if they might represent the leg rattles still worn by Latin American shaman-dancers, which are hung with the dewclaws of local four-legged animals (such as llamas in Bolivia, for example) or seed pods (such as in Panama). Drawing by Laurelin Remington-Wolf.*

The link needed to understand the shamanic body in relation to the planet is a focus on the physical phenomena of the earth itself. Since our bodies are literally cells in the larger body of the earth, we feel and respond to the experiences she registers in her body. This is religious. We can discuss it in scientific terms, using the Gaia hypothesis of interlocking systems. We can use contemporary astrology to understand that the planets affect the earth and us by extension. But the direct experience of tuning in to the earth's body with our bodies, and feeling what she feels, can be *ecstasy*. Ecstasy is a physical response of the body — energy rushing through the whole system, tingling and orgasmic sensations either localized or generalized throughout. Mircea Eliade, in his germinal work called *Shamanism,* identifies the shaman as a "professional ecstatic."[9] Everywhere in ancient times women were shamans. They were always connected with divination and with the movements and currents of the earth, as if they could not be separated. Women shamans and priestesses are frequently portrayed naked and grounded in the physical body, openly sexual, chanting, singing, dancing to make it rain, healing, birthing, playing musical instruments, weaving, planting, and doing the physical work of the world. These figures remain mysterious and embarrassing to the scholars, who can't make much of them, except to name them fertility figures and dancing girls (see fig. 15).

Our so-called reptilian brain (the one that responds instinctually) is perceived by science as the earliest and lowest of our modes of intelligence. Because we have cut ourselves off from this ability over the last five thousand years, and because we hold a progressive, evolutionary model of development as our paradigm, we pretend and believe that this mode of thinking is inferior. Yet the intelligence of the body is positively miraculous, and without it we have the capacity to exterminate ourselves. Since we have begun to destroy the planet in earnest over the last fifty years, through pollution and the various toxic assaults we are currently making on her body, we are experiencing the other end of the spectrum from ecstasy, which is illness and death. We don't understand, in our separation from life, that what we do to the body of the planet, we do directly to ourselves. It is the reptilian, or instinctual, brain that would provide us with this information, but we have learned to ignore and repress its signals. We suffer diseases in the latter half of the twentieth century that didn't exist in all of human evolution, and they are killing us in epidemic numbers. These degenerative illnesses are directly traced to the chemicals and toxins we have chosen to pump into our bodies and our environment.[10]

As science explores shamanistic phenomena, it comes to perceive what shamans do around the world as more and more in line with the newest branch of physics. Shamans seem to know things that are not available to normal people; and healers seem to be able to do things that are "impossible," because they seem somehow to know the secret laws of physics. Think of the healers in the Philippines who put their hands inside the physical body to remove tumors without surgical instruments and without drawing blood because they believe that the molecules will separate and make way for them. Physics, of course, agrees. And everywhere in the world where there are ancient, monumental ruins, the native people who live nearby have legends that the people who built the structures did so through magic. No matter how many times researchers come across this explanation for the building of impossibly large and heavy rock structures, they never accept it as possible. Yet there are witnesses, even in this century, who have seen Tibetan lamas in this process of moving large stones to build a temple through the agency of sound, geometry, and group focus.[11] It is only our disbelief that stands between us and understanding.

If we have been taught by Western science that something is "impossible," and we proceed to do this impossible thing, we then have to consciously eliminate the habitual phrase "I can't" from our speech. Last year I had the opportunity to do two firewalks with Peggy Dylan, one of the originators of firewalking rituals in the United States.[12] A firewalk is prepared by lighting a bonfire that burns down to embers measuring twelve hundred degrees Fahrenheit, across which participants walk. You don't walk on red hot coals in your bare feet because you believe it's possible. You walk on the coals because you temporarily suspend the belief that it is *not* possible.

At my first firewalk, in Switzerland at a women's retreat, I approached the fire without any certainty that I could walk on the live coals and not burn myself. The first woman to walk on the live coals had her young infant snuggly wrapped against her chest. I almost reached out to grab the baby before I realized that she fully intended to have her child accompany her across the coals! When our time was almost over, I decided to walk on the fire—even if it meant getting burnt—because I couldn't stand to miss the opportunity. The coals felt warm and crunchy, and I was disoriented afterward and not that impressed. I felt I had somehow not really done it, even though I had done it. (Peggy says some people later rationalize that the coals "weren't really hot enough.")

When I walked on the fire the second time, at a later gathering in California, I had a completely different experience. The change came about during Peggy's presentation, when she spoke about the *Kung!* Bushpeople. She said that they say you can walk on the fire without getting burned when your *num* has come up to the level of the fire. Suddenly, I understood that being an active healer always puts my *num* close to the level of the fire (witness the intense healing heat I generate during hands-on healing in my healing circles), and I knew *intellectually* that I could walk on the fire. My beliefs changed in that moment. The knowing made me ecstatic and eager to do it, whereas before I was frightened and unsure of myself. I didn't walk on the fire that night, I danced over it! It is such a relief when we let go of the false limitations imposed by our culture.

What do oracles, moving stones, and firewalking have to do with the body? Until we acknowledge and fully reinhabit the body—physically and energetically—we will not be able to understand or replicate skills of the early cultures. There is an ability that contemporary psychics have isolated and named clairsentience. It is contrasted with clairvoyance, which more people have heard of, which refers to seeing psychically. Clairsentience is knowing with the body. It tends to be more of a feeling than a visual image. When we say *I know that's right* or register impressions in the body that seem to have meaning, we are using clairsentience. Guatemalan shamans doing hands-on healing say that "the blood speaks."[13] They receive their healing information through currents of energy passing through their veins (or channels), which they have organized into a meaningful and coherent system of understanding that is passed along in a teaching tradition. (Their healing tradition is totally connected with their sacred, divinatory calendar that relates to pregnancy, and it is the same shamans who keep this calendar for the community.) Certainly contemporary bodyworkers have experiences like this all the time. My main information while healing comes through my body. Sometimes I have so much physical phenomena going on during a healing session it can be distracting. I have learned over the years to listen to these messages and observe when the body is quiet and when it is making these internal movements or sounds. I have always heard a kind of electrical "clicking" inside my head as the energy registers through my hands while I'm doing hands-on healing.

When my psychic-shamanic process of healing began, like shamans around the world, I experienced amazing, intense phenomena for which I had no rational explanations. My dreams were incredible and I wrote them all down, so later when something would happen that had been predicted in a dream, I was able to go back and find the evidence of my own precognitive abilities. At Hallomas (October 31) in 1977 I had what I understood to be a Big Dream, shamanically speaking. I dreamed that my partner, my daughters, and I were living too close to a live volcano, and it was going to erupt. When I awoke from this dream, I assumed, as I was learning to do with dreamwork, that the volcano represented deep, moving forces within myself that were opening and erupting into the outer world. And, of course, that was true. But the next spring, in the midst of doing intense yoga practice every day and delving into esoteric studies, I became ill with a large boil on my back. Again, as one does with alternative medicine, I stayed open to the messages from my back, learning through my dreams that week that my body was throwing off toxins from when I was four years old and was bitten by a dog. My parents had taken me (kicking and screaming) to the doctor for rabies shots in my back every day for ten days. I thought that my yoga practice must have stimulated a purification process, releasing the old toxins from the vaccine, through the boil. On the sixth day of my very large, very painful boil, my partner Karen was putting hot packs on my back, and I told her that the boil felt like a volcano needing to erupt. The next day, Mount St. Helens did erupt, and so did my boil!

In that moment things clarified for me: *The earth is alive. She and I are the same.* My body is not separate or different from hers. I think of this scar on my back as the credentials of my shamanic vocation. I show it to my students in my classes in shamanism. I read, study, and learn from many sources, synthesizing from shamanic and tribal cultures all over the world, and I teach what I know from my own bodily processes. I know that when *kundalini* moves in me, she is sacred and not dangerous; she is alive, and so am I. My sexuality, my healing prowess, and my abundant energies are all part of the same gift of the Goddess in my sacred body. The body is more than a sensual receptor, more than a physical vehicle, it is an instrument of superconscious awareness with a direct line to the soul. Awake, the body knows, understands, and reveals the Mystery to us and through us. The body is the vehicle for staying on the path of shamanic awareness and for communicating with the unknown, the unseen, and the intuitive forces on this planet. In the most ancient times, it was the female body that mediated between the earth and sky, the rational and nonrational worlds of information, through the use of menstrual calendars and the complex systems of astronomical observation that led to the development of Stonehenge and other megalithic structures.

The ancient "crude" carved images of Mother Goddess hold all of this within their bodily shape. Scholars theorize about the lack of precise facial characteristics on the Venus of Willendorf (fig. 16) and other figures like her, concluding that people had not yet "individuated" in those times and so they chose not to show personality characteristics in the carving. Instead they focused on the sexual zones — breasts, buttocks, and divine pubic triangle. Hands, feet, and faces were minimally expressed. Why? Because the figures are images of the earth as fertile Mother, Creatrix, and miraculous physical body (see fig. 17). In her image we are all created, these small figures seem to say. Early people didn't

▲ *Fig. 16    Venus of Willendorf, the most famous statue from Paleolithic Europe. This small Goddess (eight inches high) must have been made to hold in the hand or stand in sand on a cave altar. Her feature-less face links her to the ancient matrix figure described by Alexander Marshack, the eternal Mother Goddess at the center of the "storied tradition" passed on through the shamanic rituals of Cro-Magnon people. Her fertile belly and breasts indi-cate the mysteries of pregnancy and nurs-ing and undoubtedly symbolize as well the earth itself as an all-providing mother. Drawing by Laurelin Remington-Wolf.*

concentrate on fertility, because life was hard and they were starving. They worshiped the earth and noticed that like the earth, with her mountains and valleys, we in our strange, symbolically marked physical bodies can feel and respond to the messages of the cosmic forces, appreciating with our eyes closed, without thinking, beyond the limited rational mode within which we have imprisoned ourselves in modern times. Because we are a part of everything, we can experience everything at once. We need no special apparatus or technol-ogy—it's all here, right now, in the flesh. The past, present, and future coexist within us, and we can know them and attune to them through the body.

Equated and identified with the body, women are specially blessed in shamanic work. In and through our sacred physical vehicles we experience the most dramatic intensities, spiritual and material at once. Through the act of giving birth, we open physically and psychically more than it would seem possible. The heights of pleasure and depths of pain are there for us, often occurring in the same moment. During our menstruation we have a wide range of paranor-mal abilities and experiences available to us. These biological capabilities are natural, normal, and completely within the sphere of everyday activity for women. Our sexuality is graced with a multiorgasmic capability, which makes fulfill-ment simply a doorway through which to pass into more ful-fillment. This highly active sexual function is not linked directly to procreation and estrus, as it is in the animal world,

▲ *Fig. 17  Vessel in the shape of a nursing mother holding her nipples not only to her baby but seemingly to the world as a whole. This Peruvian Venus is Pacha Mama, the Earth Mother who represents the nourishing female planet providing life and sustenance for her children. Vessels in the shape of the female, frequently with breasts, are found all over the world from the most ancient times. Drawing by Laurelin Remington-Wolf.*

but is actually a sacred, magical world unto itself with extraordinary healing capacities known by all the ancient yogic and shamanic traditions to bring health and longevity.

Eve's knowledge in the Garden of Eden was body based. The snake who spoke to her was the ancient wisdom-totem of women all over the world, whispering the mysteries to us through our instinctual, psychosexual bodies. A Mexican scholar has shown that the rattlesnake, whom he refers to as *she* and which dominates ancient Mayan architecture, represents the calendar and the cosmos; its rattle is a glyph for the Pleiades, known to the Greeks as the Seven Sisters. Our expulsion from the Garden by the jealous Jehovah is no more than a victor's story of a particular patriarchal takeover and the exile and repression of the ancient shamanic religion of the Great Goddess in Western culture. Our return to the Garden is a matter of willingness and availability to the snake wisdom coming through our bodies once more. Can we stand to hear the oracle? To see behind the illusions? To respond to Nature's imperative? If we don't listen now with our bodies, we won't be able to save our bodies from death and extinction. The earth is crying out against the assault on her, and we women are being asked to give voice to that pain and expression to that healing release.

When I put my hands on a client for healing, I feel as if my hands have eyes and a will of their own. The hands want healing, and the body knows what is needed. The healer's hands catalyze and awaken the body of the sick person, so that her inner healing mechanism can begin functioning naturally. The movements are instinctual — how much pressure, where to touch — the hands are guided by a nonrational force that comes through the body and aims to heal. Together we join — healer and patient — and healing takes place through our union, through our unified willingness to be changed and transformed. Sometimes images and memories emerge from within the sick person's body, sometimes sound and crying have to happen. Sometimes the person goes into deep trance under the influence of the healing hands, and in that state she can access information and guidance that are wholistic. Sometimes she is flooded with pulsating energy. The body as a vessel for transformation is absolutely uncanny. Anything is possible, with the right circumstances and the sacred will-to-live. The fire that ignites through bodywork or hands-on healing raises the temperature, gets the juices moving, and gives the cells a message of hope and optimism. That may not sound like enough in an age where we have come to rely on heavy chemicals and surgical procedures, but even science now tells us that a raised body temperature can heal cancer, and that the T cells of the immune system respond to emotional states.[14] When the body opens to healing, the mind can follow. The patterns that block healing can begin to break apart and disintegrate, leaving a free space that includes belief in everyday miracles.

# Synchronicity: The Oracular Path

ABOUT TWELVE YEARS AGO, IN THE middle of my very intense three-year shamanic healing crisis, I walked one afternoon to the produce market near my home and selected some vegetables for dinner. As the woman behind the counter was packing my groceries, I wrote out my check without thinking, complete with the amount and my signature. This would be a normal enough activity, except that she hadn't yet rung up my bill. When she tabulated the amount on the cash register—and by now we were both laughing nervously, wondering what would happen—it came out one cent different from the amount I had written on my check. She said she would pay the difference. It was one of those absolutely extraordinary experiences that seem to be unrepeatable. I wouldn't know where to begin. I didn't even understand how it was possible, let alone how I did it. I am notorious for not even looking at the prices on food when I'm shopping. Even my unconscious mind couldn't have added it up! It was simply a miracle, without any particular importance to the world, and it woke me up that day. Although I still live, like everyone else, in the so-called mundane world, I always know that there is more here than meets the eye. I have come to appreciate the little miracles of "synchronicity," or "meaningful coincidences" between the inner and outer worlds. They are the pathmarkers for the female shaman— subtle signs we can count on to show us the way.

A woman shaman has to learn to trust her instincts and intuition. This is not foreign to a tribal woman:

She is raised in nature, with a body-based experience of existence that includes farming, seasonal changes, natural birthing and child rearing, music, festivals, and a shared sense of the sacred. A North American white woman somehow—in the midst of a culture that denies her perceptions of reality—has to come to believe in what she sees and knows as fact. How is she to do this? The earth is alive and the helping spirits are active, the elemental forces are there all the time, ready to mix and blend with our activities. The average person has tuned them out through a cultural reliance on a mechanistic science and worldview that doubts their existence. When a modern woman tunes into their presence, even as a mere possibility, they suddenly become visible in ways that cannot be denied, as if her eyes had a new ability to see.

One of my students recently shared a dream with me that clearly demonstrates this phenomenon. In the dream she is at a reunion at a beach, and there is a great fanfare celebrating a new postage stamp picturing two men on the right, whom she thinks are Bush and Quayle.

> But those who have shamanic powers are able to see another layer on the stamp, something embedded in the pattern in the ink. It appears to be bushes or foliage to most others. I am amazed when I look at it, it is [one of the women in the circle who is her lover] and other women dancing and laughing and waving. This section of the stamp appears alive, three dimensional and moving. In fact it appears to interact with me as I view it, they shout my name, recognize me and wave back from this "other" scene.
>
> I find those people at the reunion who see this "other" scene, using the stamp quite casually as a screening device, and know that I am supposed to meet with them. To the left of these women on the stamp there is another level, but I do not see it, only a dark shadowy area. I just know that it is there. I wonder what the next level might be and feel committed to going there.[1]

This woman's dream creatively expresses the magical ways in which we meet and "see" each other, and the ways our networks work on the mundane levels by our being attuned to the invisible world of causes next to and behind the "real world." The president and vice-president "on the right" may be more visible to most people in the world, but the hidden reality of women "on the left" celebrating the life force is strong and growing. The Findhorn people in Scotland talked about there being lights all over the planet—points of light held by various persons and groups — linking together in common purpose the great work of "reunion." It's a commonplace among witches and practitioners of magic that those who do not have the "sight" cannot recognize those who do, and that those who have the sight always know each other. We link with one another not only across physical space but also through time. Sometimes our meetings are shocking due to the feeling of familiarity that surrounds them, as if we have only been separated for a few minutes rather than lifetimes.

When a woman opens into shamanic healing, she experiences (classically) a crisis of her identity and perhaps a near-death experience involving her physical health. This is true around the world, but when it happens to a modern Western woman, the crisis is perceived differently due to the absence of a cultural base of support and recognition. The checkout woman at the produce market and I didn't have a paradigm for understanding and validating my knowing the cost of the food ahead of time. It hung in the space between us like some strange anomaly. Who ever heard of such a thing happening in ordinary, daily life? And if I have that capability (if we all do), then why haven't I been able to repeat the achievement in later encounters at the grocery store? Why can't I always call up my psychic powers when I need them, when they are so serendipitously available? What difference does it make that I said the right amount at the cash register that day? And who cares that later in my "progress" I was consistently able to score a perfect parking place whenever I needed one? I used to marvel at this ability, thinking that if I could do that so easily, why couldn't I manifest my larger, more complicated dreams with the same extraordinary success?

Native American mythology emphasizes the "trickster" nature of the universal forces. The concept of the Coyote, who appears when least expected and causes trouble more often than not, is similar to the Tibetan dakini. Dakinis and coyotes are those people or situations that temporarily embody the purposefully chaotic elements in our environment and give them form. They appear in those events that throw us off track, derail us from our goals, and make us feel out of control or fooled in some way, waking us up to the fact that there is a larger movement of which we are only a part. Knowing that there is something greater than ourselves at work in the world is a humbling experience. Sometimes the trickster provides experiences that make us feel momentarily powerful (like my cash-register event) and then follows it with a humiliating experience of helplessness or vulnerability. "I did this amazing thing, but I can't seem to do it again. So did I actually do it? Or did someone or something do it through me? What's going on here, anyway?" Dakinis and coyotes are known for messing with us through other people, especially those people with whom we "fall in love." We open ourselves to all that we imagine is available in the magical contact with this other person, and then the trickster steps in and pulls the rug out from under our feet. Trickster events serve to keep the ego from rigidifying.

A rigid ego is antagonistic to the impermanence in the universe. The more crystallized the identity structure, the more a person has to lose if there is change. Western science has built structures that are rigid and hostile to the natural fluidity of Nature. As people conditioned in Western educational structures, North Americans share a learned belief system that things in the physical world are concrete and stable. We think our bodies are solid and that a chair or table is inert or dead. This is the core of materialism, and it is our fundamental religion in the United States. We have been taught that it is demonic to see and hear spirits and that if we do, we are hallucinating and must be drugged or locked up until the problem goes away (is "cured"). We are literally the only culture in the world that refuses to acknowledge the presence of the "Little People," in the form of fairies, Nature spirits, plant devas, power animals, elves, or what have you. Even in Russia, where there is supposedly no religion, people still have a folk mythology that recognizes and takes account of these creatures who exist side by side with us. Something about the orphaned nature of our transplanted and quite young culture in the United States makes us rely on an absolutely mechanistic view of the universe, a legacy of the Europeans from whom we descended. Any philosophy or experience that lets in other information is terribly threatening to the American mind.

For example, since World War II the petrochemical industry has created incredibly dangerous and lethal chemicals to sell to farmers for putting on their soil and their crops in order to keep the pests away and to fertilize the ground. (These are the same substances used by the Nazis to fuel gas chambers in the holocaust!)[2] It is becoming very clear that

▲ *Fig. 18   Motherpeace High Priestess in line-drawing form by Karen Vogel, for ©Motherpeace. The High Priestess traditionally represents a doorway into the sacred realms, a psychic opening to the other world. She might be a Tantric priestess of sexual rites, a visionary or mantic one who provides prophecies and oracles, or a sacred woman in any role of direct contact with the divine.*

this form of agriculture is not working, since everything is dying—the soil, the seeds, the trees, the animals, and the people—everything except the hardiest of the noxious pests. So around the world a movement has been growing in response to this farming crisis. The movement in general is organic farming, but a specific and very interesting branch of it is the biodynamic farming method of Rudolf Steiner. The Steiner methods are bizarre to most Western people, using "channeled" information to prepare fertilizers and "homeopathic" crop enhancers used to regenerate and heal the soil. The methods work so well that straight farmers all over the world are being persuaded to use them, including formulas created from cow manure spooned lovingly into cow horns which are left underground all winter, removed and mixed with water, shaken in a certain prescribed way, and then spread in minute doses over the fields. (It doesn't work if you put the manure in anything other than cow horns. In the cow horn the manure turns into perfect, fresh humus. I can't help but think of Isis/Hathor and her cow-horn headdress in Egypt, where women practiced early agriculture. See fig. 18). In Australia and Europe, especially, more and more farmers are switching to the Steiner way of tilling the soil, *because it works.* The benefits outweigh whatever problems have to be reconciled in relation to the odd methods.

But in North America, according to the authors of *Secrets of the Soil,* farmers are more reluctant to take up these

**63**

strange methods, because they smack of "witchcraft." Even though a farmer in Minnesota sees and hears other farmers saying that these methods work better than the chemical methods that are slowly causing him to go broke, that farmer has great difficulty making the changeover for fear of the "demonic." The results of these unusual approaches are, in fact, absolutely amazing, just as that farmer fears. It is part of the American tragedy that he cannot allow for an intervention into the process that cannot be explained in hyperrational terms.[3] For Americans to let in the living play of the spirits, we are going to have to stretch our identities quite a lot more than those people living in other countries. This American phobia toward the supernatural, which permeates our culture on every level, makes the study and practice of female shamanism that much more complex and difficult, since women are traditionally understood as already closer to these taboo areas of spirits and magic. The public media has had a heyday with movies and television horror shows, depicting weird, grotesque, violent, and aberrant behaviors connected with anything outside of "normal" Christianity. And "Satanic cults" have actually come into existence like a wish fulfillment, a creation of this same fundamentalist focus, having nothing whatever to do with the Goddess or "witches" and yet being utterly connected to both in the highly manipulated public mind. Still, I remember in my own Protestant household, in the middle of Iowa where I grew up forty-three years ago, my mother taught me how to wish on white horses and the first star at night, to save teeth for the tooth fairy, to believe in Santa Claus, and so on. These mythological teachings had a lot more authenticity for me than whatever they were attempting to teach me in my Presbyterian Sunday school, although I must have been originally open to both.

So the question arises, Are women actually more instinctual than men? Is our relationship to the spirit world biological or hormonal somehow? Is "female intuition" really stronger by nature? Are we "closer to the earth"? I think so. I'm not frightened of what some feminists have feared would be the results of such biological determinism. Given the state of the earth at this moment, we had better hope that someone on the planet is connected to the earth, and it is women whose bodies are the vessels for future generations. When I look around the planet, I see war and carnage everywhere, most often supported and sponsored by the United States. In Latin

American countries, in Africa, in India, in the Middle East, people of different religious preferences and different political systems are being assisted by us to kill and maim each other's children daily for the sake of an abstract desire to have their own way. In all of these countries, it is women who are beginning to reach across national boundaries and religious differences to join hands and demand peace. The Australian pediatrician Helen Caldicott, who started Physicians for Social Responsibility, has given eloquent voice to this "simple" female concern for children and future generations. What we need in the United States is to do the work of making ourselves more open and available to this natural, instinctual ability of women the world over.

Female shamanic practices are those methods and techniques that awaken our natural instincts and impulses and then ground us in our bodies so that we can act from within. All shamans, everywhere in the world, rely on guidance from the spirit realms. They have acknowledged guardians and helpers in the invisible world, without whom they could not cure, teach, or lead their people. Most shamans carry on a fairly continuous dialogue with the invisible world, getting their information and processing it, then making their choices and determinations from that information. Shamans are grounded. They are not spacey or abstract in their approaches, but down to earth and concrete. They seem different from "normal" people because they have sight that normal people do not have. They are able to see into the causes behind the symptoms of illness, for instance, and then work to change the causes rather than simply dealing with the external manifestation. In all cultures that practice shamanism, the path is a long one, involving years of study, practice, and a gradual self-mastery that allows the person to be fully present in emergencies and dangerous situations requiring a calm, effective response.

For Western women shamans, the process may take even longer, since we not only have to learn our trade but have to begin by changing our minds in such a way that we allow in the possibilities of doing the work. We have to empty ourselves, as we can, of the cultural conditioning that serves as a major obstruction in the work. We have to "open the third eye," as yoga states it, in order to awaken the dormant psychic vision, and then we have to train ourselves to believe in what we are perceiving, since our culture does not recognize it as true and will lock us up if we're not careful. We have to study the shamanic beliefs and practices of other cultures in order to understand our own experiences on the shamanic path, since our own culture doesn't provide literature or tradition as a foundation for this learning. Then we have to translate those different approaches into twentieth-century Western women's reality in order to integrate what we are learning and experiencing into our own daily lives. In addition to all this preparatory work, we also have to do the practices that lead to self-mastery and accomplishment in the invisible realms. We need time to do this work and patience to uncover what is waiting for us deep within. It would be nice if each of us had a teacher to guide us personally on the path, but this is extremely unusual. More realistically, each of us has somehow to ground herself in her own dreamwork and psychic visions, to pray for help from the divine and spirit realms, and has to figure things out as best she can while she matures gradually on her path.

The work for a contemporary female shaman is to stop behaving in conditioned, habitual, unhealthy ways and begin to act from within. But as she eliminates the cultural factors that have distorted and programmed her reality, a woman is confronted with the open feeling of more space. This shift from density to lightness can be very frightening and can actually seem "ungrounding." A woman can begin to feel "out of her body" or "floaty" and insubstantial. She may begin to fear for her mind, clamping down on herself in an effort to control things, which creates added tension and pain in the body. The need here is for work that is grounding, to help this woman embody the energies that are awakening in her being, and also for a shift in attitude that makes it all right to feel these new feelings. In other words, we need to accept the inevitable changes within our perceptual and energetic fields. It is not necessary to maintain one's sense of "normal" while transforming. The ego can get very threatened by the new feelings and experiences, the new sensations and awarenesses happening within the body. Just as the ego needs cleansing and deprogramming from its old beliefs and structures, so too it needs a certain amount of reassurance along the way that what is happening is OK.

At some point in the shamanic process, the *kundalini* energy really escalates. The influx of energy into the system can be experienced as buoyancy, jubilance, rushes, ecstasy, euphoria, or overwhelming fear. Imagine that all the weight of the cultural conditioning has been sitting, like a dense cement block, on top of the coiled (latent) kundalini power. There was simply no way for that energy to free itself before now, so it has probably never been felt. When it awakens and moves in the body, it is (as the Tantrikas describe) very much like a giant cobra stirring and rising or like a bolt of lightning striking. The whole organism becomes electrified. I stopped sleeping for a period of weeks, during which time I alternately worried for my health (because it's not good to lose sleep, right?) and enjoyed the vivid dreams I was having in the weird trance state in which I found myself suspended instead of sleep. My experience is not at all unusual and has been reported by many others. The best thing to do, under these very interesting circumstances, is to give the energy a channel for expression. I instantly had healing energy to spare, and I happily put my hands on everyone I knew. I stayed up late, read books, and began to draw pictures. I did hours of yoga every day, including standing on my head for ten minutes, and practiced elaborate dreamwork. Sometimes writing my dreams took the better part of a night. I just dreamed and wrote all night. I had to keep reminding myself that I wasn't crazy to be having an experience like this, so I read esoteric texts that gave my precise experiences names and codified them into systems of thought and practice.

The experience of increased, high-voltage energy doesn't last forever. It eventually stabilizes, as do the emotions that have been aroused in response to it. The ongoing work for a female shaman is to stabilize both the energy and the emotions and to continue to grow and transform the personality without losing equilibrium. This may require a meditation practice, in which the person learns to watch the mental activity without attaching to it (without needing to act on everything); or perhaps physical (hatha) yoga will be helpful in grounding and housing the energies, stimulating the glands to function properly, and creating a trance or bliss state for the practitioner to begin altering her consciousness at will. Acupuncture might help to bring the seemingly wild energies into balance, and taking up a martial art form can be a wonderful means of grounding and channeling the lightning. The important thing, to my mind, is to keep a sense of excitement and joy about the process, to affirm the actual sensations of life-force and passion that are flooding through the body.

▲ *Fig. 19   This figure from a temple in India shows a snake manifesting from the vulva, a powerful and graphic symbol of awakened, active kundalini in a woman's life. Often perceived as phallic by Western interpreters, this image is understood in India as simply showing the natural, biological power of every woman — her "shakti." The snake from ancient times has been associated with women and healing, regenerative power. A snake shedding its skin is the perfect symbolic image of a woman bleeding each month. The snake sheds because it has grown too large, the woman because no baby will grow in her womb this month. The snake is often venomous to show the dark aspect of menstruation and to acknowledge death. Reprinted with permission of Thames & Hudson from* Tantra *by Phillip Rawson.*

Look at ancient figures of sacred women, with their wild eyes, dancing movements, yogic postures (see fig. 19). Make love, alone or with a partner. Lie down on the earth and allow excess energy to flow out of the body and into the ground. Ask the earth for healing and support, protection and helpful contact. Trust the basic goodness of the process, the positive direction of the high-voltage healing energies. If at all possible under such uncontrolled circumstances, enjoy it! If we weren't so afraid of something so foreign to our previous experiences, we would think it was ecstasy and we would cultivate it.

The experience of these electrical, high-powered energies wouldn't be so foreign to us if more of us gave birth in natural ways. The kundalini is a biological energy residing in the body, waiting to be needed. The birth process is the quintessential, natural time for it to release into a woman's system for her own use. Birth in other cultures is Initiation (see fig. 20). This is not only because it marks what anthropologists have called a rite of passage in the life phases but because it naturally stimulates and awakens the sleeping snake power. Birthing is a woman's organic opportunity to become empowered through a challenging, physical encounter with the forces of life and death. A birthing woman actually stands on the edge of life and death, at the doorway between them, and (in service to the race) brings a new soul from there to here. What could be more shamanic than this

▲ *Fig. 20*
*These figures of*
*squatting, birth-*
*ing women are*
*taken from rock*
*art in Africa.*
*Drawings by*
*Jennifer*
*Roberts.*

(see fig. 21)? No wonder Native people say that warriors who dance the Sun Dance do so in order to match the experience, and call up the courage, of a woman in labor. But since less than 1 percent of us give birth at home these days, this particular form of Initiation has become a part of our past. Artist Judy Chicago, originator of the *Birth Project,* points out that there had been no images in Western art of women giving birth for two thousand years![4] Another feminist artist, Monica Sjöö, was taken to court for "obscenity and blasphemy" when she exhibited her painting *God Giving Birth* (fig. 22) in England in the 1970s. The painting was based on her experience of natural childbirth with her second son born at home in 1961 in Bristol, which she says opened her up to the Great Mother, having "truly experienced how the Birthing Woman is the original Shaman."[5] And now Western medical methods (in which the woman is passive and the doctor "delivers" her) are being used all over the world, in tribal cultures as well as cities. Even the instinct of nursing is being deliberately eradicated all over the world, thanks to Nestle and the other makers of infant formula.[6]

It should be clear by now that the work of female shamanism, even in contemporary Western culture, takes an enormous amount of courage, commitment, and stamina. A shaman is tested all along the way and offered continual challenges to the body, mind, and spirit. A person takes up this vocation not because it looks glamorous or exciting but because she feels an irresistible call to it, and she has to maintain a kind of fierce loyalty to the imperative of the path in spite of her discomfort, doubt, or fear. All the practices outlined in this book function as stimulants for the process itself as well as grounding mechanisms for dealing with the energy aroused by the work. *The process the potential shaman is opening into is one of dying.* She will never be the same person she was

▲ *Fig. 21*   **The Crowning** *by Judy Chicago, one of many amazing images of women giving birth from the* Birth Project. *The shamanic power of the awakened and active kundalini are obvious here, as is the ecstasy that frequently accompanies such a wide-open psychic state. A woman giving birth in natural circumstances (less than 1 percent of us give birth at home anymore) experiences such a powerful state, but she is not allowed to have such a dramatic experience in the hospital. It is apparently too uncomfortable for her attendants, who would prefer that she behave in a more ladylike way. Reprinted with permission from Judy Chicago.*

before she began. She is on a path that requires her death, the end of her identity as she has known it. Yet for women this ego-death is a peculiar process, because the ego she is shedding was almost certainly false to begin with. It could be argued, of course, that all ego is false (phenomenal) and is the same for men and women. But I am speaking of the ego here as an expression of the soul in the world, a creative vehicle for the inner self to inhabit while in a body.

As Sylvia Perera described so clearly in *Descent to the Goddess: A Way of Initiation for Women*, women have developed an "animus ego" rather than an ego that expresses our inner nature. Although shedding is difficult for all of us, for a woman to shed what has falsely hidden her more authentic experience is a great liberation. The freedom felt after the loss of persona is spiritually nourishing, and the creativity released from within can be enormous, allowing her to re-

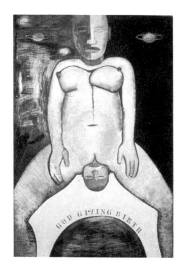

▲ *Fig. 22* God Giving Birth *from Swedish-born Monica Sjöö, who now lives in England. Sjöö created this image after giving birth to her son at home in the late sixties, and it caused a furor in England, where it was considered blasphemous and obscene. All of Sjöö's paintings are Goddess oriented and female expressive, linking contemporary women to our ancient counterparts.*

create herself in a more "true" form (see fig. 23). This is the process I am calling female shamanism—an ongoing shedding of false selves in favor of the active development of more authentic forms of expression. The snake is the ancient totem of women all over the world and speaks to the lunar nature of feminine biological evolution. A woman's natural timing is cyclical, circular, spiral, nonlinear, and nonrational. Women need to replace their crystallized identities, as these shatter or dissolve through the shamanic process, with a deliberately fluid ego-identity. If a woman can begin to appreciate and cultivate the value of an identity that is always changing, continually in flux, never completely solid, she begins to align with what shamans and Buddhists describe as "reality." Those with the sight to see into the world of energy, see that everything is made of energy, and energy is always in motion. The rest of the work is practicing to become able to accept and tolerate this vision of reality, which is in conflict with the one we were originally taught to believe.

The fundamental method of movement on the path of the contemporary female shaman is what I am choosing to call synchronicity, which Jung defined as the law of "meaningful coincidences." Walking the shaman's path is like having an ongoing dialogue with Nature or with the invisible world or with the Goddess, in which you are asking a question, receiving information, processing that information, and asking the next question. These questions and answers are like steps on the path of shamanic healing. In other times and

71

▲ *Fig. 23   Death and World cards by Karen Vogel and
Vicki Noble for ©Motherpeace. The Death card traditionally represents transformation in the shape of a
snake shedding its skin and the autumn leaves falling
from the tree. The rebirth is inherent in the knowledge
that spring will come again, just as the soul will be born
into another body. The World shows a completion of
hard work and the culmination or fulfillment one has
waited for, representing liberation from bondage or
obstacles. It shows a breakthrough for the entire
organism.*

other cultures, this method has been known as divination,
meaning to "divine" the answers to your soul's questions
through direct contact with the unseen. In our time divination
is mostly unknown, except for a few who experimentally
throw the tarot or *I Ching* or read tea leaves or palms, mostly
for the purpose of foretelling the future. All of these, including *Motherpeace Tarot,*[7] are codified oracular systems, but anything in life can be an oracle. Oracles are subtle messages
from the universe around us that teach and guide us on our
paths. We needn't have a rational system of interpretation for
understanding the messages.

There is a web that connects each of us with everything that is. It is this web that makes it possible to stay in
touch with what Arnold Mindell has named the Dreambody
and what Peter Redgrove has called the unseen Real.[8] The
ancients honored the web over everything, worshiping the
Moon Goddess as weaver of destiny: a giant spider sitting at
the center of the universe, creating the universe from her center. From her belly she spins something from nothing, everything from the empty space within (see fig. 24). In the same
way that a spider's web is infinitely sensitive to vibration, and
the smallest movement is felt reverberating over the entire

▲ *Fig. 24   This spindle weight engraved with a spider was found in the Mounds of Iowa, the author's childhood home. Spiders are frequently connected to women and our crafts because the female spider spins something from nothing right out of her own body. The spider is a form of Shakti as female Creatrix spinning universes out of herself and, in her form as Kali, taking them back again at the end of time. Drawing by Laurelin Remington-Wolf.*

web, so are all actions and reactions felt by everyone contained in the web of life. There is nothing that happens anywhere on the planet (or in the galaxy, for that matter) that does not affect each one of us and that we do not feel on some level of our being. Nothing we do is without consequence in the larger scheme of things. Each of our lives matters; at the same time, each of us is no more than a tiny speck of light in the greater whole that contains us. We simply need to become sensitive to the movements of the web in our own lives.

A woman shaman, like a spider spinning, must learn to lead from the womb. To move our attention from the head to the belly, from the mind to the body, a woman must learn to read the signals and learn to trust them. Otherwise she'll never be sure of the difference between her intuition and those little fearful voices in her head that tell her to be cautious, careful, stop, don't, and so on. Something needs to validate the intuitive movements all along the way; something needs to function as teacher or guide. That something is synchronicity as an active way of life, a path of steady observation and response to the little messages that come from the environment every day: sensations in the body, encounters and events that happen in the outer world, the way things line up in linear time, all the little miracles. A woman might use the systematic oracles like tarot as helpers in the process of becoming so centered in her own space and grounded in her body that eventually she has no more need of the outer oracles most of the time. I used the tarot for years to clarify and validate my growing intuition, so that I could more confidently act on this awareness. I would have an impulse, then check it out by drawing a tarot card from the deck, which would either agree or disagree with my initial impulse. Now I know what my intuition and instincts feel like when they're working — I can literally feel it physically in my belly. I make decisions when I can feel that feeling. When I can't feel it, I wait.

There is a deep, underlying psychic structure that the ancient people knew about and worked with in their daily lives and which we moderns have forgotten. What geomancers have called dragon lines and what the English dowsers call ley lines are part of a grid system that surrounds our planet, crisscrossing lines along which energy and force pass in regular paths that can be felt and, to some extent, harnessed by people.[9] Ancient megalithic builders (like those who built Stonehenge) knew about this grid and built structures on important points of power or current; in the Americas the people built mounds on these places and eventually (like the Mayans) erected temples on top of the mounds. In relation to these points on the planet that received and transmitted powerful forces, the ancients also used knowledge of this grid system for observing their seasonal festivals at certain precise times delineated by the movements of planets and stars in relation to the earth. The Eight Sabbaths of contemporary witches and pagans are a remnant of these important power points observed during the course of a year, and there is evidence to support the belief that the earliest of builders on this planet observed these particular points on the calendar.

These sacred holidays are universal in their meaning and in the kinds of activities that people recognize as belonging to them. They date from the most ancient times and recur throughout history in many lands; they even show up in our own secular calendar today. The solstices and equinoxes are known in our culture as the beginning of the seasons and as such appear on our calendars as the first days of winter, spring, summer, and fall. If a person looks more closely, the derivation of the two major Christian holidays becomes apparent in that Winter Solstice became Christmas in the Julian calendar, as Spring Equinox became Easter. But the four essential sacred days that fall in between the solstices and equinoxes, called cross-quarter days, go relatively unnoticed in Western culture, usually having become "children's holidays" such as May Basket Day and Halloween. Yet these cross-quarter days hold the most power astronomically and

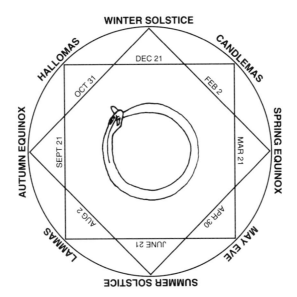

▲ *Fig. 25   This wheel of sacred holidays observed by witches and sacred tribal people all over the planet shows a snake biting its own tail. This symbol links the seasonal cycle to regeneration and rebirth, showing how the Goddess contains us within the cyclic passing of time marked by these eight special power points during each year. Celtic peoples celebrated these holidays with bonfires right up until the most recent times. In Switzerland the national independence day falls on August 1 and is celebrated with bonfires. There remain many unbroken remnants of these ancient practices of our ancestors, who worshiped these cycles with reverence and devotion. Even the groundhog looking for his shadow on February 1 is a reminder of the oracular powers available at that time and of the prophecies that were once made in the name of Brigit.*

are celebrated by other cultures around the world as sacred days belonging to the Goddess (the deep Feminine) (see fig. 25).

Perhaps my own introduction to the sacred holidays best illustrates the way in which these seasonal holidays hold us in a deep, sacred structure that actively exists in our lives whether we believe in them or not. I moved to Berkeley in 1976 with my partner Karen Vogel and my two daughters. By 1977 Karen and I were engrossed in deep research, attempting to learn everything we could about the ancient cultures of the Goddess. We delved into ancient art books, history and classics, archaeology and anthropology, trying to understand what had happened to women's power. Where did it go? And why? By 1978 we were involved in psychic healing classes and had taught ourselves yoga; I eventually taught something I called lunar yoga in Berkeley. I was healing my eyesight, writing and reading everything I could find about magic and esoterica, practicing yoga every day, and writing a novel with Karen. In early 1978 something happened to me that I understood afterward as a kundalini experience, because I found a book that described similar kinds of states. I was awake in the middle of the night for some unknown reason, hanging in a light trance state in my bed and feeling what I thought was sexual energy, when suddenly I simply flew out of the top of my head and dissolved into the black space of the night sky. Inside my head was ringing the message "I am one with all witches through all time."

This experience was extremely profound and sacred for me, and I got out of bed afterward to write about it in my journal. As a result of the experience, I totally accepted and understood the concept of reincarnation, without having to be taught. Several months later, while sitting in our room reading a book, with Karen next to me, I was leafing through Anne Kent Rush's new book *Moon Moon*.[10] In it was a simple version of the sacred calendar, done by Hallie Iglehart Austen, explaining in one or two sentences the meaning of each of the eight days of the seasonal cycle. Candlemas, she said, on February 1, was Witches' Initiation. The hairs stood up on the nape of my neck, I jumped up and ran to get my journal so I could look up the date of my kundalini experience. Sure enough, it had been the eve of Candlemas, when the Goddess Brigit (I learned much later) is said to pass and touch her devotees with healing power. I was stunned. My mind blew open and I felt pressure on my head, and an unmistakable presence in the room. Then Karen said she felt the room tilt.

At this point the walls began to undulate, and I had the shamanic vision of my life. In a period of perhaps twenty minutes, I was reinitiated into the ancient religion of the Goddess and released into my destiny in this lifetime. We had a beautiful blue tie-dyed wall hanging from Africa on the wall in the bedroom, and the center of the spiral design opened up and became a blank screen that vivid images projected onto as if someone were running a slide show. I saw three images of the Goddess—as amazon, full moon, and crone. I was shown her animals—bulls, griffins, lions, spiders—and the planets moving in their orbits around the sun, the Milky Way, everything turning, spinning, moving. All the while the tears were pouring down my face and I was transfixed, in a state of religious ecstasy, almost holding my breath for fear of losing such a precious experience. A tunnel appeared, beckoning me, and I felt afraid. A stone with letters appeared in a language I had never seen before; I was terribly afraid I was being shown something important and wouldn't be able to read it. The letters disintegrated and reformed in English: *Helena, Hell No, Heal All.* Finally, in large plain letters, the phrase I AM ALL repeated itself over and over, undulating like a snake, imprinting itself on my consciousness at the deepest level. Two spiders came together belly to belly like the sign of Cancer, finishing the show as the images slowly began to fade. I felt then, and have felt since, totally loved and held and taken care of. Never have I doubted the presence and concrete realness of the Goddess in her immanent divinity and wisdom. Never again in my life have I considered that I am alone in the universe.

More than ten years later I learned that this process is very much like that described by the Tibetan teacher Namkhai Norbu in discussing the Dzogchen path.[11] Dzogchen belongs to Tibetan Buddhism, as well as the ancient shamanistic Bon religion that predated Buddhism in Tibet, and refers to the primordial energy. Norbu describes this path as one of direct transmission from teacher to student through the use of symbols and discusses the "language of the dakini" as a form in which the ancient, secret teachings are encoded until the time that certain predestined people around the world will discover portions of them, which it is their task to translate into the cultural language of their time and place. To be a part of this lineage does not require that the person be participating in a particular spiritual form, such as Buddhism, although the teacher doing the transmitting may well be Buddhist. I have always felt a strong connection to Tibetan Buddhism and have even remembered a Tibetan past life while awake, so I have assumed that a good part of what I know comes from that lineage. Norbu describes the Dzogchen direct transmission experience as one after which the student no longer has doubt, having had the experience directly. I can still feel the presence that was in the room at the time of my vision, and its obvious protection and divinity imprinted me forever.

This was also a classic shamanic experience. To receive a direct response from the universe in this way is why Native Americans "cry for a vision." Many synchronicities followed on this vision of mine. I found Alice Bailey's *Treatise on the Cosmic Fire* shortly after at the Berkeley flea market; I read about the ancient sacred runic scripts guarded by the priestesses of the Goddess in the ancient Mediterranean area in Robert Graves's *White Goddess;* I learned about shamanism and the tunnel that a shaman uses to travel from this world to the invisible one, in another dimension. Of course, I learned more about the ancient images of the Goddess and eventually created the *Motherpeace Tarot Cards* (see chap. 7). When I was teaching *Motherpeace* years later (1982), Tarot teacher Mary Greer was in one of my classes and introduced me to the concept of the life cards from the Major Arcana. In this numerological system, everybody has a soul and personality card that is determined by their birthday. My soul card is number II, the High Priestess: she who experiences the Mystery through direct, oracular, unmediated contact with the divine; my personality card is XX, the Judgment, which Aleister Crowley called the Aeon and which Professor Durdin-Robertson says refers to Helena, the personification of the Divine Feminine through lifetimes. Remember, in my vision the words that appeared said Helena, to which I had no reference at the time. And the following spring, when Mount St. Helens erupted, so did my boil, as I described in chapter 2.

What clarified for me in my shamanic experience was total, a way of life. Candlemas, the kundalini, my shamanic vision, Helena, Mount St. Helens, the volcano dream, the volcano, my boil — I knew with a deep foundation that the earth and I are in this together, and there is an awesome choreography to it. I am not in charge, but I am not a pawn in it either. How does it work? I don't know — can't know — because it is grace-fully, mercifully much larger than my mind's limited ability to encompass ideas and concepts. This work cannot be taught, but it can be transmitted and received. Some of us get it, some of us don't. I got it through the incredible web of coincidences that vibrated through my life during that three-year period, and I continue to get it in exactly the same way today. When I understood how profoundly I was held and contained within the yearly cycle of the structure of the sacred calendar, I relaxed my grip on life. I learned to be more receptive to what Nature has in store for me as the seasons change. Our worldview sees ancient and primitive people as childlike because they watch and respond to nature. In truth, they are mature.

Although there are plenty of books describing holiday rituals with full liturgy, if a person wants to have a form, it is not necessary to do anything in particular to celebrate the sacred days. The main thing is the power of the moment. These holidays are part of an undergirding structure of forces and currents that affect us in all kinds of ways and that move and guide us spiritually, whether we know it or not. If you doubt this, simply watch the public events for a week or so around each holiday, especially the cross-quarters, and see how people go crazy! The intensity rises at these times of the year, and the door opens between the invisible and the visible planes. People respond to this by becoming upset, angry, euphoric, energized, and sick. What is needed, once you know about the timing, is to prepare a space for your own reception of the energies that are available. Give yourself time to dream and remember, allow some space for reflection and observation, stay awake! Whatever happens in your life at these particular times is oracular — it tells or shows you something. It presents you with messages, signs, and omens about your life. Big Dreams are likely to occur now, as well as other unusual psychic events. Synchronistic and magical happenings are possible, meetings with important others in your life, and so on. We often get hung up in the West on "doing something" for the holidays, when the real goal is to let the holidays "do" us.[12]

There is no one system and no particular form to shamanic work. It is earth based and eclectic, manifesting in different ways around the world. I become irritated at what seem like simplistic systems of healing and understanding cosmology, as if it were possible to put it into a box with a linear set of precepts. Discussion of the laws and principles of healing is wonderful, like circling around and around something that you love to look at and you have a passion to study. But when people begin formulating healing, narrowing the principles into prescribed forms (with do and don't, good and bad), I get suspicious and restless. The truth can only rise from within each of us through our dreams and visions, informing our conscious mind through whatever channels are open and filtering through whatever lenses we wear. In shamanic work it is necessary to have experience and then to act from that strong base of support.

A tone of superiority pervades the literature describing shamanic research. It's as if Westerners just can't help but separate themselves and feel more "right" than those who operate in other ways. So we observe that tribal people around the world (and we assume that the ancient people before them) seem to experience direct contact with their environment, and in seeing that, we feel compelled to name it: *the participation mystique.* Our naming it in this way immediately makes it "other" than our own scientific approach, which we believe to be more "true" than theirs. As a culture, we have no trouble borrowing (some would say ripping off) from native peoples their techniques and practices, even some of their beliefs (as we understand them), but rarely is a North American able to move into and join with the perspective of the people whom he is studying. (I use "he" deliberately here, since most research has been done by men or done in an accepted style that is male.) So when an anthropologist is interviewing a Peruvian or African healer, he will make comments about "animism" and suggest that this person "projects" or "imagines" that the illness was caused by an evil spirit. At best, Westerners have turned the beliefs and practices into psychologized versions of what they imagine to be taking place in shamanic healing. While the African shaman clearly states that he or she is communicating and dealing with invisible spirits, the Western psychologist who borrows the particular trance technique used for this healing will offer up a translated and paraphrased (and distorted) explanation of what he believes is actually happening. It never seems to occur to the researching scholar that he can't see what the shaman is capable of seeing because his vision is not properly developed.

Shamans do not experience their journeys or the invisible spirit world as imaginary. They don't have to. They know because they see. They experience Westerners as impossibly limited in our abilities (and our refusal) to understand reality. It is a standard joke among anthropologists that Indian people whom they interview laugh at them, tell them lies, and generally make fun of them. Is it any wonder? The more a person practices and develops shamanic healing, the less can be said about it in precise, rational, linear ways. The experiences are so direct and often so profound that to translate them into words and concepts takes an extra mental effort—a step of mediation that has to be inserted in between the experience and one's communication of it. The English language, and the Western mode of communication, work against the expression of shamanic truths by virtue of what they have left out of the picture. It has become somewhat of a truism that Eskimo culture has something like twenty different words for snow, while it is hard for us to conceive of why they would need so many. In the language of the Iroquois, there was no word or concept for rape until European intrusion. It was unthinkable.[13]

The practice of watching for signs and omens and then taking them to heart is a nonverbal work. At some point I had to stop writing in my journal because what I was saying about my experiences was somehow diminishing them while also blowing them out of proportion. What I do instead is absorb directly now, without so much mediation process of trying to figure things out. I say, inside myself, "Yes, thank you." Or I say, "OK, I will do this," or "I won't do that." I know what is advised. I know what the message means, but if I were to discuss what it means, it would become too literal, and it would start to feel contrived. The subtlety of oracles is part of their magic. The wholistic way in which they come into consciousness can't very well be broken into pieces of meaning or linear steps of understanding. The oracular is not a rational communication but comes often as a metaphor, needing to be moved delicately from one plane of existence onto another, without losing the thread of meaning. There is a clumsiness in the density of the Western approach and a literalness in our translation of things. We always seem to need to pull things from the deep to the shallow, from the profound to the mundane, as if in understanding them, we conquer them. And in attempting to conquer the oracle, we are once again trying to conquer Nature.

I was once planning an event that came to a messy, premature death. At the point in the process when I needed to let go and was having trouble doing so on my own, I dreamed of a doorway through which I and other people were about to enter. In the doorway I saw a huge yellow and black garden spider sitting at the center of a web. (More about the significance of the spider in chapter 5.) I stopped dead in my tracks, and the people I was with urged me to

**81**

knock her out of the web and out of our way. I felt completely reverent toward her and refused to go forward. I answered them, "No, this is her doorway. We won't go here." On awakening from the dream, I canceled the event and rescheduled it for later, when I could do it right.

There are those who would argue with me that this is giving my power away to something external, giving up my free will, or simply exercising a wild imagination. But I know for myself, in my body-mind, about the signs and omens. They speak to me and I listen. We dialogue. I am relieved not to be alone in the universe. I feel supported, guided, treasured by the helping spirits, led toward my destiny by the Goddess. I am grateful nowadays when I receive a clear sign like the one I just described, even at the moment that I am sad and disappointed. I spent enough of my life pushing blindly ahead, ignoring the signs and signals, going after my passion without considering the karmic consequences. It's true we have free will, and it's also true that we make karmic mistakes that take a long time to work out. When a person becomes able to read the signs and to know better, the defiant karmic choices become dangerous to her health. Innocence is protective, and mistakes allow teachings to occur; but mastery demands obedience to the laws of Nature.

Tribal people who practice shamanism, like the Huichols in Mexico, believe that a person will become ill and experience disastrous events in her life if she breaks her vow on the shamanic path to completion. The contract is between the person and Nature, so there is no easy way out of it. If a woman decides (or is forcefully called) to be a shaman-healer, she is first of all in a probationary process of opening to the path. But at some point she steps onto the path (the esotericists call this discipleship), and there is really no turning back. Shamans all over the world tell stories about the problems they incurred when they tried to get out of the contract, to go back on their agreements, or to practice old behaviors that were OK before they began their work. In our culture this is obvious in the way that foods and drinks can be abused when a person is younger and hasn't opened to the spiritual forces. I used to be able to abuse my body with alcohol, sugar, and meat without direct, felt consequences. But once I began the purification process of awakening to the energy, releasing the toxins and negativity from my past, and channeling greater healing power, it became impossible to eat fast foods without

getting immediate diarrhea or to drink wine without a headache or to eat too much sugar without the back of my neck
seizing up in a spasm. The same is true of gossiping or lying.
They used to be benign offenses; but no more. All negative
behavior has a peculiar feeling in the moment (inner stirrings,
signals, warnings) and immediate consequences that I would
rather avoid in my life. The way in which the web is holding
us makes all negativity harmful to ourselves and everyone
else. The effects of it double back on us in no time. The "punishment" comes from Nature rather than from some external
authority like the police.

To practice shamanism a person has to be ready to
clean up her act and lean toward positive behaviors without
anyone making her do it. I like to think of the ancient cultures
and tribal communities where everyone knows everyone else
and sees what they are doing in their lives. In our modern
culture we seem to think that if we don't tell, nobody will
know. We tell lies and practice chronic denial, believing pri-
vacy to be a more important right than the responsibility to
tell the truth. What a difference in the Huichol tribes, where
people are routinely asked to make group "confessions" in the
presence of the shaman and in ceremonial ritual (in the presence of the deities) about any breaches of conduct in their
lives. This group purging is a cleansing that, regularly practiced, keeps the tribe healthy and in balance. I think of the so-
called Pyramid of the Moon at the end of the Avenue of the
Dead in the ruins of Teotihuacán in Mexico. This impressive
structure sits at the end of the main street of the city, and
everything is oriented toward it. During excavations archaeologists dug up a monolithic Goddess made of stone (fig. 26)
which they believe once stood on the top of the building, looking out over the entire vista. Her eyes have the typical trance-
like, staring quality of the other Goddesses in ancient Mexico,
and she would have given the impression of a deity who was
watching you all the time, day and night. Apparently the
Spanish knocked her down and buried her when they arrived
on the scene in the 1500s.

Imagine the power of being seen in this way! The
Goddess, watching us, loving us, and holding us accountable.
Our lives are so enriched when we understand the power of
doing the right thing. When we begin, again, to acknowledge
that we are all connected and our behaviors affect each other
deeply, we are more able to give up our addictions in favor of

▲ *Fig. 26    This Mexican Goddess
was found buried in front of the Pyramid of the Moon (named by the
Aztecs) at the ruins of Teotihuacán
in Mexico. Archaeologists think the
Spanish pushed her down from the
very top of the pyramid, where she
had watched over the whole city more
than one thousand years earlier,
and buried her. Photo by the author.*

making positive choices. The feeling of being entirely alone in
our decisions, separated from Nature and other people, gives
us a false sense of inflation and permission to abuse the natural laws. This in turn makes us sick and out of balance, which
leads to further misconduct. The importation of Asian spiritual disciplines into North America has brought with it a kind
of surrogate conscience for people who become disciples of a
guru. They make a contract to keep certain behaviors and
practices, according to the code of the center or ashram,
which is a step toward developing the kind of inner authority
I'm describing. And I suppose Catholic confession is attempting to create the same sense of being seen, known, and held
accountable. But what we really need now, in this time and
place, is a means of becoming directly accountable for our
behaviors and choices and developing our own deep sense of
spiritual authority.

# Astrology: Deep Structure of Female Shamanism

ANCIENT ASTROLOGY WAS BODY based and biological. In the beginning it was a felt experience, but after the beginnings of patriarchal civilization, it became a "science" in the more modern sense of that word. Among the first artifacts from the Paleolithic strata in Europe are calendars showing that women kept track of their menstrual cycles in tandem with the moon (fig. 27). These early calendar bones are precise lunar tallies, believed to belong to a larger, more encompassing system of mathematics and science (see chap. 1, p. 17). Women shamans or midwives thirty thousand years ago used these small bone implements to record and document the passing of time in relation to their biological experiences as a group. The first language — picture symbols — is inscribed on these early objects and later appears in the weaving and pottery of the Neolithic (agricultural) period. Shamanism and astrology were not separated until very late in our evolution, when the separation from Nature and our bodies was made. The first Western zodiacs are dated to the transitional period after 3000 B.C.E. in Egypt and the Middle East. They were connected to the Goddess, as in the zodiac from the ceiling of the Temple of Hathor at Dendera in Egypt. With the rise of the Dynastic cultures in Mesopotamia, India, China, Mexico, and Egypt, astrology (like yoga and shamanism) began to be systematized and codified into the disciplines we see today.

All over the world ancient people have left us remnants of their star study. Archaeologists posit that the

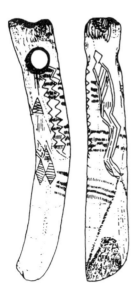

▲ *Fig. 27 These menstrual calendars show us how ancient European women midwives (twenty thousand years ago) kept track of their moon cycles on this antler, which they engraved with snakes and notches for telling time. Alexander Marshack says this notational system had to be part of some larger, more sophisticated system of mathematics and science by which our ancestors lived their daily lives. Similarly, Andean scholar Gary Urton maintains that menstruating women most likely developed a standardized zodiac from their observances of lunar phases in relation to the positions of the stars, using their own synchronized menstrual cycle as the biological standard for developing and keeping highly evolved records of nocturnal celestial cycles. Drawings by James Bennett from Marija Gimbutas's* The Language of the Goddess.

stone laid over a Paleolithic child's grave, marked with cup and ring marks, could signify breasts or might be a picture of certain constellations. The stone was laid with the picture facing downward in the grave, protective and nurturing like the later images of the Sky Goddess Nut inside Egyptian sarcophagi (fig. 28). The Anasazi pueblo dwellers of Chaco Canyon built an astronomical observatory on a high butte in New Mexico where a so-called sun dagger of light can be witnessed pouring precisely through three standing stones onto a rock face carved with a spiral. The beam of light enters the spiral and leaves it, much as one would enter a labyrinth, go to the center, and leave it, exactly on Winter Solstice each year. Later, on Spring and Fall Equinoxes, it comes into the labyrinths sideways. Furthermore, the complex, esoteric nineteen-year eclipse cycle is recorded at this site, just as it is at Stonehenge and other ancient stoneworks. Similar shafts of light enter into the chambers of New Grange in Ireland and the Great Pyramid in Egypt and so on all over the world on particular days that were intended to be marked and attended to. The ancient shamans at Chaco Canyon, as well as those in China, recorded in pictorial images the impressive supernova of the eleventh century B.C.E. The Anasazi inscribed symbols of the event, which can now be seen under a rock ledge, high up near a sacred, oval-shaped ruin.

▲ Fig. 28  Images like this of the Egyptian Sky Goddess Nut were often found on the insides of coffins (sarcophagi). She is often shown eating the Sun God every evening and giving birth to him again each day. The stars that make up the shape of her body indicate an interest in astronomy and astrology in Egypt and a connection of these ancient arts with the Feminine.

The ancients created, understood, and used these sacred places at specific times for their spiritual work. Babylonian Ishtar's name meant "Star" and her "girdle" was the zodiac, her monthly menstrual period was our first Sabbath. Ancient Mexicans kept track of the precise cycles of Venus and Mars and paid attention to the movements of all the planets as if it mattered in their daily lives. At the center of their calendar, the Aztecs portrayed the Earth Goddess in her terrifying form, resembling Medusa or Kali, with her tongue hanging out and her eyes bulging (fig. 29). Mayan shamans in the highlands of Mexico and Guatemala still use their sacred calendar today and link it to a woman's pregnancy cycle.[1] Scholars believe that places like Stonehenge and the other mounds and temple structures all over the planet were used not only as observatories — to witness and record astronomical events — but also for ritually attending to these events by being present in the body as a channel for the forces being transmitted. The energies coming from the various stars and planets at different points in the cosmic cycle have value for human beings: They heal and renew us, and we are capable of housing and channeling these energies for the benefit of the

▲ *Fig. 29    The famous Aztec calendar stone actually marked more than simply the changing seasons. Its intricate symbolism contains the exact orbits of planets in the solar system such as Mars and Venus. Modern science has probably only begun to catch up to what the ancient Mayans and Aztecs knew, as their yet-indecipherable calendars and hieroglyphs demonstrate. Notice the eight pointers on the stone, showing us the eight sacred holidays in a seasonal cycle, announcing that these ancient people worshiped the Goddess through honoring her sacred cycle. She sits at the center with her tongue out in the tradition of Kali or Medusa but has been chronically misidentified as the Sun God. Drawing by Laurelin Remington-Wolf.*

whole planet. We are actually vehicles or vessels for the transmission of these celestial energies to the earth. The standing stones, temples, and chambers that ancient humans placed in precise alignments to the planets and stars also receive and transmit these currents of force for healing and magic.

The zodiac is perceived as a pictorial image of constellations of stars having meaning on the Earth. In Euro-Western astronomy, the zodiac lines up along the passage of the Sun over the "ecliptic" (solar astrology). Peruvian Indians, however, see the Milky Way as the path of the zodiac, rather than the ecliptic, and they equate the Milky Way (the celestial river) directly with its terrestrial counterpart, the Vilcanota River flowing through Cuzco. Scholar Gary Urton says about the astronomy of the Peruvian Indians that "one cannot understand the sky without first understanding the earth."[2] The Indians also observe and honor not only the visible constellations of bright stars but also the "dark cloud constellations," which they perceive as particularly feminine. The forces of weather that accompany the rainy season in Peru (half the year) are equated with the element of water and fertility. Rainbows are serpents, the Milky Way is a river where souls of the ancestors reside, and there is a dark constellation named "the Serpent" that rules the night sky all during the rainy season. The "heliacal" rise of the head of the Serpent occurs during the first week of August (the sacred Lammas holiday celebrated by Witches) and sets during the first week of February (Candlemas). Additionally, real live serpents in the Cuzco area (above twelve thousand feet) give birth to their young from September to October, just after the rainy season begins, suggesting the natural link between the celestial animals and their earthly counterparts.[3]

In an unusually enlightened study, Urton comments on the relationship of women and the moon, which he says is "neither unique to the Andes nor is it a totally arbitrary association . . . However, it is not generally recognized that the importance of the moon for females also involves the stars." Urton points out that female periodicity would naturally lead to the development of "private lunar zodiacs," which would then evolve into a standardized zodiac, because women living together tend to synchronize and bleed together. He calls attention to the Incan "Virgins of the Sun" who lived together in Cuzco (also at Machu Picchu), performing the rituals and ceremonies of the Incan religion, and could have served as the "biological standard" for a coordinated lunar zodiac, and also as the "record-keepers of nocturnal celestial cycles." In other words, women probably invented astronomy and astrology in the Andes, as in other parts of the world. He says his female informants always tended to rely on the moon for providing a point of stellar orientation, and when locating constellations on a star map, women "were almost always disoriented by the absence of a moon on the map . . . In contrast, the absence of a moon did not seem to present a problem to male informants."[4]

Urton makes a lucid plea to scholars regarding the ways we have approached study of the sun and moon, saying "we have been dazzled by the 'sun kingdom of the Americas' and consequently have blinded ourselves to the true depth and scope of the total system. Only in recent years . . . have we been made aware of the importance of the moon in the ritualism, symbolism, and calendar system of the Incas." He suggests that we "assume that complex systems of astronomy and cosmology have existed in the Peruvian Andes since at least Chavín times (i.e., since about 1200 B.C.E.)."[5] And he states more than once that "The most important aspect of lunar astronomy and symbolism, its relation to women and the menstrual cycle, remains largely unstudied." He says this is due to the fact that the scholars are mostly men, and men can't get the necessary information from the women they are studying, because Indian women won't talk about menstruation to male anthropologists. "This is the one area of ethnoastronomical research which has the most potential for significantly increasing our understanding of the Quechua and Inca calendar system and of determining the possible existence of a standardized female lunar 'zodiac.' "[6]

The Western personal astrological chart is like a snapshot taken at the moment of birth, showing where the planets of the solar system were stationed in relation to the celestial backdrop as each of us incarnated in this lifetime. This map can be read for psychological insight into the self. But of course, after our births, the planets continued moving in the sky, and it is these ongoing movements that make a relationship to the stationary planets in our natal charts. The relationships (which are known as transits) are very valuable in understanding our life's journeys and experiences.[7] The ancients tracked the cyclic movements of the planets against the backdrop of the starry sky, and they worshiped and honored these cycles as the universal Mother ruling Time and Fate. What we call astrology was really their entire cosmological worldview and approach to life. They knew in their beings what we are attempting to piece together with our minds.

Women practicing feminist astrology today are together rebuilding a common language for communicating easily about things that defy explanation. Astrology was a significant part of my original shamanic vision (see chap. 3), and I trust it to guide me to deeper understandings of reality than I am able to perceive through strictly Western modes of investigation. Just being aware of the meaningful movements of the planets in relation to one another in the sky helps me relate to and understand the world in which I live. The planets are like characters dancing close to and then away from one another, and the ramifications of their dances are literally earthshaking. The incredible events of the late 1960s all over the world have to be linked in part to the coming together of the two most forceful outer planets in the solar system, Uranus and Pluto. When Uranus and Pluto meet, according to traditional astrology, revolution occurs.

Astrology as a Western occult science is intellectualized, so that it seems to have nothing to do with the body. But female astrology is body based and related to the intuitive processes. The use of astrological knowledge can ground us and alleviate some of our fears about being alive on the planet in these uncertain times. Although difficult to master, we can all learn enough basic information about this form to be able to use it. The mystique around it—the myriad details and things to memorize—needn't be overwhelming. It's all part of a veil that can be lifted aside, and once through the secret doorway, initiation begins. We begin with the moon, learning where we stand from moment to moment and how that feels. Once the subtle changes and cyclic movement of the lunar phases can be perceived, we can superimpose this framework for understanding the larger, "more important" planets in the sky and how they affect us. Astrology provides a means of relating to the profound structure that underlies our everyday experiences without assuming we can figure it out. The more astrology opens up to us, the less we can know in the traditional logical sense of the word. The doorway through which we pass into astrology is a doorway to the Mystery, and the most adequate response is awe.

We all have transformative experiences in our lives that could be described as transpersonal—beyond the ego or ordinary consciousness. When these events take place, they are not infrequently unpleasant or frightening. We experience the loss of a loved one, through death or the end of a relationship, or we lose a job or break a leg. Somehow, if

we're lucky, through the loss comes some form of enlightenment or understanding, some growth takes place. We are
forced to let go. We change. This is transformation. But for
many of us these experiences seem disconnected from our
daily life, like they hit us from the outside, "out of the blue,"
and they seem undeserved, cruel, fateful in a negative way.
They tend to create bitterness in us and a sense of victimiza-
tion. People who commit suicide must think the cruel experience will never end, that things will never change, that their
pain will go on, unmitigated, forever. They have no structure
that holds them in a belief in the future, a faith in the essential
goodness of life. Because we lack a true spiritual base in our
culture, this emptiness and lack of understanding is pervasive. It was the Church Council in 400 C.E. that declared that
reincarnation and any belief in cycles of existence were heretical, and anyone who challenged this view was to be annihi-
lated. Is it any wonder that we in the West lack understanding
about the way things work in cycles?

When Karen Vogel and I were first studying tarot
and the ancient Goddess cultures, we began to learn astrology
as well. As I read esoteric texts on tarot, kabala, Western
magic, and the occult, I began to think about the solar system
and made an intuitive drawing of the planets. I thought that
although things are obsessively solar (yang) here, there must
be a corresponding lunar (yin) system that relates to our solar
system. I drew pictures of another center that was an exact
counterpart to the sun, but invisible, ruler of the nighttime
consciousness, the esoteric spiritual center of the universe we
inhabit. I imagined that this strong feminine center was available and accessible to those of us who were waking up to the
Goddess in our time. Then at some point I learned that the
orbits of both Neptune and Pluto are so erratic that even
astronomers posit that these two planets may not actually
belong to our solar system but simply orbit here around some
other — invisible? — center. Mary Daly's book *Gyn/Ecology*
came out around the same time, suggesting that the "patriarchal foreground" of the visible world can be overcome by
contemporary women "moving beyond the boundaries of
patriarchal space" into the "matriarchal background" of our
re-membered ancient past.[8] And recently I read something
obscure about a Black Sun that seemed to suggest that there
is, theoretically at least, an invisible point in space that func-

▲ *Fig. 30   The image of a woman men-*
*struating probably represents the Goddess*
*creating the local river of the rock in*
*Africa, where this image was drawn.*
*Woman's sacred and mysterious power of*
*bleeding without a wound was recognized*
*and honored everywhere before patriarchal*
*culture intervened and made it taboo or*
*demonic. Drawing by Jennifer Roberts.*

tions in direct counterpoint to our solar body, just as I suspected.

Because female shamanism is body based and related to the blood cycle, the first step in learning astrology must be to reclaim the menstrual time (see fig. 30). A woman must begin to relate to her periods and to the lunar rhythm established by their presence in her life. The menstrual period keeps the heartbeat for a female shaman, and she must be familiar and comfortable with it. Start by recording the dates of your last ovulation and menstruation, and add to that notes about dreams and activities during those times.[9] See how many days your menstrual cycle normally takes, and whether or not you are regular. Get an overview. If you do this work in a group of women, you are all likely to begin to cycle together before long, so you can expect some shifting of your cycle in relation to the others. Cycles shift for other reasons as well, so just keep track and get a sense of your rhythm to begin. After you can see a regularity in your menstrual record, get an astrological calendar (there are many)[10] and begin to look at new and full moons. See whether there is any relationship between your menstrual cycle and the phases of the

**93**

Saturday
Dec. 21
set 16:38
V/C 05:23
FULL 05:23

Sunday
Dec. 22
set 08:15
rise 17:55
V/C 17:34

Friday
Dec. 20
set 06:20
rise 15:27

Thursday
Dec. 19
set 05:11
rise 14:27
♊ 06:21

Monday
Dec. 23
set 08:58
rise 19:15
♌ 06:38

Wednesday
Dec. 18
set 03:58
rise 13:38
V/C 16:28

Tuesday
Dec. 24
set 09:33
rise 20:33
V/C 18:11

Tuesday
Dec. 17
set 02:46
rise 13:00
♉ 03:10

Wednesday
Dec. 25
set 10:02
rise 21:47
♍ 07:23

moon at
perigee
WINTER
SOLSTICE
03:54

Partial eclipse
of the Moon

Monday
Dec. 16
set 01:37
rise 12:28
V/C 17:19

Thursday
Dec. 26
set 10:29
rise 22:59

In the depths of darkness
come healing and rebirth.
The Elder represents the tender care
which is needed at this time
to restore the body, mind, and spirit.
Her bird is the rook;
her color, blood-red;
she heals and purifies
the inner and outer being.

Sunday
Dec. 15
set 00:31
rise 12:02

Friday
Dec. 27
set 10:55
V/C 01:26
♎ 10:37
LQ 20:55

Saturday
Dec. 14
rise 11:38
V/C 04:32
♈ 20:06
FQ 04:32

Saturday
Dec. 28
rise 00:08
set 11:21

Friday
Dec. 13
rise 11:16
set 23:28

Sunday
Dec. 29
rise 01:17
set 11:49
V/C 01:51
♍ 17:03

Monday
Dec. 30
rise 02:23
set 12:20

Tuesday
Dec. 31
set 03:28
rise 13:37
V/C 11:05

Wednesday
Jan. 1, 1992
rise 04:25
♐ 02:30

Thursday
Dec. 12
rise 05:22
V/C 05:15
♏ 14:09

Thursday
Dec. 12
rise 10:53
set 23:28
♓ 09:19

Friday
Jan. 3
rise 06:12
set 15:18

moon at
apogee

Wednesday
Dec. 11
rise 10:30
set 21:26
V/C 16:01

*ruis·elder*

Thursday
Dec. 5
rise 06:36
set 15:39
NEW 22:56

Friday
Dec. 6
rise 07:32
set 16:29
V/C 09:18

Saturday
Dec. 7
rise 08:20
set 17:25
♒ 07:41

Sunday
Dec. 8
set 09:01
set 18:24

Monday
Dec. 9
rise 09:35
set 19:24
V/C 02:46
♒ 20:27

Tuesday
Dec. 10
rise 10:05
set 20:25

December 5 - January 3, 1992!

13th lunation

▲ *Fig. 31    The page from* The Lunar Calendar: Dedicated to the Goddess in Her Many Guises *shows how the women's spirituality movement has attempted to reframe the passage of time for us in a new visual format. Time doesn't actually happen in squares, as the Julian calendar would have us believe, but in circles, like the constantly changing phases of the moon shown here. A woman can synchronize her menstrual cycle with the changing face of the Moon Goddess and attune herself to this basic female biological rhythm. Reprinted with permission from Luna Press, Boston. Moon cycle design R. D. K. Perrens.*

moon in the sky. Many women bleed with the new or full moon and ovulate at the other end of the spectrum, and this may show in the record you're keeping. If one woman in the group is strong in her cycle, the others may synchronize with her.

Every month the moon starts out as a tiny crescent, grows larger (waxes) and becomes full; then begins to wane and grow smaller, becoming once more a tiny crescent in the early morning hours, finally disappearing from view altogether (see fig. 31). In ancient times the Sumerians (and later Babylonians) worshiped the Goddess Inanna (later Ishtar), ritualizing her lunar cycle by celebrating one Sabbath each month that represented her bleeding time. Merlin Stone told us that the word *Sabbath* comes from *sabbatu,* meaning "heart-rest."[11] The story of Inanna itself—our first epic myth—is at its simplest level a menstrual metaphor of the moon's journey through her monthly cycle of waxing, full and waning, dying and being reborn. In India there are still temples where ritual is performed in honor of the Goddess's regular menses.[12] Elinor Gadon tells us that the Hindu Sanskrit word *ritu* means "menses" and is the root of the word *ritual*.[13] We just need to understand that *the monthly menstrual period is the quintessential ritual experience,* analogous to the time of the Dark Moon — the impossibly magical time when the moon disappears from the sky and then through a miraculous rebirth appears once more; and the impossibly magical time when women, without a wound, bleed from the sacred yoni for three days.

Early Semitic people divided the month into four quarters, squaring the sacred circle and making a Sabbath each week. They continued to celebrate the lunar sacred marriage of Ishtar for so long that for the husband and wife to make love on Friday evenings became one of the Jewish sacramental instructions that stayed in the Hebrew texts. All the planets can be followed through a similar circular orbit, divided into four quarters, which allows for observation of each of these important "squares" or aspects that the planet makes to itself as it travels around the sun. The trine aspect — division of the circle into three parts (the triple Goddess: maiden, mother, crone) — and the square aspect — division of the circle into four quarters (the contemporary lunar month) — are the main patterns we need to observe in order to understand almost all that astrology will eventually ask us to know. The sacred three and the sacred four add up to the sacred twelve of the astrological wheel. Three modes and four elements equal twelve signs and houses. (Just note, for now, that this structure is the same as the tarot with its three circles of Major Arcana and four suits [elements] in the Minor Arcana.)[14]

Once you have understood how to look for the moon's phases and compare them to your menstrual cycle, there is a second way of harmonizing with the movements of the moon. Using your astrological calendar, you should be able to read that the moon travels through a different sign of the zodiac every two and a half days or so. This lunar cycle is slightly longer than the cycle of waxing and waning phases. It is just as common for women's cycles to link with this more esoteric lunar cycle as it is with the phases. If your bleeding time comes, as mine does, whenever the moon moves into a certain sign, let's say Aries, then you won't always bleed with the new or full moon but will go through changes in the course of the year. In the spring the new moon falls in Aries, so you would be bleeding with the new moon; in the fall it's the opposite, and the moon is full in Aries, so you would be bleeding on the full moon.

By watching and recording the astrological passage of the moon through the signs of the zodiac, you get to know how the signs feel, because that's what the moon is so good at showing us. You come to know the twelve signs by their element (earth, water, fire, or air) and how it stimulates you in your body, mind, and emotions. If you pay attention and record your observations over time, you will begin to see regular characteristics of the different signs that you have imprinted in your body rather than learning them intellectually from a book. You can compare what you have noticed and felt with what the experts say in the books on astrology, but by that time you will be grounded in real experience, which is by far the best teacher. Women are deeply connected to the moon, the female nature profoundly lunar at its biological base. If you can make friends with this lunar capacity, the rest will come more easily. It's one thing to read or hear that Gemini is light and airy and another to pay attention to your feelings, thoughts, and impulses for the two days of the moon's passage through the sign of Gemini. Eventually, with enough practice, you will be able to recognize where the moon is passing by the feelings and responses in your body and mind. Especially attune to the transitions, when the moon leaves one sign and enters another. The feeling of earth followed by air is quite noticeable, or water to fire. You gain an appreciation for the fact that there are no accidents but a grand choreography, and that our impulses and events happen out of what the Buddhists call co-arising.

The development of body-based receptivity to the movements of the moon and planets helps to develop clairsentience, the knowing with the body. The intellect is being used here, but it is not the boss. A larger intelligence is at work, which includes the intellect as well as feelings, sensations, dreams, desires, images, hopes, and impressions. In this process a woman can begin to follow the principles of synchronicity laid out in the last chapter. Like Buddhism, synchronicity challenges students to check out everything for ourselves — not to rely on anything through hearsay. Apply this teaching to astrology. You can read in a book that a sign or a planet functions in a certain way or means a certain thing, but don't believe it unless it checks out for you. Then you will be developing your own sense of inner authority. Once you get a handle on the lunar cycles, you can branch out into other aspects of astrology, taking in a little at a time until you really have it. Next you can begin to relate the moon, which you have come to understand somewhat, to the sun in your chart.

Now get a birth chart made for yourself. You can order one through a computer service, some of whom will even give you a printed interpretation of your planets and how they relate to one another.[15] You probably need a workbook to guide you through an introduction to the fundamental aspects of your astrological blueprint. Demetra George and Douglas Bloch have created the easy and comprehensive *Astrology for Yourself*,[16] where you can learn the steps in a linear fashion. Jonathan Tenney and I wrote the *Motherpeace Tarot Playbook*,[17] which applies the *Motherpeace* images to the study of astrological principles. Get a workbook or two and fill in the blanks, doing a little every day or every week. Don't worry if you don't understand it all or if it all seems overwhelming. Astrology is a lot of numbers and names of things for a while, and then one day, magically, it takes. Allow yourself to study it easily, without stress, and take in whatever interests you, comparing it with your observed and felt experience.

I use astrology charts every day for determining whether a student should study with me, for measuring the significance of events, for grounding myself in the deeper meaning of things that might otherwise seem random or chaotic. When something out of the ordinary happens in my life, I am immediately curious to look up where the planets are and to see how that is affecting me personally. Knowing the planets is like having a symbolic language at my disposal, a whole perspective through which to observe and make sense of reality. If you don't know how to use an ephemeris,[18] there are computer printouts that will tell you where the planets are in the sky and how they are relating to your personal chart. In ancient times the whole community had a lived experience of this art, and we need to reinstate that common knowledge in order to live well in these chaotic times. Ancient shaman women related to astrological phenomena in terms of understanding and relating to events as a whole, affecting the group at large. Even the lunar, menstrual cycle wouldn't have been personal or individualized, since before electric lighting, women bled together. The lunar, menstrual calendar could have been kept by a recorder or midwife, keeping track of cycles for the tribe in general, with whatever minor variations existed among them.

Demetra George's work *Mysteries of the Dark Moon* (HarperSanFrancisco, forthcoming) is very helpful for women attempting to come to an understanding of the structure of life through a feminine perspective. She works with the lunar cycle as the model until we understand the basic cyclic form: birth, fulfillment, and death, followed by rebirth and another cycle. Once we have a clear image of this basic female metaphor of the cyclic process, Demetra teaches the solar-lunar relationship, looking at the position of the moon in a birth chart in relation to the natal position of the sun. If you begin by imagining that the new moon phase shows up in a chart when the moon is within a few degrees of the sun at the moment of birth and is moving away from it (that is, growing or waxing) until it is opposite the position of the sun (full moon), and then waning and actually moving closer to the sun again as it dies, you can actually see characteristics or typologies in people just from this relationship. Someone with a crescent moon phase at birth has a personality, and destiny, very different from a person with a dying moon; and all people who share a crescent moon phase or a waning (basalmic) moon phase share a core characteristic that can be documented in their lives. Since we utterly lack female metaphors of growth in Western culture, these approaches are refreshing. The reemergence of female shamanism and Goddess-religion feeds a hunger in us. The difficulty in systematizing feminine process lies in the deeply intuitive, psychic way that it functions. If women come together in a circle and do this work, we are likely to experience changes in our menstrual cycle, from being together perhaps or from paying attention to the cycle itself or both, who knows? It is extremely hard to separate ourselves from the experience we are trying to observe, and the female shamanic process makes no attempt to do that but honors the totally fluid character of the female psychophysical reality. Astrology is an intuitive process of coming to understand that we are held in a deeply sacred structure, without ever trying to analyze the structure to the point where we think we understand it. As such, it is a doorway leading directly into the Mystery, and it naturally leads as well to a deep humility and a sense of trust in the universe.

Learn to read an ephemeris. Get a pocket astrological calendar and note where things are every day. Get into the habit of thinking astrologically. Record more than your behaviors and outer events; keep track of your thoughts, feelings, moods, impulses, the weather, how many sirens you heard that day, traffic jams, bird sounds, the people in your life and how they related to you. Don't leave anything out, everything counts. If you keep a dream journal, you can correlate the two records, and then add to that your menstrual record. Our separation from Nature is nowhere more apparent than in these splits between our inner and outer realities. If it seems like too much time or trouble at first, choose one planet besides the moon to pay attention to. Choose the planet that rules your chart. You'll have to learn some astrology to do that. The sign on your *ascendant* is your rising sign; the planet that rules that sign (look it up in the *Motherpeace Tarot Playbook*) rules your chart. Whatever that planet is doing always affects you in important ways. Why not begin to get to know it? Look it up in your chart first to see what house it's in; then begin to pay attention to where it is in the sky and where that falls in your chart. For example, my rising sign is Aries, which is traditionally ruled by Mars, and my Mars is also in Aries. That makes Mars my ruling planet and doubles its importance in my chart because it is at home in its own sign, although not in its own house. The descriptions of Martian personalities don't exactly fit my experience, because they are so male oriented and culturally inspired, so I have to do a little transposing. Astrologers tend to label Mars as the belligerent god of war, whereas I think of Mars as Shakti, the creative Goddess of the fiery creative will.

Try working with ritual, calling in the four directions, and thinking of them as the four elements in astrology. Figure out where you would stand in the circle, based on your sun sign, then your moon, and so on. Play with it—it's much more interesting than dogma. Jonathan Tenney has inspired me to explore astrology through movement, dramatization, visualization, and what we named sacred play. For years he met with a men's group that practiced experiential astrology in the Bay Area. Esoteric teacher Alice Bailey predicted that intuitive astrology would be the most important science to emerge at the end of the twentieth century, and this is it. We need more than anything to come back to an integrated approach to Nature and the universe, and this way of relating astrologically makes it possible. You can also help yourself learn astrology by using the *Motherpeace* images. When you work with images in addition to concepts, the concepts come into the body. You can intuitively grasp the meanings of the different planets and signs. To learn about your sun and moon signs, go to the chapter on the "People Cards" in the *Motherpeace Tarot Playbook* and figure out the two elements of each of those sixteen images. Choose the one or two images that contain both of the elements that belong to you by sun and moon, and then you have something with which to identify. You can do the same with Mars and Venus and so on if you want. So, for instance, my Mars in Aries could be represented by the Daughter of Wands or the Shaman of Wands. Both of these images are descriptive of my experience and help me to understand the elements. (All this is covered in the astrology section, second half, of the *Playbook*.)

To begin to grasp the concept of transits, it is helpful to plot the new moon each month. Find the degree and sign of the new moon in your astrological calendar, then fit it into your birth chart. The new moon is in the same degree of the same sign for everyone, of course, but that point falls in a different place—a different "house"—in each chart. Where the lunar cycle begins matters. The particular "house placement" is the seed point, the place where things begin for that month and is always worthy of note. Then add the degree and sign of the full moon for that month. The full moon—and the house in which it falls—show how the lunar cycle will express itself in your life for that month. Whatever seed was planted at the beginning of the cycle will flower at full moon then whither and die (come to conclusion) by the end of the month, leaving room for something new to begin with the next new moon. If the new or full moon falls on a planet in the personal chart, this is particularly significant. You know this by being exact and noting any planets in your birth chart that fall within three degrees of either the new or full moon. Then you can spend the rest of the lunar cycle observing what happens and how it feels, and from this you can extrapolate some meaning about the astrological characteristics of the sign, house, and planets in your life.

For example, I was invited to teach at a weeklong conference in Canada where native and nonnative women would be coming together to heal themselves. I noticed the new moon that month fell at a very important place in my chart called the North Node. This spot in the natal chart points the way to destiny and new directions. At the same time Mars (my ruling planet) was "returning" or coming back to the point of its beginning at my birth, which it does every two years. So although I couldn't predict how that conference would affect me, it was very clear to me it would be important because it was happening at such an auspicious time for me. Another time I was watching the planet Mars making a "retrograde station" (seemingly backward) over a significant point in my birth chart in its own sign of Aries. When Mars exactly reached that point, I had an unavoidable car accident that day that wasn't my fault—a car ran into the back of me and pushed me into another car in front, and my back and shoulder were injured. Mars in traditional astrology often rules accidents and injuries.

At some point this stuff takes. All of a sudden it makes sense. You have to trust that although astrology can't really be taught, it can be learned, and at some point you will get it. When it becomes integrated into your practice of observing and responding to the cues and signals from Nature and the universe, you have another tool for helping guide your choices and actions. When you can feel the workings of the planets in your daily, monthly, and yearly cycle, you become more able to surrender to those powers that are bigger than us. When you can effectively make that kind of surrender or offering up of your ego, your spiritual life expands to include more than it could when you were hanging on to your ego-fixations. You have to be able to feel some kind of support under you in order to give up being in your head and to realign with your belly, your instincts, and your movement center. You can't make that change in the abstract, or you will feel too ungrounded and afraid. Learning body-based astrology is a concrete way of making the shift from the mind to the body, from your thinking process to a larger, more encompassing part of your total intelligence. You can still use logical methods of making choices, but in addition to the rational mind, you will also be employing invisible aspects of your reality in discerning the path of action.

When you really understand the cyclic process—
from the seed point to the flowering to the dying and distilla-
tion and the rebirth—you can transfer this understanding to
the yearly cycle of the sun, using the eight sacred holidays as
your points of observation (see fig. 25). Winter Solstice is the
dark phase, the seed point, like the new moon; Candlemas in
February is the crescent phase, the quickening; Spring Equinox is the first quarter, like the waxing moon; Beltane is the
gibbous, growing light; and Summer Solstice is full expression. Now the dying must begin: Lammas is the disseminating
phase, creative; Fall Equinox is the last quarter, time to gather
in; Hallomas is descent, the balsamic phase, when we reenter
the dark, bringing us back to Winter Solstice again, when the
light is born out of the darkest night. The period of time from
Hallomas to Winter Solstice is like the disappearance of the
moon from visibility in the sky for those mysterious three
days. This cycle—this orbit—applies to all the planets in the
solar system and provides a reference point for understanding
the various phases in the two-year orbit of Mars, or the
eighty-four-year orbit of Uranus. Like Chinese boxes, the
same cycle happens in bigger rounds. All of astrology is built
on these phases and on the aspects they create when they
interact with each other and with your personal natal planets.
The ancients knew this and used the number eight to represent Ishtar and her girdle of planetary bodies. The eight-
pointed star was significant in many early cultures and can be
seen in the later sacred calendars from different places. The
so-called Aztec calendar wheel, for instance, shows clearly
these eight points in the cycle, referring to the eight sacred
holidays in a year and the eight sacred phases in planetary
cycles (see fig. 29).

Once you have begun to understand the phases of the
planetary cycles, you can begin to look at their transits in the
sky. Having learned to feel the differences between the ele-
mentals (earth, water, fire, and air) by paying attention to the
movements of the moon through the signs, you can begin to
translate this knowledge to a larger screen of awareness. The
moon is watery and related to the emotional experience, so
begin to watch the sun in its yearly cycle through the signs of
the zodiac. Remember that in ancient times the yearly cycle
was divided into thirteen lunar months. The "thirteenth fairy"
of our Sleeping Beauty myth is the lunar month that was left
out of the patriarchal reckoning. The crone's spindle that

pricks Sleeping Beauty's finger on her sixteenth birthday is her first menstruation, which becomes a curse on the whole kingdom, causing everyone to sleep for a hundred years. Since Julius Caesar we in the West have paid formal attention to only twelve months every year, calling the extra Full Moon a blue moon and creating superstitions around the sacred number thirteen. Still, you can notice how a fiery planet feels as it moves through each elemental sign and assimilate this information into your storehouse. You have approximately thirty days to pay attention to how Aries feels, compared with Taurus and then Gemini and so on. Watch other people too. Begin to understand the cycles of your culture through the lens of astrological awareness.

When you have spent "a year and a day" learning the feeling of the moon passing through the signs thirteen times, and the sun passing through each sign once, then you are ready to begin working with the other planets. The method is the same, just watching the ephemeris, noting as the planet moves through each sign and paying attention to how that feels and how it affects your life. In general you can observe Mercury, Venus, and Mars in the same way you have already looked at the sun. But you can also start to notice the movements of these planets in relation to your birth chart. As the moon moves around the zodiac during one month, track its exact movements by degree in your chart. Do the same thing with the sun for a year. In a year's time, the sun passes over every planet in your chart, catalyzing some sort of experience that can be felt and observed. All the other planets do the same thing but in different amounts of time. Mercury is fast, hitting all your planets quicker than the solar year; Venus takes a little longer than a year. Mars takes two years and Jupiter takes twelve. (Jupiter was the sky god that ruled the "new time" of the Julian calendar, with its twelve Jupiterian months.) Saturn is much slower, taking almost thirty years to complete a cycle. The "Saturn return" at around age twenty-nine is about growing up and becoming mature.

The comforting thing about keeping track of your transits is that everything literally has a beginning, a middle, and an end. The transiting planet approaches whatever planet in your chart it is going to be affecting, and it makes a conjunction. Planets frequently have a retrograde period in which they appear to go backward, and during this period the transitting planet will hit (conjunct) your natal planet a

103

second time. The third pass of the transitting planet over your natal planet completes the transit, until the next time the two planets come into relation with each other. You can know in advance when the transit encounter starts, how long it lasts, and when the last pass of that planet will take place. Then as you go through the experience, you have a deep sense of the meaning and purpose of it, even if you don't like the way it manifests. So, for instance, you become ill with some disease that incapacitates you for a period of time, and all your resources have to be directed toward your healing process. Any shaman can find meaning in this, and must, in order to work with it properly. But astrologically, if you see that Chiron, the planet of the shaman or "wounded healer," is transitting a personal planet in your chart, or Neptune or Uranus, this knowledge provides a framework or context for meaning to develop in your personal mythology.[19] Or you fall in love and get married and have a baby, all in the course of a very short time, let's say a year. This could be high drama, a woman who loves too much, or Pluto over your sun — a death and rebirth experience, connected to past lives and reincarnation, bringing power and transformation and a permanently shed skin.

When you have mastered astrology enough to be able to use it, you discover hundreds of ways to entertain yourself with what you know. You can look up the planets of every significant person who comes into your life from that moment on. You can do couple charts, baby charts, charts for events, group charts, and so on. It is endlessly fascinating, always educational, and profoundly meaningful, even on the simplest levels. You can watch the transits on your marriage chart, keep track of the movements of the planets in relation to your women's circle, track all the important phases and aspects of the outer planets (Uranus, Neptune, and Pluto) to your personal planets for your whole life, asking yourself: What happened to me when Uranus made that important aspect to my sun, moon, Mars, and so on? What was different when Neptune did something, or Pluto? You can have the computer make a list of the dates when the outer planets square and oppose themselves in your chart (like the first quarter, full, and last quarter moon phase superimposed on a much larger cycle).[20] In chapter 7 on shamanic art, I describe a process of making a doll with owl wings and talons from a road kill near my home many years ago. The doll took me several years from start to finish, and during that time I was having some extraordinary planetary transits, first from Neptune (the image came like a vision) and then from Uranus (I finished the doll and understood it in larger terms). The transits were happening to an esoteric part of my astrological chart called the Black Moon Lilith, which was related to the owl and her wisdom (see chap. 7 for more details).

Looking back over our lives is illuminating in the context of astrological transits, helping us to assimilate and understand the archetypal meanings of the outer planets, Uranus, Neptune, and Pluto. These planets rule the Major Arcana in the tarot, referring to forces in the universe that are larger than we are and to which we can only respond. These are the planets that represent Fate and require some kind of surrender from us. Their contacts with our personal planets tend to feel annihilating and overwhelming without some understanding of their purposeful activities. They all represent some aspect of the death process, and when they come around, the first thing to go is the ego. Whatever attachments we have in the area of the personal planet being affected are going to be loosened up in the course of a year or so. Each of the outer planets works in a different way, through a different approach, and these characteristic approaches can be felt and responded to. Uranus — the electrical planet — shatters structure, so its effects in our lives are shocking, disruptive, and upsetting. Uranus makes the nervous system hyperactive, either energizing us or driving us crazy. Neptune, by contrast, although it also wants to bring about change, does it in a completely different way through dissolving. Neptune is watery and fogs us in, making us disoriented and unclear, confused, disillusioned, sleepy, drained. And Pluto — the outermost planet with an orbit that takes 240 years — works so deeply to disrupt our ego-patterns that we experience being pulled, like Inanna, into the underworld and left to rot. Pluto transits are depressing and can be debilitating, but when they are finished, the planet under attack becomes more powerful and expressive than before. A deeper authenticity is reached, and like Inanna returning to the upper world, we feel more real.

The transitting planets seem also to have greater or lesser effects on our personalities, depending on how familiar they are to us from our natal chart. So, for example, Uranus is strong in my chart (squaring my Venus) and Uranus transits feel familiar to me, although they can be uncomfortable.

A Uranus transit may keep me awake at night, but I can adapt. Neptune, the watery planet, feels strange to me in transits, making me feel unlike my normal Aries self, diffuse and under siege in some way. If an outer planet manages to work on several planets in our charts in the course of a few years, the purpose of that planetary energy takes over in the life for a while, until the desired effects are achieved. They wear us down and finally we surrender. They work on us until they can work through us. They bring transformation and growth that we couldn't have calculated, might not have invited, but ultimately couldn't resist. Their effects in our lives makes us into the people we become as we mature. They temper us and hammer us into shape. Our evolution depends in part on our creative responses to these great bodies moving in the sky, and as we come to relate to them and reflect on their direction in our lives, our lives feel that much more in balance.

In ancient times the planets were personified as the Goddess in her many guises: birth, sustenance, death, transformation, regeneration. Eight of the ten planets used in modern astrology are male. The male sun represents the person's conscious identity; the feminine moon represents the unconscious. Mercury is a male god, representing the trickster. Venus, the only other female force in the tradition, is the sweetheart and represents our creature comforts, our desires and sexual attractions. All the rest are considered male: Mars, the god of war and passion; Jupiter, the great "benefic"; Saturn, the fearsome but Wise Old Man, Father Time; Uranus, the Destroyer; Neptune, the god of the sea with his trident; and Pluto, god of the underworld who raped and abducted Persephone. There is another planet known to orbit beyond Pluto, and some contemporary astrologers have tentatively named her Persephone, but in traditional computer charts it is called Transpluto. It's as if patriarchal culture has imagined a world of men alone, with two necessary auxiliary female figures, the mother to give birth to the male and the sweetheart to mate with him.

Recently some astrologers have begun to work with the asteroids. This belt of planetary bodies moving in an orbit between Mars and Jupiter is composed of the remains of a larger planet that apparently exploded in the past. (This is very interesting in light of the worldwide theme of the dismembered Goddess. She was dismembered by her brother, the war god, who scattered her parts to form the earth or to mark sacred shrines on the earth. If an earlier humanity did blow up the world, as esoteric science teaches, maybe it was the Goddess planet that they exploded.) The larger four asteroids are all given the names of Goddesses and present us with immediate and useful ways of integrating the feminine into astrology. Ceres, the mother and grain goddess; Pallas Athene, the amazon and wisdom aspect; Juno, the wife and committed partner; and Vesta, the temple priestess, are now included in computer programs that create charts. These asteroids were "discovered" and named in the last hundred years, and they have been found to correlate to the myths they describe in their names. Ceres relates to nurturing issues in a chart, as well as food disorders; Pallas Athene relates to work and independence; Juno to relationship patterns and commitments; and Vesta to autonomous sacred sexuality and focused work. There are hundreds of smaller asteroids that can be tracked and located in space and that have ephemerides, so that they can be studied and worked with.

When Demetra George first calculated my asteroids on her computer a few years ago, we were both pleased to learn that the asteroid Victoria fell right on my ascendant. Is it an accident? Fate? Luck? The probability is highly unlikely, and the synchronicity is wonderful. Her book *Asteroid Goddesses* will get you started with very deep material on the main four asteroids.[21] After that, with Demetra's help, you can delve into the three Liliths — the asteroid Lilith, the Dark Moon Lilith, and the Black Moon Lilith — and come to understand the shadow material in your life, the presence of the Dark Goddess, your connections to the Old Religion, and how the process of anger and resolution of conflict works out in your life.[22] I learned that Asteroid Lilith squares my lunar nodes, directly affecting my destiny and that Dark Moon Lilith opposes my sun exactly. Black Moon Lilith is conjunct my Juno at the top of my chart, making me a very "heavy" wife, to say the least, and they exactly conjunct my husband's Dark Moon Lilith, adding betrayal to the age-old intensity of our relationship.

I discovered that the asteroid Bacchus is conjunct my moon, along with Merlin — both male aspects of the old Goddess religion, relating to magic, Tantra, and ecstatic religion. I've been obsessed with how the ancient people moved the great stones that created their temples and stone circles, and it is Merlin who was said to have built Stonehenge in one

▲ *Fig. 32   This vessel with breasts is
from Old Europe around 6000 B.C.E.
and shows the fundamental archetype
of the Feminine as container and pro-
vider of nourishment. The female
body cannot very well be separated
from the body of the earth, in which
our bodies function like cells. What
she feels, we feel, for better or worse.
Drawing by Laurelin Remington-
Wolf.*

night through the use of sound and magic. The asteroid Arabia is exactly conjunct my sun, and I have spent my entire
adult life unearthing material about the ancient Goddess
whose roots have led me again and again to the Middle East
and the Neolithic cultures that spawned Inanna, the first
writing, poetry, weaving, agriculture, priestess temples, and
pervasive images of the divine Female. Arabia is also one of
the places where astrology began. I learned through astrology
that my Pluto (transformation and power) sits on the ascendant of both my daughters; that my Down's syndrome son's
Chiron (healer) sits exactly on the North Node of my destiny,
and that Uranus was transitting my South Node (past lives)
when my husband, Jonathan, came into my life, and I married him at once. Doing astrology is deep fun, sacred play,
profound study. Every avenue leads to new questions, every
"answer" opens a whole new world to explore. You cannot
possibly exhaust it in one lifetime, so there is never a need to
feel overwhelmed or behind.

The whole process of the female shaman is one of
opening and becoming a larger vessel. In ancient times the
women spent a good part of their time making sacred vessels
of all types, large and small, many with breasts and a divine
triangle (see fig. 32). It must have been comforting to have
the constant presence and reminder of these sacred pots, linking to the female body and our deep, purposeful being in the
world of form. In our magical vessels women produce life.
The sacred enclosure of the womb guards and nourishes the
new life then activates to push it out into the world. Every

month, like the moon, we die and are reborn as our vessel fills and empties to celebrate this event. Contemporary Western women have so much available to us that we don't know how to bring into the world. We have all the experiences of every lifetime, distilled to the essence, ready to bring into this incarnation. Yet the forms facing us in this particular century are so limited, so tightly circumscribed. We are told we can be either a wife or a spinster, either a mother or remain unfulfilled. We can work or we can raise our children.

Astrology is the perfect discipline to help us learn to stretch and accept paradox. To master astrology you have to let go and not know. To learn to understand the planets you have to be willing to let them work through you completely, and you have to yield to what they want, at the same time making creative choices and decisions regarding your life path. You have to study a lot and think only a little, letting what you know surface through your life experience, your intuition, and your dreams. It's as if there is this river flowing that is your life. You are in a kind of boat with an oar for steering, and it's your job to run this river creatively. Your goal is to enjoy the ride, not get hung up anywhere, not sink or drown, and when you come to where the river meets the ocean, to let your little boat sail right on out to sea. It's my profound belief that astrology is a central tool for making this life a joyful, exhilarating ride without fear.

# The Dreamer and Her Path of Power

IN THE ANCIENT WORLD DREAM-
ing was sacred, providing an opportunity to touch the spirit
world and obtain advice, direction, healing. Cave paintings in
old Europe and rock art in Africa and Australia show us that
early people were able to merge with the world of animal spirits and dream helpers, no doubt calling on them through what
we would now label vision quest or initiation rites. The most
remarkable paintings and drawings are found in caverns difficult of access, requiring the initiate to crawl on his or her
belly for long distances in the dark. The incredible hybrid animal and human figures inscribed on the walls of the Lascaux
or Peche-Merle caves in France may have been inspired by
sacred dreams and visions of the ancient shamans, either individually or as a group.

Later, during transitional times—when worship of the Great Mother changed to worship of a Sky
Father—in Greece and other places, temples were built for
initiates to enter in order to sleep there and "incubate" healing
dreams. Such temples were presided over by priestesses of
the Goddess Hygeia (fig. 33) or later the priests of healing
gods, such as Asclepius. In Malta statues have been found of
a sleeping Goddess (fig. 34), a dreamer perhaps, or one of the
priestesses who, like modern shamans, would have incubated
a dream for the petitioner who came to the temple. These
images, from 3000 B.C.E., have an antecedent in the Paleolithic era (ca. 25,000 B.C.E.), where one of the ancient caves
has carved into the rock on either side of the entry the figure

▲ *Fig. 33 Hygeia, the Goddess of health, is the last remnant of female healing once so common in the Greek world—her shrines usurped by male deities. Pictured here, she has her snakes for prophecy and magic. Eventually these snakes became the symbol of the American Medical Association, which is ironic given that Western medicine was created over the dead bodies of European healers and wise women. Gynecology and obstetrics were invented by men after they created and patented forceps. Drawing by Laurelin Remington-Wolf.*

of a woman "reclining" (fig. 35). Archaeology discusses this symbology in terms of feminine indolence, whereas certainly the images were sacred and represented a state of trance, dreaming, or giving birth which must have taken place in the interior of the cave temple.

Throughout history dreams have been seen as avenues to the spirit world and ways of getting divine guidance or sanction for certain actions. Roman, Chinese, and Aztec emperors tended to follow the advice of their magical consultants who dreamed for them. Even as late as the twentieth century the czar of Russia was listening to the advice of his Merlinlike magician Rasputin. Only in industrialized Western countries have we forgotten how to dream and how to respect and listen to our dreams. We don't take dreams seriously in the West, a result of the so-called Age of Enlightenment when "science" replaced the nine million women healers ("witches") who were burned to death during the Inquisition for dreaming, visions, and other "works of the Devil."

At this point in human history, especially in North America, people are so drugged and media overloaded, it is unusual even to remember that we dream. Is it any wonder we don't take our dreams seriously? It is not unusual to hear North Americans say that they don't dream, which is biolog-

▲ *Fig. 34   This sleeping woman from the island of
Malta is probably incubating a dream or perhaps — as
some scholars think — waiting for the spirit of a dead
ancestor to enter her body as a new child. This waiting
was done four stories underground in the* hypogeum,
*where the dead were entombed and which was also,
according to Elinor Gadon, apparently used for oracles,
prophecy, ritual, and ceremony. Drawing by Laurelin
Remington-Wolf.*

▲ *Fig. 35   This may be an earlier version of the same
archetypal woman lying in wait for a child to enter her
womb or incubating a dream or vision or even, as
Marija Gimbutas suggests, giving birth. This figure was
inscribed in the rock leading into a cavern in France
during the Paleolithic period. Another similar figure
was drawn on the other side, so that as a person entered
the cave, she was flanked by these female images. The
cave itself was used for ritual. Drawing by Laurelin
Remington-Wolf.*

113

ically impossible. Part of any shamanic awakening must include an opening of the dream channels and the uprushing of amazing and illuminating material from the unconscious. Becoming aware of our dreams is a healing process in and of itself, bringing us into direct contact with the inner planes. Something usually stimulates such an awakening—a cleansing of some kind, a period of retreat, a healing process. Whatever is blocking the dream process, or the process of remembering, must be removed in order for the dreaming to begin in earnest.

In 1976 I made a dramatic shift away from prescription medicine and a dependency on chemicals to treat my tension headaches, and my dreams opened very rapidly, without effort or conscious intention. Discontinuing the chemical medications I had been putting into my system for ten years was such a cleansing, it released my unconscious process into the daylight. Most of us have no idea what kinds of effects are caused by the chemicals we ingest daily. The average intake of "ordinary" tranquilizers like Valium is so high among the general population (especially women) that tribal shamans would be horrified. We are drugging ourselves into a national stupor, completely blocking the natural healing process that the dream life provides for us. Add to this the huge amount of alcohol, marijuana, cocaine, and sleeping pills Americans consume, on top of whatever prescriptions are given to us by doctors for our various ailments, and it becomes clear that we have a serious collective crisis on our hands. The inability to dream creates further tensions that are often "cured" by prescriptions for more complex drugs in larger and more frequent dosages.

Another major blockage to recalling and relating to our dreams is the fast and unreflective pace at which most Westerners live. At night, after a dinner of meat, much of America sits in front of the television for several hours, drinking beer and eating sugar, potato chips, and other chemical-laced substances. Americans go to bed late, sleep only a few hours, and are rudely awakened by an alarm clock. People jump out of bed, shower, rush through dressing and breakfast, get in the car to drive somewhere to work all day, repeating the whole sequence the next night. Is it any wonder we don't think much about our dreams and that we laugh at the suggestion that they might matter? For most of us, to begin to remember our dreams and use them creatively requires a revolutionary transformation in our approach to everyday life.

To dream well it is wise to eat little before bed and go to sleep well before midnight. How many modern women are able to keep this kind of schedule? Moreover, to remember dreams it is best to waken naturally at the end of a dream sequence, slowly, and write the dream down before even going to the bathroom. This gentle approach to awakening stimulates the dreaming consciousness to remember deeper dreams that occurred earlier in the night—the dreams behind the dreams—and to recall more details that would have otherwise disappeared into the unconscious on rising. There are special techniques that can further the dreaming process, such as sleeping on the right side, drinking mugwort or saffron tea before bed, burning incense, and using crystals and dream pillows. All this creates an optimum situation for dreaming in order to stimulate and relate to dreams in a sacred, healing way. We can use techniques such as a short meditation practice of clearing the events of the day before sleeping, which allows dreaming to start at a deeper level and produces more significant, bigger dreams before morning.

Clearly, if it were possible, all women would take a break from the normal routines to do our sacred dreaming. I remember how upset I got with my young children when I first began to remember and work with my dreams. They didn't know how much it mattered, and they would come into my bedroom with their morning agendas and interrupt my process of awakening, causing me to lose the dreams as if they were sucked down a tunnel. I couldn't follow the dreams and couldn't retrieve them. I had to create a serious boundary between me and my children first thing in the morning, a definite rule that they could not bother me until I was awake and ready to interact with them. It took a while to get it working, but without such a boundary I was going to be angry with my daughters every single day. The payoff was worth the effort, as I was able to begin writing down my dreams and having them for myself, which was extremely nurturing.

For several years I kept elaborate dream journals and worked on my dreams every day. Since I didn't have a teacher or healer with whom to apprentice, this process was important in my learning. I read books about dreams, using their suggested methods, studied Tibetan dream yoga (along with other forms of yoga and Tibetan practices), and nourished myself with esoteric treatises and philosophical tracts, learning to read the tarot cards and finally creating the *Motherpeace* cards during this time. Many mornings as I came out of a dream, I would write it down and discover in it information pertaining to the particular Motherpeace image I was working on that day.

The power animals that appeared to me in my dreams became the deepest stimulants for dreamwork and held the most continuity in the process for me. My first power animal as an adult, after my shamanic healing crisis began in 1976, was a giant Mexican orange-kneed tarantula as big as me. As a child I had been terribly afraid of spiders. I couldn't stand to be in the room with one and would scream until someone took it away or killed it. At night I had recurring nightmares of spiders climbing all over me, under the bed, on the walls. My parents and sisters were quite forgiving with me about this phobia, "taking care of" the problem for me whenever they could. I learned to rely on others for their help with this enemy.

When I was about nine years old, I carried on a horrible secret compulsion for a period of several weeks. We had moved from a small town to a city in Iowa, and in my backyard I would catch large yellow and black garden spiders, although I was terrified of them, and put them in a jar. Then, for some reason that even now I cannot fathom, I would make little bonfires in our garage and drop them onto the flames, hissing, until they were dead. I carried out this obsessive activity, over and over again, with a terrible fascination that expressed itself nowhere else in my life, before or after. Clearly I was possessed.

The activity eventually passed, and I went on with my very normal Midwestern, suburban life, adjusting to the neighborhood and our move. I remained hysterically afraid of spiders until my first marriage ended in 1972. When I decided to leave my husband and live with my young daughters by myself, I began to have a different relationship to the terrifying creature of my childhood. One day, after driving the children home from day care to our small house in Colorado Springs where we had lived with their dad, I went to open the garage door while my daughters waited in the car. As I opened the door, a very large, shiny black spider greeted me at eye level, hanging before my face from her own sticky thread. I knew immediately it was a black widow, although I had never seen one before, and instead of my typical response of screaming and running away, I thought clearly of my situation. My children and I lived there alone. If I let her go, she might hurt them. I took off my shoe and gently knocked the spider off the door, killed her thoughtfully without squashing her body, turned her over, and called my daughters over to educate them about their first black widow spider. "Don't ever touch one of these," I said calmly, "they can hurt you."

This event changed my life. From that point on, in the daytime, I was no longer hysterical at the fact that spiders shared the world with me. Five years later, when my shamanic path opened and they began to visit me in numinous dreams, it seemed cosmically right to me. The first vision from my Mexican tarantula was positively demonic in its impact on my psyche. She was enormous, dark and hairy, with knees of orange crystal, gemlike and fantastical, and she danced and jumped in the dream, taunting me. I was in awe of her, dwarfed and frightened by her, and I awakened hysterical and in a cold sweat. I was to enter into a dreaming confrontation with her over and over again in the years to come, in a gradual process of healing and rebirth. I always dreaded her return yet paradoxically looked forward to each opportunity as an initiation in which I might teach myself to rise to the occasion in more courageous and creative ways. Over the years my dreams were visited by black velvet tarantulas, some black with red interlocking rings on their backs, and finally one that was my pet and drank milk from a cup I put on the floor for her. Finally I danced with them.

The spider was Shakti for me, a teacher in the yoga I practiced daily and had begun to teach in the community. I imagined her as dancing, creatively and endlessly active, going about her business with power and authority, as I needed to learn to do. I witnessed in her a dark jewellike sexual power, a raw potency I recognized as Tantric and that I would later come to understand as shamanic, female, and arising from contact with the Dark Goddess. I manifested her artistically as part of a collaborative theater piece in 1980 with Cassandra Light, Karen Vogel, and other Bay Area performing artists. I created her in clay on an enormous spiderweb frame in red, black, and white, the colors of the Moon Goddess. My artistic representation of her finally died one day in

1983, during my High Priestess year, when I was moving the piece from one house to another, at the end of a relationship. Driving down the highway, she fell from my car and broke. During the same period a student in one of my first Mother-peace classes brought me the cast-off skin of her live Mexican orange-kneed tarantula named Gertrude. Only then did I comprehend the symbol: tarantulas — like snakes — shed their skins. Now when I find I am sharing the house with black widows, either I live in harmony with them or escort them politely outside to a more appropriate place for them to live. I feel blessed by the presence of spiders and understand them to be messengers of the Great Goddess in my life. They no longer come as opponents in my dreams; they are allies now.

The material in our dreams lends itself to a wide variety of interpretations and analyses. All the techniques for understanding and working with dreams can be interesting and useful in terms of psychological development, growth, self-understanding, and so forth. But on a deeper level dreams are not to be understood, not to be grasped. Shamanically they guide us and provide us with direct wholistic information to which we do not have access in the daytime. We may not ever actually come to understand the creatures in our dreams or the real meaning of their visits. I could write pages of Jungian interpretation about spiders or about Native American myths and cross-cultural stories with spiders and Spider Woman as the subject, but it wouldn't really explain the *why* of the dream. The only thing that really matters in the dreamwork is the personal experience — the tactile, vibrational experience that stays with me forever.

The orange-kneed tarantula never changes in my dreambody. It is always as powerful and numinous as the first time I saw it. I know she is a real being, alive, existing in another dimension, awake to me. I am always moved to the same sacred place when I think of her or picture her in my mind. Every now and then the red and black velvet spiders return to my dreams, reminding me of some new aspect of my process with the Shakti work. In recent years the yellow and black garden spider has made regular oracular appearances, as in the example I mentioned in chapter 3. It is interesting to me to make distinctions, to understand, for instance, that tarantulas don't spin, they dance and jump and shed their skins. Or to contemplate that the garden spider sits very still and spins webs that shine in the sunlight, creations she makes from her own substance, that catch her dinner. But these discriminations only point me to the deep, sacred truth of the experience as I felt it directly in the dreams. They don't speak of the numinous presence of the creature herself. The interpretations I make even remove me to a certain extent from my relationship with the animals or dream characters, which in the final analysis, is all that matters.

As complex human beings, we might deal with our dreams in myriad ways, all of which are fun and satisfying, leading to healing and empowerment. But the important thing to keep in mind as we dream and pay attention to the dreams is the inscrutability of the Mystery. Dreams come from the Mystery. They are manifestations of the deep unknown, of spirit, and even beyond spirit. They speak to us in a language that is cross-cultural and without racial bias. They allow communication with anyone, anywhere, of any species. They put us in touch with everything at all times, telepathically and completely. Dreams are totally beyond our ability to understand with our brain consciousness. Any dreamwork we do is for the purpose of simply penetrating the first few layers with our rational understanding, so that we can integrate and assimilate material from the archetypal realm into the everyday waking consciousness. The Mystery itself can be felt as a giant web that holds us all in contact and in undeniable connection with one another, as well as with other selves throughout all our lifetimes.

When I first dreamed of the Mexican tarantula, I went to the San Francisco aquarium, where they keep a live one in a cage. I stood and stared at this living embodiment of my dream creature for a long time, sort of thrilled, fascinated, and revolted all at once. I wanted, of course, to get over my fear and terror, to make friends with it, and come away a better person. I couldn't get past my horror of it for quite a while, and then, suddenly, it moved. Chills ran down my spine; my skin crawled. Visceral, tactile reactions, creepy and scary: How did a creature get so hairy? How could an insect be so big? Of course, spiders are not insects, and this one seemed to have the consciousness that we think of as characterizing mammals. It was an animal! I watched it and thought on it for a long time, and at some point I surely made contact with it, because it began to relate to me. Then the most extraordinary thing happened. My heart opened. My chest got warm and tingly, with waves of warm energy flowing out from the

▲ *Fig. 36A I made this line drawing at the beginning of a five-year process of dream-work in relation to the taran-tula, a frightening image of Shakti or the dynamic, creative Feminine.*

▲ *Fig. 36B The tarantula dances, leaps, and sheds its skin regularly. During the Middle Ages in Europe, women went somehow "wild" and together danced a dance called the Tarantella until they dropped, a practice reminiscent of the earlier Maenads, who went wild in relation to the ecstatic God Dionysus. Photo by Catherine Allport.*

center in response to this creature that I was attempting to love. It made me sweaty and brought tears to my eyes.

The next time I went to visit, I brought my art tablet with me and drew its picture (fig. 36A). After that my dreams were more friendly, and the spider visited me in smaller, more lifelike forms instead of as the enormous, larger-than-life giant it had been in my first dream. Finally its Mexican origins began to prod and stimulate me, awakening a deep passion for that country and its people. In 1983 I married my husband in Mexico after traveling there for several weeks in search of what we felt to be a strong past-life connection. I had been working on a book about the Goddess in Mexico, which took form that year while we were there, called *La Diosa Escondida (The Hidden Goddess)*. Now I travel and teach in Mexico and have learned to speak some Spanish. I am certain that the orange-kneed tarantula, my shamanic awakening, and my roots in ancient Mexico are all linked in some esoteric way, part of the unfathomable Mystery of life and death and the Goddess (see fig. 36B).

Another power animal who appeared early in my dreams and has remained as a personal guardian for me is the giant snake. The snake is linked to creation and healing from the earliest times, carved in wet clay on Paleolithic cave walls thirty thousand years ago (fig. 37) and found everywhere in the world since that time. In India the snake is the Goddess Kundalini, she who "rises" through the chakras, bringing healing, enlightenment, and spiritual attainment to yogic practitioners. Her worship has continued unbroken in India since matriarchal times, and she is directly connected to the female body and biology. In general the snake can be said to be the totem of women.

My first visitation from the giant snake came on Candlemas in 1981. For five years I had kept myself in intentional male-free space, giving myself a much-needed rest from the dramas and struggles of the sex-role battle. During that time Karen Vogel and I created the *Motherpeace Tarot Cards*, and I healed myself of major physical and emotional illness and more or less raised my young daughters. But at Winter Solstice of 1980, I met a man who would become my lover and creative partner for two very intense years of growth and sharing. Six weeks later, on Candlemas—the day that we would become lovers—I woke up from the following dream: I have unconsciously stumbled into a giant cobra's nest, and before I can escape, she raises up—huge and green—and strikes at my heart. As I awaken, I feel the sting in the center of my chest, and I understand that I am dying.

To make love to a man again, after such a long time, and with a great deal of passion and depth, was, of course, a major death to my identity. The energetic influx that came with the relationship, which had the distinct feel of a past-life connection and opened my sense of myself as a temple priestess, was directly connected to kundalini energy and Tantric practices. (Astrologically my Vesta is on his South Node, connoting past-life Tantric connections.) I wrote passionate poetry and felt an arousal of energy in my system that was both erotic and creative. During this time I went to the San Francisco aquarium, where my friendly tarantula lived, to visit a giant reticulated python that had always fascinated me. The python—thirty feet long—had always been coiled and asleep (or in trance) when I had visited the museum. But on this particular day, when I walked up to the cage and looked at the great animal, she suddenly roused her giant self and

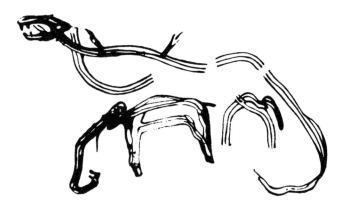

▲ *Fig. 37   This is surely one of the oldest dragons ever created. It was finger painted with wet clay during the Paleolithic period in a European cavern where ritual was performed. The Chinese still refer to the currents running underground in the earth as dragon currents, and the geomancers in England have discovered the "dragon lines" running between all the old stone circles built by ancient Goddess-worshiping people. Drawing by Jennifer Roberts.*

came right over to the window to meet me eye to eye. I was almost blown away. As I stood there facing this amazing, beautiful, powerful creature in her awake state, the kundalini energies were swirling through my whole body, up and down, like a wind rushing through me. The experience was beyond eroticism, yet it contained something akin to sexuality, and I realized that the snake was not relating to me — Vicki — but was responding to and communicating with *my snake!* In that moment I understood in my body what anthropology has so weakly named totemism or animism. Aboriginal people say that when a child is born, so is her totem (somewhere in nature), and that the animal's life parallels that of the child as she grows. My snake, as I felt her in my body that day, was very real and tangible and was clearly visible to this physical snake in the cage.

Although I have had many, many snake dreams since that time, one other one stands out as directive in my life. During the same relationship I just described, toward the end of our two-year period together (which not only started on Candlemas but also ended on that holiday), I was engaged in a deep struggle with my emotional and nurturing needs, while trying to figure out how to make a sufficient living. This dream helped me more than all the thinking in the world: I am standing on wet red clay which suddenly begins to move. I realize it is alive and I feel threatened. I hastily attempt to get away, climbing up a huge cliff as fast as I can as the red clay turns into a huge red snake. As I look back over my shoulder, the red snake has become much larger and has turned white. It towers over me, laughing a huge, deep belly laugh (male), saying, "When are you going to let me take care of you?" On awakening, I feel so totally held by the universe that I am able to stop worrying and begin the always-necessary process of letting go in faith. Again the tangible presence of this totem made my life easier to handle by giving me an irrefutable and direct contact with the natural world and its cosmic forces.

Most women have had snake dreams. Many women are afraid of them, considering them bizarre or wishing they would go away. But when women learn that the snake, which has been demonized along with the Dark Goddess, is the ancient totem of women and healing, they begin to integrate its positive qualities into their lives. When I have snake dreams, I always feel cared for and close to the Mother. I often dream of rattlesnakes, which are friendly to me, and other small snakes, which I am holding or caring for in some way. In one dream I wore snakes around my neck as jewelry, which demonstrated my shamanic power, and I frequently use snakes in my dreams as power tools—pointing them, shooting them somewhere with purpose, or using them in some way. Recently when I was ill, I dreamed of a medicine man with white hair like mine, wearing skins and carrying a snake; he was "very rattlesnake."

The third totem animal that has always visited my dreams is the owl. Owl medicine seems to relate specifically to female group work, especially shamanic healing, and has to do with a certain kind of authority or leadership in that area. When I first began to study yoga, a male guru visited my dreams with an owl as his messenger, and since that time the owl has become more mine, and more feminine. Most recently I dreamed that I was in a field where there was construction work and noisy machinery, and the owl came down and lighted on my back, blending and merging into my body, until we were one, and we flew away from the noise and the static of the physical plane. This signified a transition I would soon be making in my work life, moving into a slightly more

▲ *Fig. 38 This figure of Lilith, the Night Hag, was sketched by Coral Cadman from the original relief at the British Museum. Lilith is part owl, part woman and represents the demonized Dark Goddess in Western culture. She was Adam's first wife but refused to be subservient to him, so God replaced her with Eve. The story goes on to say she spends her time copulating with demons near the Red Sea and having grotesque demon children, a hundred per day. All over the world the owl that pertained to women's magic and healing power has been made inauspicious and unclean. Even native people on the North American continent seem to feel an aversion to owl medicine, although it is still just as firmly connected to women as ever.*

transpersonal plane, doing less administrative work and more creative "flying." Although I have dreamed of many other animals over the years, these three—the spider, the snake, and the owl—seem to be my guardian animals who come again and again when I am in need or when the universe needs to get a message to me. All three, interestingly enough, belong to the demonized realm of the Dark Mother (see fig. 38).

# Dreamwork

I use a simple system for coming into relationship with the dreams, easy ways of working with them that fit many different needs and impulses. I hope, ultimately, that my students will come to experience their dreams as numinous realities or messages from the invisible world, as guides for living and preparation for dying. Life itself, with all its seeming concreteness, is really a dream in which we have the possibility of making choices in every moment and changing the dream: flying, making love, shape shifting, experiencing the impossible. The amazing synchronous connections between what we dream and what we experience in the daylight hours should be enough to confuse the rational mind about its clear-cut separation between dreaming and "real life." The constant interpenetration of the dream life into reality, and vice versa, should successfully teach us that they are one and the same experience, with only a slightly different texture.[1]

It's amazing how much information, feeling, and meaning come through in telling a dream in the first person, present tense. Sometimes just this change (from past to present) will open the dreamer to the deeper levels of her own dream, without having to do any work. In the same vein, the first level of dreamwork I ask people to do is the shamanic level of "real information." How much real information is in this particular dream? If I dream of my mother, I might take the dream at face value and call her to find out if something from the dream is really happening to her. If I dream I am having a fight with a good friend, or someone in my community, I need to tell the dream to that person, as a completion and as a form of communication of something that may be going on between us on the unconscious or invisible level. Bringing it to our consciousness may be the main purpose of the dream.

At the next level, I might begin to associate around the symbols in the dream. For instance, maybe I would write down everything that came into my mind about my mother in this dream — what she is wearing, how she looks, what she says, who she is with, what she reminds me of, how old I am in relation to her in this dream, how old she is, and so on. I flesh her out as a symbol, feel into her as someone appearing

**125**

in this form in my dream at this time. This is more of a psychological approach to the dream, which allows the imagination and the associative mind to be very active. What does this person (this symbol) stand for in this particular dream? What does it make me think about, feel, want? What does she represent to me? Sometimes we wake up knowing what a particular person or thing means in a dream—it just pops into our mind. Other times it has to be worked a little.

The deepest level of technical dreamwork is to embody the dream characters and objects. Probably the simplest way to do this is the "gestalt" approach, where I put a pillow out in front of me to represent my mother or whomever I am wanting to understand from the dream. I begin to dialogue with this person or object. I do this by speaking to her (out loud or silently) from my position as myself. Then when I am ready to hear from her, I go over and sit on her pillow, and I let her speak through me. I become her. This sounds silly to the uninitiated, but it works so well and so quickly. There is nothing to say but try it. While the associative method brings expansion and clarification to the mind, this third method brings the dream into the body. Whatever person or thing seemed "other" than the dreamer becomes one with her now. What was inconceivable or incomprehensible in the dream experience becomes understandable and forgivable now. We blend into the other characters, we become one with them, they become part of us. We know what they experience, what they think and feel, what they would say. We can complete the conversation, finish the dream action, make peace, open our hearts.

This is the most difficult level of dreamwork because it frequently needs to be done when there is an adversary or opponent in the dream, someone with whom we do not ordinarily identify. To the conscious mind of the dreamer, for example, a rapist in the dream is unforgivable, entirely corrupt, without hope, without room for compassion. To the deeper self of the dreamer, if she is willing to try the painful process of literally moving into the rapist's space for a time, it will become clear that she contains parts of herself that not only understand but are like him. She will actually feel him—his pain, his confusion, his suffering. It is completely healing and heart opening to come into contact with these cast-off, unacceptable parts of ourselves. It is not that the dreamer would enact this shadow part of herself; she simply needs to contact it, which immediately brings a visceral understanding and compassion. This body-based compassion flows out of us into the world and affects others. Our ability to identify with all sentient beings opens the way for us to free ourselves and others from the terrible collective pain of life on our planet at this time.[2]

The deep truth that dreamwork teaches us is that we are all the same. All humans here on the planet are having essentially the same experience, with minor variations. There are different levels of consciousness, quite different external material circumstances, and different "karmas" working their way out through each of us. But our feelings, hopes, dreams, fears, pain, and suffering are very similar—a collective experience. We try to be individuals, wearing different costumes and personnas, but inside we are not that different. This is a spiritual maxim that sounds abstract until we begin to practice identifying with others. In our very mechanized, isolated reality of the twentieth century, it takes intentional work to come to this level of response-ability, to be able to identify or empathize with other human beings in different circumstances. Americans are used to joining groups and clubs based on our external similarities. We group ourselves by income, neighborhood, race, job level, religious preference, and whether or not we have children. We actually come to believe that others are completely different from us, and therefore, secretly at least, they must be against us. Then, of course, we come to fear others as threats to our well-being.

Dreamwork puts us in touch with the collective mind and its images. Doing the work in groups is especially healing and evocative, but doing it on our own is a good beginning. When we practice coming into contact with the deep reality our dreams are wanting to express to us and through us, we open to an invisible level of life that contains much of what is missing from our daily routines. Following our dreams over the years leads to a deeper understanding of our inner selves than would ever be possible by only tracking our conscious developmental level. Allowing the process of our dream to unfold naturally, but following and keeping in touch with it, is very exciting. By paying attention to the dream level (what Arnold Mindell calls the secondary level)[3] we begin to respond to the unconscious parts of ourselves. We can allow these parts to live in us more fully, responding, expanding, growing into our real complexity.

Finally there is active, intentional dreamwork that involves going back into the dream and intentionally changing it: completing it, reworking it, making it stronger or more powerful in some way. A natural, organic healing is available through our dreams. When we have a nightmare or a recurring, disturbing dream of some kind, we can reenter it either in trance or in another dream and make different choices, try different alternatives, to bring about a different outcome. The dream state is more fluid than everyday life seems, allowing for quick changes and magical actions. In a dream we can decide—on the spot—to evaporate or disappear, to fly, or to change into something else. We can dematerialize other people or things, throw them away or physically overpower them, or turn them into friendly characters right before our eyes. We can, like the Senoi people of Malaysia, confront the opponent and get a gift, making a shamanic ally out of them. Practicing empowerment can occur in the dream state, which is then mimicked in "real" life, where things are denser and take longer to change. Eventually the changes we have made in our dreams begin to spill over into our waking lives in visible, demonstrable ways.

In this way shamanic dreaming is empowerment work for women, who have been disenfranchised from the central workings of our culture and who are so often the victims of violence and aggression. It is possible through dreamwork to build a strong psychic defense that actually keeps away danger and protects against violation and makes us physically stronger. Dreamwork can teach us to stand our ground, to speak out when we have something to say, and to fight back when we are threatened with annihilation. In a nightmare I had early in my process of shamanic healing, a man tried to rape and kill me. In the dream I was terrified, trying to scream but unable to make a sound come out of my throat (a common female dream). I entered back into the dream in a meditation, determined to face the rapist-murderer and fight for my life. After I was successfully able to do that— viscerally, with my whole being—I never had to practice it again. I practice nonviolence as a way of life, but in order to ground myself even to begin to stand on my own feet, I needed to respect myself enough to protect me. Having done that, the product of that experience has stayed with me in my psychic field all these years. It seems to be a permanent part of my dreambody.

As a shamanic student progresses in technical dream-work, it becomes less and less necessary to work on dreams actively. Like yoga or other forms of meditation, after practicing the skills for a while, the dreamwork "takes." It becomes a flowing experience of continuity with the other parts of the shamanic life. The dreams, like the waking states, are filled with signs and oracles, messages and truths, paradoxes and challenges, which need to be attended to as soon as they are perceived by the dreamer. I no longer get up most mornings and write my dreams for forty-five minutes, as I once did; but I live my dreams in a deeper way than I ever have. They heal and guide me, and I use them to live well. In my marriage, dreams have been very important in resolving conflict, because they speak from a level beneath the struggle of our two egos. Oftentimes my husband and I dream for each other, bringing healing messages and truth to what would otherwise be a blocked or painfully conflicted conversation. When we reach a stalemate on the conscious level, our relationship becomes more active on the dream level.

My students frequently dream real facts about me and my life or experience me visiting them and teaching them in their dreams. We share these dreams and work with them when we can. We often have group dreams, on behalf of and for the benefit of the entire circle. This is classic shamanic work, dreaming for the community. I have made some of my most important structural decisions about my school and classes from these kind of healing dreams. When the conscious mind doesn't know what to do, the unconscious mind can unlock the solution. We just have to be patient and wait, rather than acting from fear or impatience. It sometimes takes the dreaming consciousness a few days to come to an expression or the waking mind to remember it. And it seems that when we are in transition in our psyches, our symbols and our internal language begin to change. As they change, the waking mind can't recognize them, so it forgets the dream as it wakes up in the morning. It takes dreaming the new dream a few times, practicing it, for the waking mind to become familiar with the new images and remember it consciously.

Isn't this a wonderful metaphor for shamanic training in general? *It takes the conscious self a little while to catch up with profound changes taking place on inner planes.* In times of radical transformation, the brain-consciousness gets tired, dull, befuddled, disoriented. It only knows the old, the familiar ways. It fears and recoils from the new and unknown. In those times we are tempted to contract and pull back from the changes, as if they might be dangerous to us, threatening disintegration. Our fears loom up in front of us, taking the form of possible terrible outcomes or consequences that we imagine might happen if we continue to grow and change. The conscious mind begins to rationalize why this growth isn't good for us. We fantasize about the good old days when we were more comfortably unconscious, more peacefully asleep. So it is as important in waking life as in dreaming to dream our new dreams over and over again and to tell our visions more than once in order to give them energy through sharing and embodying them. We rehearse them until they become real enough to us that the old pictures can fall away.

# Trance Journey and Spirit Flight

SHAMANISM IS DEFINED BY THE ability of the shaman to enter a trance state and travel in a body different from the physical one we see with our eyes. The purpose of this shaman flight is healing, although the individual methods vary from culture to culture. Often the trance journey is enacted because the soul of the sick person has strayed from its home—the body—and the shaman has to go and retrieve the wandering or lost soul. Sometimes the journey is for the explicit purpose of communing with powerful beings who live in a different reality from the physical, in order to get their help in a healing process or conquer them in a shamanic battle on the invisible planes. The shaman, or the shamanic patient, can use the trance state to obtain information and advice from teachers and guides who are available on other levels. Telepathy happens in trance states, allowing for long-distance communication to take place between people, and knowledge of the future (divination) can often be gained while in trance. Esoteric science says that physical healing of the body can best be done by focusing on the physical body from another plane of consciousness, through the trance state.[1] Methods of entering and achieving trance states vary from culture to culture and include a spectrum of diverse practices from quiet meditation to wild drumming and dancing, from fasting and purification to the ingestion of psychotropic substances (see fig. 39).

▲ *Fig. 39   This contemporary
Siberian shaman woman is
enacting what may be one of the
oldest shamanic ceremonies on
earth, a female dancing with bird
feathers to the beat of a drum.
This might be for the purpose of
making it rain or for healing
or divination on behalf of her
tribe. Drawing by Laurelin
Remington-Wolf.*

We have pervasive archaeological images of women
in trance states, eyes staring, often singing, chanting, or praying; sometimes they dance, often they wear skins or feathers.
Frequently they are pregnant or giving birth. Stories behind
the use of sacred medicinal herbs and plants that grow wild
on the planet often include something relating to pregnancy
and birth, leading me to think that the earliest uses of these
plants might well have been for calming and relieving the pain
of women in labor. Peyote, for example, was supposedly discovered by a pregnant woman who was wandering lost in the
desert, about to die from lack of food and drink, when she lay
down near a shady plant to rest. Here she saw the tiny peyote
plant, which told her (telepathically) to eat it and it would
take care of her and her baby. She did, and the rest is the
history of the Huicholes in Mexico. Every year the Huicholes
return to the "land where their Mothers dwell" in order to
pick the sacred peyote for the ceremonies their community
will share during the coming seasonal cycle. The Peyoteros
walk (and nowadays ride in buses and trucks) for three hundred miles to the place from which they descended, from the
time when their central deity was Grandmother Growth, the
first shaman and creator of the world.

The Huichols see incredible sacred visions when they
eat the sacred peyote and stare into the fire, and they chroni-
cle their visions in their now-famous artwork. The women
embroider fantastic bags, belts, and clothing; the men create
startlingly beautiful stories in their newly developed art of
yarn painting. Their famous earrings bear the "peyote stitch"
and the traditional pattern of the peyote flower. In more
ancient times they also ceremonially ate the *Kieri* plant or Tree
of the Wind (a form of sacred Datura), which is now consid-

ered more dangerous (and taboo) than the peyote. In their seasonal ceremonies the Huichol shamans honor the cornfields with the sacrificial blood of a slain bull (and in earlier times, a deer), which is a remnant of the much earlier times when the women in ancient Mexico invented agriculture and probably offered their menstrual blood to fertilize the fields.[2] Even today, the Huichols revere many female Goddesses of nature, including Eagle Mother, the Goddess of the Ocean, the Goddesses of the Rain, of the Corn, Beans, and so on.

Almost everywhere that shamanism has existed it seems to have at some time been connected with hallucinogens or consciousness-altering plants (see fig. 40A). In another part of Mexico the famous shaman Maria Sabina practiced her sacred mushroom ceremonies for fifty years in the local tradition of the indigenous people of that area (fig. 40B). Gordon Wasson's documentation of the "mushroom cult" and the healing power harnessed by Maria Sabina, as well as his scholarly work about the ancient "soma" of the Siberian shamans, gives us a contemporary glance into an ancient practice that seems exotic to us but has been an almost universal form of trance induction.[3] The thousands of female figures found in the cornfields, graves, and temple sites in ancient Mexico attest to the pervasive female shamanic trance ability and to some of the powers accrued through that practice as well. These figures with the wide, staring eyes of the "other world" dance, drum, play musical instruments, sing, chant, and practice yoga postures. Although scholars arbitrarily relegate them to the realm of "magic" and oppose them to "religion," the figures themselves clearly represent sacred activity and a consciousness focused somewhere other than the mundane (see fig. 41).

The whole issue of whether or not a shaman needs (or uses) hallucinogenic plants in order to enter altered states of consciousness is a heated one in the West. Since the sacred plants exist and have been used since the most ancient times for the most sacred work, one can hardly argue that they are bad or should be avoided. Yet since they have been made illegal in our culture, one can hardly recommend them either. The fact that Americans are materialistic and consumer oriented and make almost everything into commodities for our personal, selfish, instant gratification, without taking responsibility for the consequences, adds to the problem. I don't recommend taking recreational drugs, since in America it tends

▲ *Fig. 40A    This ancient mush-room stone was found in the highlands of Guatemala, one of hundreds, and refers to the ancient, sustained practice of shamanizing with the help of what Gordon Wasson called the wondrous mushroom. Drawing by Jennifer Roberts.*

▲ *Fig. 40B    Maria Sabina is probably Mexico's most famous shaman in the twentieth century, brought to public attention through the writings of Gordon Wasson. She, like so many women in Mexico and Central America, performed the sacred mushroom ceremonies for curing until her death in the 1980s. Photo courtesy of The Wasson Collection, The Botanical Museum, Harvard University.*

to lead to chronic addiction from which it is terribly hard to break free. Marijuana is the best example of this problem, being a totally sacred herb with a long history of sacred, ritual use in cultures around the world. Marijuana and LSD were the great liberators in the 1960s in this country, breaking people free from their mental constructs and shaping a visionary

▲ *Fig. 41* *This ancient Mexican shaman is Maria Sabina's predecessor from a much earlier strata and through her accoutrements, indicates the power and authority vested in healing. Ever blind to the power of the woman, archaeologists usually tag figures like this "noblewoman" at best and simply "female figurine" at worst. She radiates so much shamanic power that one is practically healed by looking at her! Drawing by Laurelin Remington-Wolf.*

culture, the ramifications of which are still being felt. Yet look at the number of people who became paralyzed from overuse of "weed," almost totally unable to act, spinning their own narcissistic little bubbles of isolation and lethargy, or the poor souls burned-out on LSD, who can be seen on street corners in Berkeley, still hearing voices and lecturing crazily to whomever will listen.

I took up smoking marijuana in the mid-1970s, long after many people of my generation had experimented for a decade with drugs. The tension headaches I had suffered were relieved temporarily by use of the plant; and more importantly, when I began occasionally to smoke alone, a whole world opened up within me that I had never known about. I learned about sacred play in this drug-induced state and began to spend time with myself being quiet, imagining, relaxing—all things I had not done since childhood. Being such an extroverted personality, I had simply never experienced the inner world, except when I was deeply in love or in some way "altered" by outer circumstances. I began to draw pictures and eventually made the *Motherpeace Tarot Cards*, all related to the psychic doors I learned to open through the use of the herb (see fig. 42). "Grass" was OK while I stayed at home and didn't go out into the world to work. But after my self-imposed retreat, when I wanted to participate in my culture again, I found it absolutely impossible to do so. Being chronically stoned and trying to do anything were mutually exclusive states of reality for me, and I

**135**

▲ *Fig. 42   Motherpeace Priest-*
*ess of Discs, a line drawing by*
*the author for* Motherpeace.
*The Priestess (or Queen) of*
*Discs traditionally shows a fer-*
*tile woman, close to the earth,*
*relaxed and healthy. In this*
*image I added a marijuana*
*plant as the tree that keeps tele-*
*pathic contact with her child*
*while she practices her yoga.*
*Marijuana, like other psychotro-*
*pic plants, has been a sacred*
*part of ceremonies in Mexico*
*since ancient times.*

gave up the drug for good. By that time my psychic awakening had thrown open my doors anyway, and even one toke
completely blew me away. In only three years it had gone
from a helping plant to a very unhealthy reliance on something other than myself. I have since watched the same pro-
gression in other North Americans. The combination of our
addictive tendencies and our lack of a spiritual base for our
lives often makes drug use a disaster. We lack the proper
resources for correct use, both as individuals and as a
community.

When the Huicholes enter the trance state together
through the collective use of their sacred peyote plant, they
experience something that is grounded in an ancient group
reality. From the time they are small children, babies even,
they take peyote and travel with the shamans to other worlds,
where they are initiated and taught the tribal wisdom. The
same is true for other tribal people around the world who use
psychotropic plants in their religious practices. They are
grounded together in a shared reality that is based in a sacred
set of values they hold dear. They are grounded in their bodies, and they have elders to lean upon. Our use of hallucinogens and psychotropic chemical substances here in the
United States has often been more for the purpose of shaking
up our realities, loosening our grip, and forcing a little of the
disintegrative process we need to undergo in order to get out
of our conditioning. When we ingest sacred substances in the
West, we may or may not touch the spirit, but the chances are
we will realize that things are not as tidy and normal as we
were taught to believe. When our mental constructs begin to

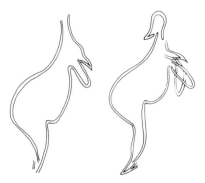

▲ *Fig. 43* *These pregnant dancing women are from the cavern of Peche-Merle in the south of France, dating from 20,000 B.C.E. or earlier. Drawn in wet clay on the inside wall of the cave sanctuary, they danced headless or birdheaded with other animals, in shamanic ecstasy. These may be the earliest shamans portrayed anywhere on the planet. Drawing by Laurelin Remington-Wolf.*

*Trance Journey and Spirit Flight*

break down, we are freed a little to open to the possibility of other realities, which is very helpful. For a people schooled to believe that spirits don't exist and are figments of their imaginations, that there is no reincarnation, and that healing can happen only with a prescription drug given by the doctor, these openings can be quite advantageous. However, as a shamanic way of life, drugs don't represent the best way of getting a consistent hold over ourselves. The key is in the integrative work. Can you bring the information and knowledge gained from the substance experience into your real life and ground it? If not, you will find yourself taking more and more of the substance to escape from your life into "bliss," which leads to a fairly serious (although false) separation between spirit and matter.

Dance is probably the oldest and most widespread form of shamanic trance-inducing activity. Shamans in many parts of the world dance to raise the energy and change the consciousness. The headless and bird-headed women dancing, pregnant, on the walls of the cavern at Peche-Merle are the oldest dancing shamans on the planet. Merged with the animals, drawn in wet clay with someone's fingers as much as thirty thousand years ago (fig. 43), they embody the ecstasy and freedom that characterizes shamanism and the trance state. Similarly African women run and dance on rock cliffs in what is now the Sahara, as do Aboriginal women in Australia. In ancient China, Joseph Needham tells us, the female shamans—called *Wu*—danced with bird feathers and rattles. The *Wu* were able to make it rain, among their other healing powers. Think of the Chinese arts of acupuncture, geomancy, and meditation, and you have some sense of the legacy left by the *Wu.* They were originally "spirit healers," whose name

▲ *Fig. 44 Gabrielle Roth is an "urban sha-man," author of* Maps to Ecstasy: Teachings of an Urban Shaman, *and well-known teacher of shamanic movement and trance dancing. In this photo she and her drum blend into one expressive elemental sound through the power of the trance. Photo by Robert Ansell. Reprinted with permission.*

was later changed to mean "witch" or "wizard." In Africa the *Kung!* Bushpeople dance to heal illness in their tribe. While the women clap the rhythm, the men dance, and when the heat is properly raised, healers lay their hands on the sick person to disengage the "demons" or spirits of illness and bring the soul back to the body. The healers describe the experience of going into trance with yogic-bodily manifesta-tions: The *num* boils up the spine of the dancer in trance, and when it reaches the head, he (or she — some of the best healers are women) puts his hands on the patient to transmit this energy into the sick body.[4] Some Ojibway shamans describe a process of trance induction that includes dancing and shak-ing wildly to raise heat and being able to control weather and other phenomena.[5]

Aside from psychotropic plants, the drum may be the most powerful single instrument for inducing trance in a per-son. The steady rhythm of the drum basically forces the con-sciousness to change, actually causing the brain waves to decrease to what our scientists call the alpha level or deeper, which allows normal thought patterns to be interrupted and even to cease. When the rational mind is interrupted from its ordinary mental processes, visions can happen, the inner eye can open to the invisible world, and a new perspective can be gained (see fig. 44). Even Westerners have been able to access this form of the trance journey, which has become the most popular in North America among Anglos. Among Sibe-rian and Lapp shamans, the drum has been used to put the shaman into such a deep trance state that he or she "dies" to this world and enters the "other." The shaman literally drops his or her physical body and journeys in another body—lighter and invisible, the "soul body" or "spirit body"—to the upper world or the underworld. The physical body is guarded by one of the shaman's human helpers, who makes sure that it is kept intact for the shaman's eventual safe return. It seems, in this deep trance state, as if the physical body is deeply asleep or comatose, to the point of being like a corpse, and that the enlivening force of the shaman's soul is truly at work somewhere else. The drummer holds the rhythm, keeping a steady beat that carries the shaman on the journey and brings the soul back to the body on completion of the task.

This kind of deep, cataleptic trance state is not necessary for healing work, but it is a serious form of ancient shamanism practiced around the world. In Japan the shamans used to be women who did this form of trance journey, as well as raising heat through more active practices and channeling information mediumistically. Then with the arrival of Buddhism in Japan, the tasks were divided into male and female roles, and women became passive mediums while the men became the more active healers or "shamans."[6] Nowadays in Japan the women who are left practicing this ancient form are usually blind, blindness being one of the criteria for membership in this particular vocation. In Tibet Buddhism fused with the ancient shamanic Bon religion, and the shamanic practices were incorporated into the practices of the monks. Tibetan lamas use drums and horns and chanting to induce trance states, which they focus into detailed visualizations that, when practiced correctly, can change consciousness and regenerate the body in miraculous ways, just like more "primitive" shamanic practices in other places.

It is possible to enter a light trance state and not even know it, as I believe we all do every day. In our culture we tend to call this form of trance daydreaming, fantasy, or just "spacing out." Every long-distance driver has experienced trance, as have moviegoers and music listeners. Children easily enter trance states and seem to enjoy them immensely, until their elders tell them enough times that they are wasting time, being lazy or bad. Babies are in a trance state almost completely in the first few weeks, and with the proper environment, so is the mother of a newborn. I remember sitting in the rocking chair, nursing my son, for hours each day, entering into deep, peaceful states of consciousness in which

I watched, amused, as my impulses and ideas floated past without impact. It was as though I was watching other possible realities arise, live briefly, and pass away without manifesting, while I sat on and on in the rocker, transfixed and blessed by a pervasive state of nothingness. I felt I was finally experiencing the Buddhist state of emptiness, and then later I learned that Buddhist lamas have a derogatory name for the period of time when a mother is nursing her child: "milk mind." They don't want her teaching or doing dharma work during her nursing years, a serious loss to Buddhism! Lovers also know this empty state, especially if they have learned the Tantric art of relaxing together after orgasm and allowing the bliss state to permeate their energy fields and expand their consciousness into the void.

The most important mistake Westerners make about the whole subject of trance is to assume that it is merely a meditation or a guided visualization, that the whole experience arises from the mind and is related to the "imagination." While it may include each of these forms, the shamanic trance journey itself is an actual movement out of one body (the physical) and into another vehicle (the energy body, the light body, the spirit body) and another dimension. Where the spirit body travels to is up to the individual shaman, who slips through a crack between the worlds to enter another time zone or another plane. Or, as in astral travel or lucid dreaming, people have experiences of seeing their bodies lying on the couch or bed while they fly around the room or around the world. It is possible to have an experience of going somewhere yet be able to feel sensations in the body the whole time, enjoying an encounter that simultaneously includes both the here and the not-here. Shamans are "shape-shifters," who learn to change their form at will, becoming free of the normal constraints of the physical plane. They have unusual sight and hearing, as well as the ability to transport themselves in unusual ways.

I first learned that trance journeys were not the same as imagination when I was working with children who had eyesight problems. The kids with whom I was working were preadolescents from a local alternative public junior high school where I was teaching yoga. After we had worked together for a while with yoga and the *Motherpeace Tarot Cards,* they came to my studio individually to work on their particular healing processes. In particular, one young girl and one young boy taught me about the actual realities of the trance experience. Since the kids had no preconceived notions about trance and didn't know what I was doing, they were open vessels for the organic experience to evolve and show itself. I had them lie down on the floor on their backs, while I sat at their heads and put my hands over their eyes very gently, to shut out the light and to transmit the healing energy I knew to exist in the hands. Then I would begin to suggest relaxation and rest to them, until their breathing had become regular. At that point I began to help them imagine they were walking down a road, looking for an opening or a tunnel through which they would travel.

I had done this work with adults, following a format I had invented after my own experiences and what I read in books. But these kids, having no concept of guided meditation, didn't know to wait for my "suggestions," and they began to take me on trance journeys rather than my taking them! They would enter the opening, which they saw immediately, as soon as I suggested it, and then we would be off and running, on trips that made my head spin. I had read enough shamanic anthropological literature to know what some of the prevailing experiences were in various places and had studied yoga, meditation, and past lives. They consistently experienced and described classic shamanic travel, archetypes, beings, places, and things. It became more and more clear to me that they were actually going somewhere. And the places they were visiting were the same places visited by shamans and travelers from other cultures and other times. I began to understand that there is a particular terrain in the other world and particular beings who inhabit it, and we can see them whether we are African, Chinese, Peruvian, or North American.

One day the boy student had an encounter with himself in another lifetime (without even knowing that he was experiencing and describing such an event, and basically being too young to absorb the concept of it after the journey). I knew I was getting into something that was broader and more interesting than I had at first imagined yet that contained within it a set of structural procedures and norms that I would come to understand as the universal principles of shamanic trance. Slipping between the worlds altered our relationship to time and space. Gravity no longer ruled there, and the laws of the physical world did not bind the traveler. One could be present in this life and in another lifetime at the same time and be having an encounter between two aspects of the self. The teachers and healers that presented themselves there were powerful and compassionate, with wisdom and teaching that was way beyond my students' rational minds (and barely within the framework of my own). The animals and plants they encountered there gave them information that checked out in the physical plane later, and I could tangibly feel the transmission of energy and power that came across the planes from those beings. My students took this in stride and went back to being normal teenagers after they left my office, leaving me overwhelmed with the power of the Mystery. I began to have a different kind of respect for the organic process of trance and for the kind of directions I gave to people with whom I was working.

I began to trust with more certainty that the only thing necessary to provide someone in order for that person to have a successful, healing, trance journey was the structure: a tunnel, a guided entry through it to the other side, a few simple suggestions about what might happen there, and a guided return back to "normal consciousness." The going and coming seem to be the places where trouble can happen, as when we are deep in a trance or dream state and the phone rings, shaking us out of that reality and too quickly and unceremoniously into another. It's jarring, like coming up too quickly on an elevator, getting what deep-sea divers call the bends. The transitions are best made in a relaxed manner or with a sustained focus like that achieved by steady drumming (even if the drumming is wild). It's the continuity that counts. I began to experiment with letting the person I was directing give me hints and ideas about what to suggest, having them speak out loud while they were journeying, telling me what they saw and heard, and then I could enter into the trance with them and literally help in the moment. I noticed that having the person tell the journey as he or she went kept them conscious, so they could remember afterward. Finally I began to see things myself before they would say them and to suggest things just as they were beginning to see them — a mutually satisfying and exciting experience!

When I read some of the texts and how-tos about shamanism that began appearing in the 1980s, I wondered about the frequent rigidity of form and technique. The tone is that

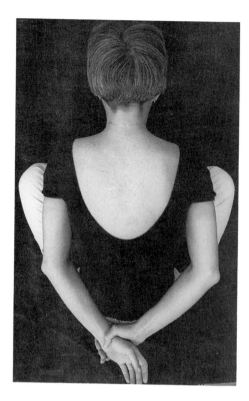

▲ *Fig. 45    The author doing yoga mudra during shamanic apprenticeship period, 1976– 1981. In this ancient pose from hatha yoga, I would go into deep trance for fifteen minutes, leaving the conscious world and journeying to places where I received help and guidance from my teachers and guardians. Photo by Craig Comstock. Reprinted with permission.*

of an expert telling us what is OK and what is not, what is a good way to have the experience and what is not. I feel suspicious when someone makes too great a distinction between real shamans and mediums or between magic and religion. The authorities often proclaim, for example, that if you don't remember what happened in your trance journey, it is not really shamanism, and you don't really have control of yourself. Yet I have had many ecstatic trance journeys in which I have not remembered the content, although I have clearly traveled somewhere and received a teaching from beings I could just barely distinguish in the liminal state between the worlds as I came back into my body.

When I used to practice yoga for long periods every day, I always finished the session with the yoga mudra, with my legs in the lotus posture and my forehead on the floor (fig. 45). I would hold this posture for fifteen minutes exactly (without consciously timing it), and at the end of that time, almost as if a bell rang, my trance would end, and I would

**143**

find myself rushing (whooshing) back into my normal consciousness from somewhere else, with visions of a circle of ethnic women (Native American? South American?) disappearing, their voices still vaguely ringing in my ears. It was very soothing to me, and I knew I was being taught what I needed to know. My power was increasing, and my abilities were keeping up with my practice. Although the contemporary literature makes it seem as if it is totally necessary to be in conscious, rational control of your process at all times (if you are really a shaman), I tend to appreciate those ecstatic moments when I am not "doing it" myself. Granted, it is very exciting to be lucid in a dream or in a trance; but it is certainly not necessary for doing good shamanic work. I suspect that underneath this contrived distinction is a difference between how men do it compared with how women do it. It may very well be that women tend to be more trusting of the intuitive processes, seeming to go unconscious, letting things happen, and being tagged as mediums rather than true shamans. (Remember that in ancient Japan, women were the shamans; and then with the influx of Buddhism, the men took over the dynamic aspects of the practice, leaving trance mediumship to the women.)

My work with people in trance journeys is structured clearly through a series of simple steps, including the things that seem necessary for a satisfying visit to the invisible realm for healing. Other than this simple structure, I don't intervene much in the person's process, allowing them to experience the place and the beings there in their own special way. Contemporary Americans have their own ideas about the other worlds and the use of psychic techniques for accessing healing power, and they apply these interpretations to their journeys as they see fit. I simply guide and steer a bit, as if I were taking the person down a river in a boat at their request and for their own purposes. I take us through some kind of opening, which can be anything—a keyhole, a window, a rabbit hole, an opening in a grove of trees, a cave with an underground spring, an elaborate doorway. Once through the opening to the other side, I ask them to describe the landscape, especially focusing on their physical senses of smell, touch, sight, and hearing. I suggest they will hear or see water and guide them toward it. (Often when I suggest the water, they have already found it.) I have them immerse themselves in the water and allow it to cleanse and heal them. This can be extremely profound for most people and doesn't need any embellishment. Women especially will often cry during this phase, feeling both the pain they are releasing and also the nurturing presence of the living Goddess in the form of water.

After they have refreshed themselves in the water, I ask people to step out and find a garment waiting for them on shore. They put it on and describe any feelings or memories associated with it. I ask them to make an altar from objects and items they find around them. Then I let them sit or lie quietly in front of the altar for a while, making their prayers, setting their intentions. When they seem ready, I suggest they begin to explore the terrain, especially paying attention to the plant life. I tell them a particular plant will catch their attention in some way, and they might sit down and relate to that plant by touching it, merging consciousness with it, listening to it, and so on. When they are finished with this work, they can ask the plant or tree for a piece of it to take along with them as medicine. Often the plant suggests exactly the herbal remedy they need. They go exploring then, with an eye toward the animals inhabiting the place. When a particular animal catches their attention, through outrageous behavior or appearing more than once, they connect with that animal as their friend and guide and go with it on a journey or a dance. My experience is that generally the animals will want to show them something, demonstrate some power, or teach them about something in the body. The experience is frequently one of wild dancing, running, or flying.

When the animal experience begins to end, I ask the animal to lead them to a sacred enclosure, where I suggest they will find an ancient guide waiting for them, some being who has known them for lifetimes and loves them very much. They leave the animal outside the enclosure and go inside to meet the guide or teacher. Naturally this is powerful for everyone. Some people see the guide, others feel her, sometimes the guides talk, and sometimes they simply make extraordinary contact through touch or telepathy. I ask the person to give a gift to the teacher and to accept a gift from her. I suggest that they ask for advice in any way that feels natural, and I give time for this communion. When it feels as if the person has had enough time and is relaxed and complete, I tell her to end the encounter by saying thank you and good-bye, perhaps making a contract about how often to come for visits, and to leave the enclosure, find the waiting animal, and return to the place where she began.

At this original place they leave the garment near the altar and complete anything that doesn't feel finished. They ask the animal if it wants to come along, and if it does, it jumps into their body right away, often taking up residence in a particular place. If the animal doesn't come along, it gives them something of itself to bring back. When they are completely ready, I have them take a deep breath and once more enter the tunnel, returning to this side of reality and to their ordinary consciousness. I remind them that they will remember everything they need, and they can return whenever they like. I help them reenter the bodily experience by stretching and moving slowly, making a clear transition between there and here. Generally a person likes to take a little time to write down the trance experience in detail, while it is still fresh in the mind. We might then discuss it for interesting content — what kind of animal, the experience's meaning for the person's life, and so on. I always suggest that a person manifest the animal in whatever ways she can, by getting photographs of it to keep on an altar at home, drawing or painting it, or creating a "fetish" or image of it in some magical way (see chap. 7). Often the animal from the trancework will appear in the outer life in some way, through picture postcards that come in the mail or visits while the person is out walking in the woods or something.

Trancework brings the other world a little closer to us. What goes on in our dream lives, in the invisible and unconscious realms, becomes more accessible to us through this technique. Our facility in moving between the worlds grows as we practice, and this faculty is the central defining characteristic of shamans everywhere (see fig. 46). Individually it is a relaxing way to heal the self, getting us in touch with teachers and guides for living a better life. As a consistent practice, it allows for more fluidity in the ego structure, so that eventually a person can begin to use the beings and forces of the invisible world for healing others in the family or community. A shaman is eminently sane but experiences an expanded reality; she may appear to be eccentric, but she is grounded in a real orientation to time and space. Unlike a schizophrenic person, a shaman knows the difference between here and there and is able to move back and forth

▲ *Fig. 46   This priestess from Crete is in trance, indicated by her open, staring eyes that seem to see into the other world. The doves on her head may represent the passenger pigeons that carried oracular information from one center to another in the ancient period, as Robert Temple asserts. Probably her oracular trance is the result of ingesting the sacred poppy, which is shown on the headdress of a figure from the same place and time. Women are, as Monica Sjöö suggests, the original mantics (prophets). Drawing by Jennifer Roberts.*

between the two places at will. This knowledge of boundaries, and the ability to pass through them, distinguish a shaman from someone lost on the astral plane, at the mercy of ghosts and fantasies, frightened, and disoriented.

As a shamanic healer, I use the trance state with clients on its own terms, without adding much. When a person has a conversation or encounter with an animal, plant, or guide in the trance state, I simply hold them there and allow that to happen in the fullest way possible. I often feel the power of the healing force that is transmitting from the one plane to the other. In a way it transmits through me—literally through my body, my vehicle, my hands. That transmission of power, intensity, information, and guidance is my main objective in doing the work in the first place. My individual work with clients changes their circuitry: It's as if there were a wire from the sky, available but not hooked up, and the person I'm working with is the other wire. I take the two wires and connect them, creating a working circuit. It's kind of like jump-starting a car, recharging their battery. From that point on, the person is more likely to be able to make contact for herself, which is the purpose of my work with her. But a therapist, for example, could use the trance state to reach deeper levels of information and meaning, and then work on them in ongoing therapy sessions. Doctors and nurses could use the trance journey for extra information in the healing process, in addition to whatever techniques and medicines are

**147**

already being used for the particular patient. People in relationships or in families might use trance states with each other for reaching closer contact with their sacred powers as well as each other. It is a very versatile medium.

In groups, rather than the usual beating of a drum, I use the sacred sounds of some other ancient and ethnic instruments from around the world, like gourd rattles, seed pods, bells, drums, whistles, and shakers of various kinds. Bells from Peru sound completely different from those from Tibet, "rainsticks" from the Amazon have a totally different effect than a drum, and drums of every possible type are available. I have collected a variety of instruments to orchestrate group trance journeys. Since we have no particular shamanic tradition among North Americans of European background, I feel no sense of ownership of these instruments, they do not belong to me (or to my people), which gives me a lot of freedom in choosing and using them. I use them with the utmost respect and hope that none of their original owners or makers would regard my use of them as sacrilegious or offensive in any way. I don't attempt to replicate the ceremonies or liturgies that belong to the instruments but simply use the magical, sacred sound they make in a prayerful approach to the sacred state of trance. They are extremely effective in changing people's ordinary consciousness and facilitating the trance journey. I have used this form of trance induction in a variety of situations, including a large rally at the Nevada nuclear test site a few years ago.

I use a microphone with large groups so that I can speak quietly and still be heard. I ask people to relax and find a comfortable position for sitting or lying down, since we will be doing the exercise for about ten or fifteen minutes. I lead them in breathing deeply and sinking down into their bodies, making a connection to Mother Earth, helping them to contextualize the experience as one of healing. I make it very clear that there is no right way to do it and that everyone will be able to have an experience of some kind. I ask them to use whatever perceptive functions work best for them—for one person it will be sight and images, for another it will be sound or a feeling in the body. I use all the same steps of the structure outlined above for individual trance induction, but I don't ask them to respond verbally. I simply allow a little time after each suggestion, along with the hypnotic sound of the instruments, to allow each person in the group to have his or her own experience. At the same time, I know the group energy is a powerful enhancer and facilitator of the trance experience, so I trust that each person's experience will be heightened by simply going into trance together. I have put a hundred women in trance together in a room where babies were crawling over their chests as they lay on the floor, and still everyone was able to enter an altered state and have an experience. The power of the experience is in the sounds made by the various instruments, which carry the souls in flight and choreograph the individual dance that takes place for each person. When people share their experiences afterward (as they do in my workshops), they often have the same animals and remarkably similar experiences.

To use trance in a group you can use as few as one instrument (a drum, for instance) or as many as half a dozen, alternating them and playing with the ways that the sounds align with the various parts of the experience. For instance, rainsticks obviously make the sound of water and are a wonderful accompaniment to the immersion in water described above. Drumming or hard rattling is good when the animal is taking the person on a dance or a journey, and soft bells are great for sitting at the altar or greeting the teacher. It is totally intuitive and fun, without rules, and it offers the possibility of never repeating yourself. It takes a little practice to be able to speak to the people and use the instruments at the same time, without losing the continuity of movement so necessary to a successful journey. Yet the instruments hold the focus very strongly and make for a powerful trance experience, especially for someone who has never done it before. I never tire of this presentation, and I've never had an audience who didn't enjoy the experience and feel it was valuable. Once someone has been initiated into trance through the group process, it is much easier for them to enter into the experience on their own.

One quiet word of warning: As a shaman-leader, you are helping to bridge between the worlds for people, and you must have built a strong enough vehicle to handle the karma of that work. This is not to frighten anyone who would try this method but simply to advise that you start with individuals and work up to large groups slowly, allowing your psychic system to develop the appropriate boundaries and openness necessary in the work. There is a magic in group work that helps to open the healer, but since you are carrying the focus of the forces coming through, it is necessary that you grow into the ability. The first few times I worked with trance in groups, I had some unpleasant side effects afterward, from a slight headache to not being able to go to sleep that night. I have learned always to take a bath after group work and to take a little time for clearing my aura of any extra energies. There is the problem of merging with others, and there is also the problem of high-voltage energies opening the system in ways that are uncomfortable at first. Rather than going to elaborate lengths to protect against the effects of having someone else's energy in your field, I feel it is wise simply to practice and accept a few uncomfortable consequences, assuming a certain amount of cleansing will be necessary over a period of time, as you learn to be a clear channel. The negative effects don't last.

The redeeming power of trance by itself is minimal. In shamanic cultures the trance state is used in the context of many other healing practices and concepts. Just going into trance is nice, but so what? I think we need to combine trancework with meditation, yoga, journal writing, making shamanic art, drumming, and ritual. When you meet an animal in a trance state, it will be deeply grounding in your life if you make an image of that animal and use it daily in some physical way. "Dance the animal" is Michael Harner's advice,[7] and this can be expanded to include any form of giving the animal body and form. The forces and powers make an exchange with us through the trance channel. They lend us their powers, and we lend them a body for expression. When a guide or teacher makes a meaningful contact with you in a trance state, you need to recharge yourself through continuous contact with that guide and use the power of the guidance you experienced until it comes easily into your daily life. Otherwise the trance experience becomes an exotic way of "getting off" during a weekend workshop or a way that a healer or therapist "gives" you an interesting experience, rather than the deep practice it really is. It's too easy for Westerners to begin to think of ourselves as special after having unusual experiences like trance. The ultimate value of trance as a tool is, we hope, to loosen up the ego structure a bit rather than to reinforce our ego drives of self-importance and narcissism.

The trance state, in its most profound sense, provides an opportunity for the ego-personality to get out of the way

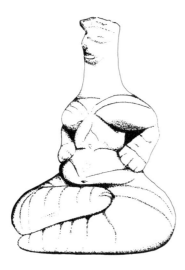

▲ *Fig. 47 This crowned Snake Goddess in meditation is one of my all-time favorites. Although yoga originated less than five thousand years ago and Buddhism much later, this early figure from Crete was clearly practicing both yoga and meditation in 6000 B.C.E., leading to the obvious conclusion that women invented the yogic arts. Our early unsystematized shamanism was refined during the patriarchal transition and codified into what we now call yoga, whose texts have saved and transmitted the material down through the ages. Drawing by Jennifer Roberts.*

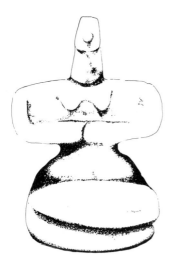

▲ *Fig. 48 This figure similarly comes from the Aegean area also around 6000 B.C.E. and shows a woman in deep yogic meditation. Her snake legs are crossed in an asana, allowing her to commune more effectively with the invisible world and raise her own kundalini. Drawing by Jennifer Roberts.*

and make itself available to a higher power (see figs. 47 and 48). It is possible, through trance, to relax and enter states of consciousness in which there can be an acknowledgment of other forces coexisting with us here in the world. When we are working toward goals, the trance state can cut below the ordinary brain-consciousness that thinks in habitual, conditioned patterns, aligning the personality with the soul or self. While in trance we come into contact with our deeper selves, the real me, the essence behind the form. This experience is immeasurably healthful, providing a kind of well-being that can't be quantified by Western science. If we can then integrate the information and experience of the trance state into

**151**

our waking reality, through concentrated effort of ritually focused intention, the goals can be attained more easily.

In shamanism the trance state is used then in combination with shamanic art and dreamwork and the enactment of ritual and ceremony. All these practices are more powerful when shared in a group or collective way. Shamanic communities are tribal: everyone knows everyone. You don't apply your newly learned techniques of consciousness and ecstasy to your problems in private; you enact your dreams and visions in front of the whole family, the whole world. There is a kind of grounding missing from the modern urban Westerner's use of shamanism, which has to do with our lack of continuous community. Even our circles and groups only meet now and then, leaving us to our own devices the rest of the time, often without any real contact or support in between. Or we process our material with a therapist in a private office once a week, which can't help but lead to the feeling that what we are experiencing it unique, "my problem," rather than a shared experience. In a tribal situation, when someone is ill or in crisis, the whole community tends to get together to banish the illness and take part in a celebration of renewed health. In the smallest sense, the family of the sick person is generally included in whatever healing process is undertaken. No one is ever alone.

There is no foolproof solution to this very deep problem of isolation in Western culture. But I like to work more and more in groups and in progressively larger groups over the years. The one-on-one healing modality can become addictive, a fix needed by each individual every week in order to keep her alive and functioning. It sometimes leads us to such an introverted focus on self that I think we forget the relative quality of our own suffering. For example, although certainly women suffer terribly in Western culture from male dominance, we sometimes get so involved with healing the pain of our childhoods and so on that we lose track of the fact that we are actually quite privileged in comparison with people in other cultures around the world.

Ultimately trance and other techniques of healing need to be for the good of the community and not simply for the expansion and deepening of individuals. Shamanism is a service occupation. Shamans learn practices and techniques of sacred work not because we are special or set apart from the rest but because we are called to carry a little more than our own load. Shamans do their own job in the community — farming, mothering, making art, whatever — and they do shamanic healing work as well. A "wounded healer" learns to relate in a healing way to her own problems in order that any solutions she comes up with might be applied to the greater whole of which she is a part. A person who correctly uses the trance mode in her life becomes tangibly grounded and available for helping others, and others respond to this. The psychic field around her changes in response to the amount of time she spends in trance, and this change has an impact on her community. She becomes more balanced, more aligned with her inner purpose in her outer life; she has equilibrium. We should all take up the practice of opening ourselves to trance states, not so that we can have exotic experiences that make us different from other people but because we need the contact the trance state provides with the unseen and the spirit realm. The practice of trance, if it were to catch on in Western culture, could actually facilitate world peace by creating large numbers of people who are not explosive and reactive without thinking but peaceful, contemplative, and (therefore) more effective in response to the problems facing them.

# Shamanic Art: Manifestation of Creativity

THE MAKING OF SHAMANIC ART IS one of the oldest forms of giving expression to the sacred. Like so many other attributes of ancient culture, much of the earliest art appears to have been created by women in a ritual context. The so-called Venus figures from the Paleolithic period in Europe, the calendar bones described in chapter 1, the first fabrics, pottery, baskets, and so on all came from women's hands. As so many archaeologists have pointed out, the early artifacts all seem to have been imbued with "magic," which I take to mean sacred intentionality. Academics disagree. A scholar of ancient Mexico, writing in the 1950s, went so far as to make a distinction between the early art, which she defined as "magic," and the later art, which she called "religious." In truth the only distinction is that the earlier images are female and the later ones male. She and others call the earlier ones pretty ladies and discuss their animism, and they call the later ones gods and refer to them in discussing the origins of religion.[1] Her methodology is based on an accepted but inaccurate theory that "archaic" cultures could not, by definition, have a central abstract concept of deity, therefore the female figurines could not be Goddesses but merely represented women or perhaps corn and other growing plants. The elaborate work of Marija Gimbutas should put such an outdated theory forever to rest.[2]

Sometimes scholars describe the transition period between the ancient women-centered cultures and the later male-dominated ones in visual or artistic terms. Sigfried

155

Giedion, for example, a noted art historian, describes early Paleolithic and Neolithic art as the most beautiful, fulfilled artistic expression the world has known and clearly delineates a change that occurred five thousand years ago. He defines the earlier art (e.g., cave paintings) as "spatial" and discusses its naturalistic and "zoomorphic" perspective in contradistinction to transitional art (of the Sumerians or Egyptians, for instance), which became "vertical" and "anthropomorphic." The humans no longer mingled among the animals on the walls but were separated and distinguished from the animals and any animal roots they might have experienced earlier.[3] The shared shamanic experience of the earlier art in the caves, where the human and animal identities are merged, changed to an egocentric fixation on form and human perspective. Of course, this change coincided with the attributes of the patristic or patriarchal cultures that took over at that time. Warfare suddenly became a subject of artistic expression, weapons were created instead of calendars, written scripts began to document amounts of grain owned by the king, and so forth. Government became centralized, women's roles were domesticated, and class stratification came into being.

The power of images is undebatable. The presence in our time of these ancient images that belie traditional archaeological theories so widely held by scholars is of great benefit to women attuning to our innate power. The unearthing of ancient female figurines that were clearly sacred and of central iconographic importance to the civilizations that made them is indeed "worth a thousand words" (see fig. 49). Figures of women in trance, chanting, and praying are liberating images for modern women who are generally not allowed to be priests or rabbis and who are not accustomed to assuming religious authority. The undeniable fact that ancient women made sacred art in their own image, and used these images in their religious practices, is of immeasurable importance to contemporary women. Marija Gimbutas describes her experience of beginning her important dig at Thessaly in Greece, where she bent down and picked up a small female figurine even before breaking ground.[4] A rainstorm had exposed the tiny figure of a *yogini* or priestess from 6000 B.C.E., predating the Greek Olympian gods and city-states by several thousand years. All her professional life, Gimbutas had dealt with "weapons, weapons, and more weapons" from the Indo-

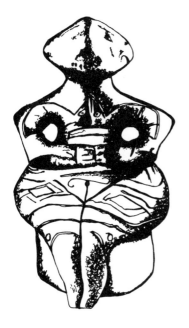

▲ *Fig. 49    Buffie Johnson identifies this figure from Bulgaria as the Lady of Pazardzik, dating her from the mid-third millennium B.C.E. The patterns on her body are part of the ancient tradition that Marija Gimbutas defines as the Pregnant Goddess or Earth Mother. Like the other figures in meditation, this one is a profound example of female authority, right down to the birthing stool on which she is enthroned. Drawing by Jennifer Roberts.*

European cultures that overlaid ancient indigenous cultures, which were discovered at a deeper level of the archaeological strata. Gimbutas had come to perceive these earlier cultures as peaceful, egalitarian, and matristic. The project in Thessaly confirmed her research and allowed her to document fully the early cultures of the Goddess in her beautiful book *The Language of the Goddess.*

One of the most natural outlets for the awakening of snake power in contemporary women is art. The making of shamanic art is a way of ritually coming into contact with the spirits of the unseen world and enlisting their support in our lives.[5] All artists experience some level of this contact with the invisible realm in their artistic process, calling it the muse or inspiration. And in a general sense all artists are shamans insomuch as they are channeling images or concepts on behalf of the collective, which images (one hopes) are healing and aim toward the higher good of the community. A shamanic healer can make art without being an "artist," however, and in a sense it is best to eliminate any artistic expectations from the work, since so many women feel intimidated by the art establishment and what is considered to be art. For our purposes, the less a woman knows about art, the better off she will be in this particular process of awakening the expression of shamanic art. The fewer rigid preconceptions, the freer her

**157**

▲ *Fig. 50* Motherpeace
Six of Wands, the first
Motherpeace Tarot *image
to be drawn by the author.
This image traditionally
means a creative burst or
coming into leadership,
bursting forth with energy
and power. It is the quintessential Shakti image of the
Motherpeace deck, liter-
ally marking the beginning
of a creative project.*

mind and spirit will be in coming to the work. The closer she
can be to a child's mind (the Zen "beginner's mind"), the truer
the work will be. So the first thing that needs to be released,
before a woman can begin to make shamanic art, is the widely
held and oft-stated belief that she "isn't artistic."

When Karen Vogel and I made the *Motherpeace Tarot*
images in 1978–79, neither of us had drawn pictures before.
We had started to draw when I began healing my eyesight,
because someone told me (or perhaps I read in a book) that
drawing was one of the best ways of relaxing and bringing
into balance the two eyes so that they could see naturally,
without glasses. I had worn contact lenses since I was fourteen years old, and I took them out when I was twenty-nine
(during my shamanic healing crisis in 1976) and never put
them back in. I was determined to end my reliance on drug-
stores for my ability to see, and the "Bates Book" *(Better Eyesight Without Glasses)*[6] assured me I could succeed. I had to
get some books on how to draw the human figure even to
begin to sketch what looked like a person. My beginning pictures were attempts to create, imaginatively, what ancient cultures might have been like, especially for women and
children. I drew people involved in activities like ritual,
chanting, dancing, cooking, gardening, and healing—all the
kinds of things I was missing in my own modern life and part
of an ancient heritage I was trying to piece together. It was
these playful, positive images that led to my drawing the Six
of Wands one day (fig. 50). And it was the Six of Wands—
Shakti in her wheel of fire—that made us think of making a

round tarot deck. Karen and I spent the next year drawing pictures practically every day and enjoying it immensely.

During this time we enrolled in a psychic class, where we met Cassandra Light, who is now director of the Way of the Doll School in Oakland and who was then making her first dolls. Casey came every week to the house I shared with Karen and informally showed me how to make art. We started by working with clay, making hand-built clay pots and masks. Under Casey's wise tutelage, I came to understand my artistic talents as a playful, childlike gift of the spirit — something unschooled and free, an expression of aspects of myself that weren't necessarily in form. Unlike my writing, with which I was ego-identified, art seemed refreshingly outside the territory of anyone's control, including my own. I made pictures from passion and experienced ecstasy every day in the process of making my drawings. I believed then (and still do) that the Little People coming through the drawings actually lived on the other side and wanted to come into form, and that they had chosen me as a vehicle. Over the years I learned that practically every culture in the world knows about the fairies and elemental beings and honors them in some way, including our European ancestors, who somehow left them behind when they migrated to the North American continent. It is only we — the orphan culture of the United States of America — who deny and banish their existence. (It seems that a part of the motivation for travel to this land was the effort to leave behind in the Old Country such "superstitious" beliefs, in the name of "religious freedom.")

Making art was the most surprising ecstatic form I have ever discovered. It made sense to me that sexuality is Tantric (ecstatic and otherworldly), and I understood that psychic powers would naturally entail altered states of consciousness. But I never knew that the simple act of making something could be a doorway to religious experience. Every day I would stand in front of my drawing tablet, look at the empty page, consider the tarot card I was going to work on that day, and begin. Hours later I would emerge from what seemed like a journey to another land, a trip that made me lose track of time and space, allowing me totally to merge with my material. It was only the fact of evening — the darkening of the light — that would cause me to end my work for the day. In the mornings I practiced yoga; in the evenings I studied and contemplated the images I was working on, making decisions about the animals that should be in the various pictures, and so forth. It was easily the most interesting, exciting work I had ever done, yet people around us seemed to agree that it was wasteful, if not impossible, for us actually to make a new tarot deck. One artist told me it had to be GREAT ART, and it should take at least ten years. "You're making what?" people would ask, speechless with distaste, "a tarot deck?" Or someone would look at the images we were making and tell us, point blank, that the bodies didn't "look right," and we didn't know how to draw (which we didn't). Somehow it all seemed beside the point.

Finally we completed the *Motherpeace* cards and Karen had them printed; I wrote the book to accompany them, and now they are happily out in the world, opening doors to that same realm for the many souls who resonate with them. Shamanic art remains shamanic, even after the process is completed and the result is set free into the world. Made in a state of healing trance, the cards transmit the healing power to whoever uses them. That is why tarot cards work so well, even for those who don't necessarily believe. The healing intention that comes through the trance experience and the artistic process is passed along to the viewer, who is transformed. All healing images are *yantras* in the Indian Tantric terminology—sacred enclosures in which the *Ishta-Devata* (tutelar deity) resides.[7] When a person meditates upon a yantra of the Goddess in any of her myriad forms, or that of the power animals or elemental beings, the energy of that being is eventually incorporated into the body and soul of the meditator. We become one with the being at the center of the image, who is ultimately a representation and embodiment of the One.

"Fetish art" is the general name of what we think of as shamanic art in our culture. The making of a fetish is a sacred task, and it is one of the first assignments I give to my women students when they take up the study of female shamanism. A fetish is a conglomeration of found objects, feathers, bones, rocks, beads, hair, leaves, twigs, and anything else that pleases a person and represents the variety of materials found in Nature. It may take a representational form, looking like an animal or a doll, or it may not. Some fetishes look like mobiles or a piece of abstract art. Some take the form of shields. I ask the women to spend time in the wild gathering anything that attracts them, without necessarily having a system of correspondences to explain the intuitive attraction. Choose anything that Nature sends you, including found objects from city streets. The gizmos, gadgets, and whatnots that fall from cars or bikes, or that someone discarded as junk, can become magical when they take a shape or form that appeals to your inner mind and reminds you of an archetype or process in your life. I have made evocative pieces of artwork that include copper rings and metal pieces from auto mechanic shops as well as feathers, beads, and bones of animals found on trails in the hills.

The purpose of a fetish (or yantra) is healing. Probably everyone has seen Zuni fetishes, generally small ceramic or stone sculpted animals that function protectively for the owner. In Africa women make pots that become homes for the spirits that originally made them ill and that will be captured in the pots to be mastered and harnessed for healing.[8] You can set your healing intention and then use the fetish to focus your mind or will on that vow. In the sense that I am describing it, there is no right way to make your fetish. Just enjoy the process and be aware that everything counts. Every knot you tie is a wish made; every stone, bead, bone, or feather means something. But you don't need to know the meaning in some literal, linear way. It's enough just to love the sacred process, trust the magic, and let the artwork begin to speak to you as you produce it. Before you have finished the work, you may have a sense of its name, its purpose, and how you need to relate to it. For instance, some fetishes might "want" something specific, such as to be placed on an altar and given flowers or incense daily. Others will hang in a room and remind you of their purpose every time you pass by. You can make a fetish for protection then carry it with you or keep it in the room or house you wish to protect. Maybe your fetish will have some other instructions for you. The fetish itself is created as a means of contacting and making yourself available to guidance from the realm of the invisible spirits.

The difference between a fetish and the new-age practice of creative visualization is that the fetish uses materials of the earth that are charged with the vibration of whatever they came from. The animal hair or bones you use in your amulet actually empower the amulet with the knowledge and instinctual nature of that animal. Usually the process begins before you ever start working on the piece of art, when you find the particular feather or bone or tooth and realize

161

what animal it belongs to. Already you are in a process of communication with the spirit realm, and the animals are talking with you, guiding and directing you, and in some sense, lending you their power. When you make an amulet or fetish using the found feather of a red-winged blackbird, for instance, you might take some time to observe these birds and their habits or read about them in a nature book to understand on a deeper level what they are teaching you, what it is that needs to be brought into your life at this time. A hummingbird feather has a different impact and purpose on your life than an owl feather. The animals whose dropped feathers or dried bones you find have healing medicine for you, and this must be respected and observed for best results. It doesn't mean the bird is telling you to do such-and-such or the coyote is guiding you to a certain particular action that you can figure out through some intellectual system of what things mean. (This kind of thinking, and the glamours that surround it, are the bane of the new age!) It is more of a dual event: You find the coyote tooth, and the coyote has meaning in your life as an archetype in some way. Both things are happening at once, the dual event has meaning, and one didn't cause the other.[9]

Here we are dealing with what Rupert Sheldrake has called the morphogenic field of invisible energy that surrounds all living beings and gives them a particular, specific vibration that can be felt and acknowledged by other living beings.[10] When a migrating bird drops a feather, it can always find its way back to that very place by the personal vibration given off by that feather. Scientists think birds track their entire migratory route by such leavings as feathers and feces. All animals do this. This in itself should make us aware enough not to hoard and grasp at every animal part that comes our way and to understand the power and sacredness of the animal parts that we use in any artwork or protection charms. This is the scientific basis of the magic of so-called witches and sorcerers who use animal parts, fingernails, hair, and the like. A healer wanting to heal a patient by long distance can focus healing power on a fingernail or lock of hair from that person or, better yet, a doll made in the image of that person, and healing will be accomplished; the same is true, unfortunately, for the negative power to do ill. Just remember that witches also have a saying: What you send out comes back to you three times over. Don't even think something about someone that you wouldn't want someone to think on you.

Doll making is an elaborate version of creating a fetish. It is more complex and powerful, I think, and very deep work for women learning to heal themselves. A doll can embody the various aspects of a person and can be the form for a process of coming to understand some parts of yourself that have previously been invisible or hidden. In the work of Cassandra Light, students make life-size dolls with a whole internal structure of chakras and joints; with faces, hands, and feet sculpted of porcelain; with costumes created to express the personality of the doll or a myth or a story that came from a dream or vision. I have made many dolls, but the most interesting one took me several years to complete and involved an amazing process of self-revelation and unfoldment. In 1983, when I was first married to my husband, Jonathan, I became pregnant during a fairly serious illness that I contracted in Mexico that had lasted several months. One of our housemates was riding her bicycle in the Santa Cruz Mountains one day and found a freshly killed juvenile great horned owl in the ditch on the side of the country road. She brought it home to our household, and we asked our friend Karen Vogel to skin it because of her instinctual shamanic connection to animals and her equilibrium in regard to dead ones.

Owls everywhere represent death. They live and hunt at night, they see in the dark, and they have always been connected to magic and healing power. Shamans everywhere are connected to owls, but the animal has become a symbol of evil in most cultures since the patriarchal transition, no longer holding the numinous power once associated with it. Native people—whether on their own or because of Spanish (Catholic) intrusion is not clear—universally seem to associate the owl with ill will and bad luck, avoiding it whenever possible. Yet in ancient times the owl was a main attribute of the Goddess. She had a snake and a bird, and the bird was generally the owl. Her wisdom, her night consciousness, and her shamanic flight (trance journey) were honored and revered. The owl was the attribute of Lilith and Inanna in Sumer, of Athene and Medusa in Greece (and earlier in North Africa, where both originated). There is a sculptural image from India of a Goddess riding an owl, who looks remarkably like the Sumerian Lilith.

Within a month of our ceremony regarding this particular owl, our housemates' relationship had fallen apart and
I had miscarried on Winter Solstice. The presence or appearance of the owl in our lives was like the wail of the Gaelic
banshee—an announcement of impending death. Yet clearly
the owl didn't cause the deaths and wasn't responsible in
some external, evil kind of way. Both deaths needed to happen. My body couldn't carry a child to term in its weakened
condition from illness; and our friends' relationship had been
nearing the end for some time. I kept the wings and claws of
the owl as a gift and reminder in my life of the numinous,
healing presence of this being who arrived on the scene so
propitiously.

The next year my husband and I moved from Santa
Cruz to the Arizona desert and found ourselves pregnant
again, this time with me in good health. We were tremendously excited about carrying this birth to term, and I consciously practiced healthful ways of living to ensure our
success. About midway through my pregnancy with Aaron
Eagle, as we neared Winter Solstice, I began to have very
compelling interior images of a large doll with the wings and
talons of the owl. I began to feel guided to make such a doll,
and the very thought of doing such a thing while I was pregnant made me ill at ease. I argued with my inner voice: But I
am afraid to use the owl parts that I associate with my mis-
carriage a year ago. My inner mind reassured me: The owl is
a protector for this pregnancy; make the doll. Jonathan and I
found a branch from a favorite tree in our desert yard near
the creek where we walked every day, which would be the
body of the doll, and I began. I crafted a dress for her from
white leather someone had given me and used the porcelain
face I had made years earlier in one of Casey's ritual art
classes. As I continued, I received more information about the
doll and its purposes. It was to hang over Aaron's crib with
its wings spread, as a protector in the night.

I knew the story of Lilith. I knew she was the Goddess from Sumer with the owl feet and wings and the stealer
of children from their cribs in the night. I had to trust that
there was some earlier version of the myth that my psyche
was relating to. It was several years later that I learned that
Lilith was originally the protector of women in childbirth and
afterward of the newborn infants. She was demonized only
after the patriarchal transition and turned into a wicked child-

stealer.[11] Meanwhile, in Arizona, we heard about a woman who got arrested for possessing an owl carcass. She was prosecuted for having the carcass of an owl hanging to dry on the porch of her rural Arizona cabin, and the fine (were she found guilty) would be five thousand dollars. Somehow that stopped my artistic work in its tracks. I couldn't bring myself to complete the doll, large as it was going to be and hanging in the living room of my little adobe house in the desert. The pieces of the unfinished doll went into a box and waited until years later when I moved back to Berkeley and could complete her with some peace of mind.

Completing the Lilith doll coincided with meeting Demetra George and studying her research and teaching on the Dark Moon Liliths. First Neptune had transitted my Black Moon Lilith during our sojourn in Arizona when I began the doll. Then several years later, when I completed the doll in Berkeley, it was Uranus who was transitting the same astrological entity. I told this story in chapter 4 on astrology and I repeat it here to stress the importance of following one's inner guidance when making artistic images. The impulse comes from another dimension, another place in time. We generally don't know the whole story of what we make. Art communicates, and the channel for the communication is sometimes the last to know the details.

The art just wants to be made. It pushes through the creative vehicle (the person) into manifest form. It has healing and awakening in mind, stimulation of hidden and forgotten information, evocation of lost archetypes and images for healing in the present. For Anglos, especially, shamanic art can be a profound opening into the nonrational realm, the world of not knowing and being guided, the world of the awakened child. We can reclaim the lost natural childhood we regret not having had in our mechanized, high-tech twentieth-century American consumer culture. Through magical art we can tune in to the world of spirits and invisible beings that native and tribal people around the world take for granted. We can get a sense of something that might be expected of us from Nature, Gaia, the "Great Spirit." Certainly, in general, Westerners are clumsy and insensitive to the subtleties that an earth-based person would understand intuitively, and we make gross mistakes from this dense consciousness we have inherited. But when we practice earth-based art and healing with integrity, we can find ways of paying back, coming into

▲ *Fig. 51 "Regina,"
the witch, the first doll
created by Cassandra
Light in the 1970s and
owned by the author.
She has a magician's
table in front of her,
and she holds the tarot
cards for the day in
each hand. Photo by
Craig Comstock.*

alignment with Nature, and righting the wrong life-styles we
have been forced to exist within. Everything in our everyday
teachings from school and family denies this invisible reality
and the cosmic power that is its foundation. We can't believe
on the intellectual level that these things are real, that they
matter. But when we make art and it talks to us and our life
changes, we begin to have a shift of our belief system that
takes place in the body and in the psyche. We know the owl
spoke to us, and we feel that the conversation was sacred, so
we have to reevaluate the old information that said any such
experience belonged to the realm of superstition or was evil.

The first doll that Cassandra Light made was an old,
old woman named Regina (fig. 51). I fell in love with her at
once and bought her from Casey before she was finished.
When she came to live at the house I shared with Karen
Vogel, we had just begun to make the *Motherpeace* images.
Regina was set up inside a wood and glass case in our living
room, with a small magician's table in front of her and a deck
of tarot cards. She was the original gypsy, kind of a mythic
combination of Tibetan and Mexican shaman. After we had
her for a while, Karen decided to make shoes for Regina —
little moccasins that she had started beading in a tiny pattern.
Casey had suggested that if we wanted to "activate" Regina,

we needed to put shoes on her. In our innocence we thought, Why not? Then one day an older, wiser teacher in our community came to our house to visit, took one look at Regina, and asked "What do you do for her?" We didn't understand the question. "Do you bring her fresh flowers and incense every day?" Hmmm. We made a note to begin the practice and then visited with our friend about the new shoes. She advised us to wait a long time before activating the doll, whom she said was contained safely inside the case without her shoes and could help us in benign ways to practice magic. If we were to set her free, she said, Regina was a trickster and would "meet us on the street" and do other pranks, causing us no end of trouble. It was humbly illuminating to consider that the physical product of someone's hands and artistic vision could actually be a vessel for an elemental spirit with its own impulses. I have been appropriately respectful and cautious in relation to all my shamanic art since that day.

One of the most valuable artistic exercises I have my students do during the first year (and often repeat again after that) is the making of a "treasure map." Treasure maps come from the Western magical tradition, and I first read about them as a form of creative visualization. The idea is to cut out images from magazines and other sources and mock up what you want, what you desire, to manifest on the physical plane. You want a new car? Put a picture of the exact type on your treasure map. Want a new house, money, a trip to New Guinea? Put up a picture of it and concentrate on bringing it into your life. On one level it is crass and materialistic, fitting right into the modern American mind-set. (The most self-indulgent, narcissistic, and abusive level of the new-age movement is the bland assumption that you can have it all and the tendency to spend your life focusing on yourself and your material existence in this way. If it were true that you can have it all, why wouldn't everyone on earth be fed, housed, clothed, and well taken care of? Is the creative visualizer so precious in the universe, so special in the eyes of the Divine, as to deserve to have it all? I doubt it.) However, on a deeper level, a treasure map can be a form that allows for the everyday persona to get out of the way and the inner mind to speak through you. If you can choose images without thinking about it and select everything that appeals to your inner child as you are playing with your magazines, you end up putting things on your treasure map that you didn't know you wanted and that you may even be a little bit nervous about. It ends up being an opportunity for you to make commitments and vows to the "high self," or the "greater power," or the "universe."

Women in my classes mock up images of world peace, abundant food for all the world's children, sacred and fulfilled personal relationships, loving time shared with their children, and so on—as well as taking responsibility for life on the physical plane. Yes, we want a comfortable home, enough money to pay the rent, and work that is meaningful and not oppressive. Who wouldn't want these necessities of life? Perhaps the deepest form of creativity facing a Shakti woman is the invention of her own life, the actual determining of her own destiny. Rather than being a victim, a Shakti woman needs to raise her vibration and channel her creativity into forms that pay the rent and support her children. She needs to get out from under the oppressive control of the corporate system, where she works as an underpaid drudge, a cog in the patriarchal machine, and begin to actualize her creative expression and her healing power for the good of others in her community. We need to take conscious responsibility for creating our lives and making the lives of our children more abundant, so that we can be freed to do the work of global service. We actually have that capacity, because so many of us in North America are not starving, are not homeless, and are not in the kind of unspeakable pain that our sisters in other countries are experiencing. When women in the healing arts end up spending time complaining and feeling contracted, hurt, wounded, inadequate, and somehow not taken care of, we are wasting our time and our lives in what I call princess-consciousness.

Women in my classes making treasure maps mock up images of the power animals they have recently contacted in their dreams or trance journeys. They may not know what the animal means, in some interpretive way, but they trust that by looking at its image on a daily basis, something will progress in the work of dialogue or communication that has been catalyzed. Sometimes they juxtapose a power animal with a photo of their child and thus perform sympathetic magic for the protection of that child. They might make wishes about their marriages or their spiritual work, asking for guidance or praying for direction. Sometimes the treasure maps, which are magazine pictures pasted on poster board, turn into elaborate mandalas, beautiful artistic expressions of something beyond the individual woman that has spoken through her and her particular desires. Much like the Tantric form of yantra, the mocking up of evocative images that are intended to heal and lead to divine growth in a person's life is a magical, meditative act. The spirit speaks through the ego, the soul has its say through the choosing and seeing of what is wanted.

After the treasure map is completed, I have the women watch to see what manifests and how. Sometimes manifestation begins immediately. I remember once putting up a picture of a beautiful ruin somewhere in South America and then getting a piece of mail from a travel service that wanted to give me easy travel arrangements for any trips in the next year. I just laughed at this superficial synchronicity. Then, although I had never traveled internationally before, I received a serendipitous phone call inviting me to teach in Chile for two weeks, which I accepted. As the items on the treasure map materialize, I paste a gold star over the images as a kind of a thank-you to the universe. I encourage others also to formally acknowledge the accomplishment of a successful manifesting task, giving thanks and recognizing our co-creativity. The creativity in this work is in allowing yourself to have wishes that you can't imagine being fulfilled. When I put up the image of South America, I had no idea how I would get there. Had I stopped myself from having the wish for that reason, wouldn't that have been too bad? I just let myself feel how much I wanted that experience, and then it came true for me in ways that were more interesting than I could have invented myself.

Esoteric science talks a great deal about the need to align the personal will with the greater spiritual will in order to lead a life of active and effective service. Most Western women don't really have much experience in using a developed personal will, let alone aligning it with a higher one. So we begin by accepting and allowing the personal desires to become known to the self as they materialize from within. We trust that there is an organic connection between what a person wants on the inside and what is wanted from that person on a higher level, from the soul level or from the universe. If we can practice forms that get us in touch with and liberate into consciousness what we want for ourselves and those we love, and ultimately for the planet, we can begin to open the channel for that manifestation to occur through our individual desires, which naturally and organically align with the desires and needs of the planet. I believe it is the suppression of women's deep, integral desires (for self and others) that has led to our being sacrificed in our daily lives and being used for the gratification of men's desires, as consumers of products we don't want or need and as pawns in the machine of our male-dominated culture.

Women's internal images are important in the process of breaking through into a new world. We must let ourselves express what is inside us, even if it makes us afraid. One of the simplest and most revealing methods of bringing inner images out onto paper is what I call left-handed drawing. What I really mean by this is nondominant drawing or uncontrolled drawing, which corresponds to what other people have called drawing with the right brain. My system is simple and basic. I just pass out white paper and black ink pens and ask the women to use the hand they normally don't use to write with. I give them a little time to become still, and they begin to move the pen on the paper without any particular intention. It's like a mini-psychic reading. As the lines unfold into pictures that weren't intended by the ego-consciousness, the person doing the drawing begins to see something in the picture. Sometimes it's perfectly clear, a representational image that anyone would recognize as an animal or person or house or whatever. Other times it's just messy lines, taking an abstract shape or form, but with a particular feeling or meaning to the artist. I have the women draw their current feeling state then listen to music and draw what they hear, make pictures of each other, and so on. You can do anything. Using the pen with the hand that doesn't have the proper control to "make art" allows the judging faculty to give up in utter futility and go away. Once this intrusive part of the personality is out of the way, a significant freedom can be felt in the body and in the movements.

I did left-handed drawings for several years after stumbling on the form during my healing-eyesight period, described earlier. I would draw pictures of everyone in my life, creating interesting psychic readings about my children, my partner, my teachers, or acquaintances in classes. It's really "intuitive drawing," opening up the larger perceptive field and making it accessible. I kept journals and would occasionally show a picture to someone I had drawn, and it would always make sense in terms of whatever was going on for them. It helped me to understand that we have enormous powers of perception that are mainly untapped and that perceptive powers are mysterious. It isn't as if I could make something happen with my drawings or get them to be the same all the time or in any way control them or even use them. Anytime I attempted to exert some form of control over them, they became elusive and nothing happened. The clearest example of this was when I executed some drawings that when I turned them around and viewed them sideways or upside down, they had writing that could be read! Letters I had made with my left hand, upside down, not thinking about it, turned into words that I could read when I turned the page over. It was almost too much for my brain-consciousness to handle. I was never able to "make" it happen again. But since I had done several pictures that way over a period of a day or two, I could never negate the experience. Finally, my left-handed drawings became as clearly executed as my right-handed drawings—the accumulation of control that comes with constant practice at anything. After making over a thousand drawings, I lost interest in the practice because my rational mind seemed to have become the boss of the activity.

What I have described so far is art in a particular sense—shamanic, healing art—but does not fall into the recognized categories of Art as the culture defines it. I am not an Artist in the establishment sense of the word: I don't paint, sculpt, or assemble regularly, and I don't sell my work. This is generally true for my students too and probably for most people in our culture. We are not artists in the sense of a destiny to create works of art that will sell to the public and go out in the world and herald change. Artists are channels for cultural feelings and creators of images that the culture is hungry for and doesn't even know it. Some artists are visionaries, reaching into the future and making pictures of who and what we might become; some are political activists, showing us our problems in exaggerated, larger-than-life expressions. But in the sense of the process I am describing, everyone can be an artist, and in a truly shamanic culture I think this would probably be the case. In Bali, for example, I'm told that all the people either make art or music. In Huichol tribal culture, in the western part of Mexico, almost all the people are either artists or shamans. It's what a person does to express life. It's a natural, organic form of being a human and an expected way of perceiving reality and sharing your perceptions with the community.

A part of what we're doing as Western adults when we make shamanic art for healing ourselves or others is healing the wound of our separation from Nature. Hearing art teachers tell us we weren't drawing it "right" and music teachers telling us we weren't singing it right inhibited natural freedom of expression. Children love to express themselves through drawing, painting, sculpting, or making sounds. What a debilitating hurt most of us carry around, thinking we "can't make art" or "can't sing" or can't do whatever we were told we couldn't do. Women especially seem paralyzed by a lack of confidence about what we can do, what we can make, and how "good" we are at things. I often think that in making the *Motherpeace* images, I was lucky not to know how to draw. Had I been correctly schooled, I don't believe I could have let those Little People show themselves!

I grew up in Iowa farming communities, near the famous Indian Mounds, in a totally nonintellectual environment. When I first traveled to the nearest big city, Chicago, at the age of sixteen, and later on several short visits as a young adult, I found myself drawn to the Art Institute, where I would wander around in awe of the paintings and sculptures, wondering how a person could tell what was good and what wasn't, what was great art and what wasn't. I never figured it out, although I did take one art theory course in college. I attended the University of Iowa for a year before I got married and had children, and the first thing I did was pledge a sorority (Pi Beta Phi). There were two distinct sides to the campus, which was divided by a river. In a more or less covert but clearly understood system of rating, the "good girls" stayed on this side of the river, and the "bad girls" crossed the river to take art and theater classes. My art theory course was more interesting to me for this reason than for the content, which I can barely remember, although I liked the slide lectures. The girls in black leotards and tights or pants (Pi Phi pledges were not allowed to wear pants on campus) totally fascinated and attracted me; they seemed somehow freer than I was, in a dangerous and unspeakable way. I carefully married a soon-to-be air force officer and continued to stand enraptured in front of the Impressionist paintings at the Art Institute whenever I visited Chicago. I decided, in a classically Midwestern approach to anything intellectual, that although I really didn't know about art, I knew what I liked.

When I began to awaken to the Goddess and started reading and learning about the ancient cultures that worshiped her and lived according to feminine principles, I also began to appreciate art in a new way that corresponded to my original experience of the awesomeness of it. I read a book called *The First Sex* by Elizabeth Gould Davis in 1973, and my mind flew open.[12] In some fashion this taboo knowledge of ancient matriarchal cultures became my central spiritual quest, and when Karen Vogel and I met (she an anthropologist, me a feminist historian), we shared a driving need to learn what happened to women? How did we lose our power? When she and I moved to Berkeley in 1976, we spent the first year checking out art books from the Berkeley Public Library and looking with awe at the ancient figures of women and Goddesses in every part of the world. No matter what the scholars said about the images they were discussing, the images themselves always told a more interesting story. I began to understand that images actually communicate more truth, in a certain way, than language. The same way that body language tells the secrets that we try to hide in our daily personas, so images tell the underlying story of every historical and prehistoric period in the world. Since archaeology is based entirely on artifacts unearthed, the images of these long-lost pieces of disappeared culture and civilization are open to interpretation. Archaeology views the artifacts from within a narrow theoretical framework, but there is no need to do so. One can simply look at the female images from ancient Sumer or Crete, for instance, and become ecstatic and almost mystical in response to them. They are sacred, and in our very secular world there are not many scholars who are able to translate into language what the images tell.

I would read the standard histories about what supposedly happened in Crete or Egypt or the Middle East and then look at the images and try to figure out what else was going on that wasn't being discussed. As I looked at these images of women in their power — women who obviously had self-esteem and some kind of important position in their culture — I felt an indescribable numinosity. The fact that the men writing the scholarly books called them dancing girls or slaves or temple harlots became less and less important. (I may not know about art, but I know what I like.) The evidence was everywhere. I became infatuated with reading all the traditional texts and seeing clearly from the images that the theories were nonsense. I began to track history myself, adding up the details, following the migrations of peoples during the transition period through the artifacts and images of women that showed up in different places at different times. Karen and I, at one time, considered making an elaborate time-line with artistic images from ancient times pasted on it, which would run in a complete circle around the wall of a room. We were determined to figure it out. Now, of course, the brilliant work of Marija Gimbutas has documented and grounded in impeccable scholarship what we were intuitively perceiving and being moved by. Her *The Language of the Goddess* is a scholarly systematization, giving structural form to the life-view, the entire paradigm and way of perceiving reality, that characterized the ancient matristic (female-centered) cultures. And the *Motherpeace* images, which is what we actually ended up creating out of all this passionate investigation, are available to ordinary women and men to use in daily life in many ways.

A person can read the *Motherpeace* suit of Wands if she wants to attune viscerally to what life might have been like in Africa before the dynasties that unified upper and lower Egypt into one country. The priest-scribes who controlled the country also introduced slavery, clitoridectomies, and class stratification. Someone could read the suit of Cups if they wanted to understand intuitively what we felt Crete might have been like when it was female centered and when they still buried their dead in round communal tombs, with priestesses facilitating ritual and ceremony. Each small tarot image is a potpourri of information about history and shamanic healing traditions, based not only on research but also personal experience with yoga and healing. A shamanic artist can say so much in so little space by simply allowing the picture to develop from the concepts and knowledge one is attempting to communicate. The pictures end up with the ability to transmit, rather than being merely something to be looked at. All shamanic art has this magical ability to make a direct impact on the viewer through a transmission of the energy that went into the image in the first place. The person looking at or working with the particular image actually participates

▲ *Fig. 52* Motherpeace *Moon tarot card, drawn by the author. Notice the winged gate at the back of the image, signifying the successful navigation of the unconscious realms of initiation and freedom into the light. But also notice how it can become a whale's tail, which causes the labyrinthine entryway to take on a more threatening meaning as the whale's open mouth. The devouring Mother invites the initiate to enter if she dares.*

in the shamanic energy and experience that originally catalyzed it. So if you want to know about trance states, you can spend some meditative time looking at the Son of Cups, for example, and you will begin to participate in the trance form itself.[13]

Of course, the images done by a shamanic artist while in trance also have the capability of channeling information not available to the rational mind of the artist under ordinary circumstances and can become part of the education or training program being undertaken by the shamanic student in general. One writer has discussed this in regard to the hieroglyphic shamanic language of the Mayans.[14] Because of this, the *Motherpeace* images continue to bring information to me and Karen that we didn't know when we drew them. Some revelation will unfold that shows us why we put a certain plant or animal in a certain tarot image. We're able to continue learning about what we channeled through our drawings into the physical forms of the cards. When I made the *Motherpeace* Moon card, for example (fig. 52), I had in mind certain intellectual constructs that I was working with about ancient cultures and female initiation. I made images of a woman entering the ocean (the unknown) voluntarily (descent form of initiation, like Inanna), having to use senses other than the rational, daytime consciousness (bats, using sonar) for navigation, with a boat ready to be ridden in (the night journey) as the initiate proceeded to move through the ancient, magical labyrinth found in Crete, India, Arizona, and elsewhere in the world. Phantasms from the astral realm are

flying about (psychism and intuition), adding to the glamour
and illusion normally associated with the card. Last but not
least I made an image of a winged gate from Erich Neumann's
book *The Great Mother*,[15] which was to represent the doorway
at the end of the process through which the initiate would
triumphantly emerge into the light at the end of the tunnel
after the dark night of the soul. All implying a very conscious,
intentional process of initiation, right? But in my first Motherpeace class, when one of my students voiced her assumption that the winged gate was obviously a whale's tail, I was
able to perceive that I had also created an image of someone
being ineluctably, fatefully drawn into the open, labyrinthine
mouth of the whale (the Great Mother in her devouring form,
according to Neumann) for a shamanic descent that may not
have been intentional or voluntary at all. No wonder the traditional tarot scholars voice fear and trepidation about the
Moon card!

This is one of infinite instances when what we
thought we were doing in making the images was one level of
reality and what was being done through us was another. Fortunately we were available for that kind of process, and even
today when I learn something new from the images, I feel a
renewed sense of appreciation for the Mystery and respect
toward the invisible, shamanic world. There is so much we
don't know and can't understand, so much real magic. As
Westerners we belong to a culture that tries to quantify and
codify everything into systems that are simple and black or
white, when nothing in the shamanic world is like that.
Everything is metaphorical and consists of several levels happening at the same time, all of them equally important but not
necessarily of interest to all of us all the time. The ego is
threatened by such layering, such ambivalent symbols, as the
scholars say. You almost have to be a poet or an artist even to
be able to begin to handle such fluidity. Art offers a direct
approach to communing with and having a conversation with
the beings and the consciousness of the Mystery, even though
it doesn't allow any of us to get on top of it with our intellectual minds. I remember the most important thing Cassandra
Light taught me about art: There are no mistakes. What happens during the process of making something is sacred and
organic. When something breaks or goes outside the line or
comes apart, it's part of the process of the thing that is wanting to happen through you. The only appropriate response is

to get out of the way and appreciate the intelligence of the process itself and delight in the unexpected and occasionally extraordinary beauty that presents itself through our "mistakes" or involuntary movements. Once the artwork is "done," it lives on to heal and impress the psyche because it has become the dwelling place of a living being who has chosen to inhabit it and who — if we could see — probably inspired the project in the first place.

*Shamanic Art: Manifestation of Creativity*

# Female-Centered Sexuality: Return to the Garden

ALTHOUGH SEXUALITY MAY NOT logically seem to be related to shamanism, it is. A woman practicing shamanic healing arts will experience the arousal of the sexual energies at some point in her process and must learn to deal with and master those energies as much, or more, than any others. How a woman relates sexually in her life is deeply connected to her groundedness, her sense of self-esteem, and her ability to receive and transmit powers and energies of transformation. One of the main observations made about the ancient archaeological figures of women is how sexual they are, pointing us to a way of expression that was both sacred and actively sexual at once. And since women are primarily defined in Western culture as sex *objects* and/or vehicles of reproduction, any process that turns a woman more clearly into a *subject* (with sovereignty over her own life) brings her sexual role into question. A woman of power (shaman, healer, teacher, leader, medicine woman) is often confronted with the inference that she is no longer a "real woman." Her integrated power is suspected of bringing with it hatred of men, castration intentions, or "black magic." The underlying accusations here are basic: lesbianism and witchcraft. The worst epithets used to keep women in line are related to her sexuality: "dyke," "whore," "ball-buster," "pricktease," "witch." Male fears of women's power run very deep, having been built up over thousands of years; and women's fears of our own power are fairly incapacitating as well. A woman expressing her own sexuality — based totally on her own innermost experience and essential way of being—is something unknown nowadays, since we are all conditioned in a male-dominated society that uses women primarily to whet and satisfy the distorted sexual appetites of men. In this sense it is ludicrous to think we could know what the Feminine is, aside from our instinctual groping toward it.

We live in a culture that perceives rape as sexual. One out of eight Hollywood films depicts rape, and research proves that men who watch rape on the screen are desensitized to the fact that such an act includes female suffering.[1] We are inundated with imagery and advertising that use women's bodies and our erotic energies as lures to sell products and to lull people to sleep. Pornography, as bad as it has always been, is becoming more horrible every day, going to the inevitable limits of a culture that equates the male orgasm with death. Few can bring themselves to speak against it because they don't want to favor "censorship" and "repression." The absurdity of a liberal culture that sanctions incest, child molestation, rape, and wife beating because of not wanting to seem repressive is obvious. From this perspective, when people look at ancient images of sacred women, they are disturbed by what they see. Our culture is repelled by what it imagines as sexual license, naked women under no one's control, something totally aboriginal and primitive. But look at their eyes, their stately posture, their ingrained sense of dignity that can be felt several thousand years later. Some of the earliest figures of snake women and owl women actually look like people hard at work, concentrating, doing something. Their nakedness and their sacredness are almost more than we can bear at one time; the paradox is too much. We call them temple harlots, temple prostitutes, and dancing girls, and that makes us feel more comfortable. We put them in their place, in a hierarchy of male over female, women paid for and delivered.

In the ancient caverns of Paleolithic era thirty thousand years ago, the vulva was the first religious symbol, representing the doorway, our entry into life, our leave-taking at death. Our ancestors carved vulvas on cave walls, on rock, over doorways, and finally in temples. In India a whole religion exists around the symbols of the yoni and the lingam. Indian theology conceptualizes the entire universe as a manifestation of the activity of Shakti, whose creative womb is incessantly active, continually spewing out all forms, all that lives and dies. This living womb, which is the creator of the universe and all forms, holds within her the mysteries of time and space. If you touch her yoni as you enter the temple, you will have good luck in your life. Until only about thirty years ago, temple priestesses called *devadasis* still actively practiced the ancient forms of worship in the temples of India: they cooked the sacred food, they danced for the Goddess (or the God), and they performed the sacred sexual rites. The British came to India, took one look at the *devadasis*, called them prostitutes, and within a short time had extinguished them by making them illegal.

Scholars tend to project their own ideas about sexuality onto the figures and paintings of early people expressing a kind of sexuality we know almost nothing about. Women in ancient cultures were free in ways we can't imagine. Their sexuality was innately connected to their spirituality. How can this wholeness be understood by a people in whom the two are irrevocably split? We can begin to reclaim those earlier images and apply them to ourselves in hopes of coming into some form of contact with that original religious sexual expression. We can dream it, fantasize it, attempt to formulate it through our concepts and practices, but we cannot have it back. We can grieve for it, and through our longing for it, we can begin to move in the direction of creating a world that includes a whole expression of sacred sexuality once more.

I'd like to share a dream from a few years ago:

There is a cenote that resembles a geyser I visited in Wyoming as a child. The cenote is boiling hot and very attractive to me. There is another woman there with me, and I tell her I have to keep overruling an urge to jump in, because I'm so attracted to it. She is too; she understands. I watch the cenote-geyser steaming, appreciating its natural beauty, depth, and mystery.

The scene changes; it's later. The cenote is cooler, the temperature now is moderate. We are in it, swimming under water, a tank, and there are bizarre fish in it, very unreal, strange colors and patterns, with polka dots like balloons. I don't know who put them there, but they push up against us. I tell the woman I don't like them, they aren't natural.

The scene changes again. People are emerging from the cenote-tank. Someone has cleaned it out or opened it up, and aliens are emerging from it as from a UFO. Men. They wear business suits, they stand waiting. I decide to greet them; they are so stiff. I walk up deliberately to two of them, saying "Welcome," and reach my

**181**

arms out to hug them, even though this is very odd for them, and they remain stiff in it.

Last sequence: I go to the cenote and they have turned it into a small cement-lined pond out in the back-yard of a large white house turned into apartments. I stare at it for a long time in shock and disappointment. The woman understands my reaction; she nods in sympathy. There is nothing to do. I simply stare at the way the pool has been shaped and made smaller, totally controlled and man-made like a lily pond, landscaped and with sidewalks around the edges. It looks almost nothing like its original wild state. I stare in wonder and horror at the domesticated pond. I can hardly remember the original. I wonder why they had to do this.

I awake from the dream crying.

I was working at the time on a process involving my sexuality, and the dream was an obvious reference to what has been lost and is unreclaimable. All my life I have related to my sexuality as sacred, as I'm sure many other contemporary women have done. But rarely have I been able fully to come home to what I know is possible, to what lives within me, wanting a field of expression. It is very frightening to be a woman in a patriarchal culture. We all manage, and most of us get by, so we sometimes forget the incredible effort it takes just to keep ourselves together in the face of the male violence that threatens us every day. A recent look at the fears men have of women and women of men show an astonishing gender-based difference in the quality of experience: Women are most threatened by rape and murder; men are most afraid of being laughed at by women.[2] For many women rape is not an abstract threat but an enacted reality. For others, just knowing the possibility exists is enough to keep us in our place most of the time. If we haven't been raped, we feel lucky, and we make internal decisions to keep "being careful." If we have been raped or molested as children, we make the best possible effort to forget, to repress the memory and get on with our lives, even perhaps to heal ourselves of the wound caused by this unforgivable violation. In any case we attempt to forgive men in general, because it would be unfair to blame men in general. Yet we live in a war zone, with the ever-present reality of rape, violence, and murder in the back of our minds. Robin Morgan elaborates on this now-universal female experience in her book *The Demon Lover*, describing a woman walking on any street or path anywhere in the world who hears male footsteps behind her and feels afraid.[3]

At the same time, women are forced to market our-selves sexually at all times. If we want to get ahead in our culture, it is clear from the start that we must be attractive sexually to men or we will not make it. Whether or not a woman actively takes this on as a challenge she wants to meet or actively resists it in reaction to its degradation, it is a fact of our existence every single day. And what is considered sex-ually attractive is defined by men, promulgated through male-controlled advertising and movies, and dutifully noted and responded to by women. We are required to be puppets, dancing in response to strings that are being pulled by some other mind, with other intentions. We are not autonomous. I would say this is particularly a problem for women in the West, but then I remember Chinese foot binding or Middle Eastern clitoridectomies (which mothers did to daughters in the name of erotic love), and I know the problem is universal and worldwide.[4] I leave to the psychologists to discover why men would prefer dancing puppets to real live women, and I will move on to discuss the inner experience of women in this condition.

Women naturally become the suppressors of our own internal sexual experience anytime it threatens to externalize and expose us. We have internalized the cultural hatred toward our natural sexuality, as well as the sensible fears we adopt in order to survive, and this leaves us with two experi-ences: One happens on the inside and in secret, the other is expressed. Our inner reality is a garden, where we can come to know the Goddess and her ancient ways, in our dreams, fantasies, visions, and time alone in nature. The outer reality is more a performance, however you want me to be. What-ever is in style tends to mold us, at least subliminally. We behave as we are conditioned to behave as "good girls" or rebel against society and behave as "bad girls," which also leads to our oppression. Think of the popularity of movies like *Waiting for Mr. Goodbar* or *Fatal Attraction* (women standing in lines around the block, waiting to get in!) and you know con-temporary women have internalized something false but binding, to which we respond like Pavlov's dog. The fact that even supposedly hip feminist women dress up in French-whore negligees, garters, and boots for their male partners or that lesbian women have taken to imitating the worst of het-erosexual sadomasochism together shows a remarkable degree of collusion with the oppressor.

▲ *Fig. 53    Two women together — whether sisters, mother and daughter, or lovers we will never know. This image comes from a temple in India, but in ancient times women were often shown together interacting in loving and beautiful ways. Only under patriarchal rule did women become estranged from one another, isolated and competitive in relation to men. Courtesy the Los Angeles Museum of Art. Used with permission.*

Yet the garden within is always calling, and our longings for a return to our divine nature are strong enough to emerge through artistic images and to permeate the whole field of Western psychology. Western cultural beginnings are tainted with the story of Adam and Eve, and the "original sin" that led to expulsion from this very garden that we each privately and painfully remember in our cells. In the beginning Eve, like Lilith before her, was kin to the serpent, who whispered heresy in her ear. The heresies of "snake power" are reincarnation and sexuality, and on account of Eve's allegiance to these truths, all women in history are bound to painful childbirth and a forced exile from the garden.

When Karen Vogel and I were first uncovering and rediscovering the Goddess, we posed our question as a sexual inquiry. Looking at the ancient images of women (see fig 53), seeing in them an expression of sexuality that does not freely exist nowadays, we asked, What happened? How did women lose this power, this amazing expression of self-esteem and the sacred? What could have taken that away from us, and why? In our personal relationship, she and I were experiencing a released kundalini or energetic expression, causing "rushes" through our bodies that were continuous in our first year together. I had experienced a glimpse of this in my earlier relationships with men, but there was some new quality present for us that caused us to look to the past for answers. We bonded together in a highly creative alchemy that allowed the *Motherpeace* images to be born through our soul contact.

And although our sexual relationship didn't last more than a couple of years, our bonding process connected us in a family or kinship way. Karen, who helped raise my daughters during the years we lived together, was later present at the birth of my son and lives with me and my husband now in our extended family.

When I first opened to women sexually, my mind awakened as if a light bulb had just gone on. I was twenty-three, had read and understood Kate Millet's *Sexual Politics*,[5] and being with a woman implied that there were no limitations on my sexuality. I felt certain that this was "the solution." How simple! If all women would simply stop relating to men and start relating to each other, our problems would be solved, because we wouldn't be "like them," and we could create our own little paradise where we would be gentle, loving, connected, free, and totally together. Without THEM. But even a little time spent in lesbian culture is enough to understand that there are problems with making an identification based on who you sleep with. It's just too tenuous. Not only that, but identity itself is tenuous and always changing — the self is impermanent and unstable. How could any group aligned around a single identity issue possibly become the blueprint for a new world? It was very disappointing and disillusioning, in my own primary relationship with the woman I loved and "married," when we found ourselves acting like heterosexual married couples. Shock. Our inner conditioned tapes keep right on running, no matter who is on the receiving end. Karen and I liberated each other through our stark experience of what psychologists call projection and codependence: Please be there for me in the way I'm used to, OK? And as a trade-off, I will be here in the way that's familiar to you as well.

I spent two full years after that in a celibate state, relating to myself. It was really a relationship with the Goddess, and I spent hours stimulating myself to cosmic orgasms and a deeper understanding of sexuality than I'd ever realized. I figured out that no one could really be my lover the way I wanted if I couldn't be. My sexuality was so sacred, able always to lead me into contact with the Divine, that I simply stopped believing sex and spirit were separate. I studied yoga, including Tantric and Taoist sexual practices, and I finally decided that even yoga was primarily a male system that worked for men, focused on "keeping the organ down"

**185**

and saving the "vital forces." What did this framework have to do with women? Women, after all, are multiorgasmic, as Masters and Johnson told us in the 1960s. We have the insatiable capacity to be stimulated to one orgasm after another, with the entire process building on itself in intensity, no peak in sight, and without any apparent loss of vitality. There is no "little death," no sacrifice of arousal, no spending of one's energy. Obviously this means that our yoga in the sexual realm demands a different approach. The ancient figurines show us this approach.

Most Tantric texts are written by men for the male student of yoga, leaving the presence of the female in doubt, except in her usual function as object of desire. Most of the practices seemed to be aimed at having a woman there and then avoiding any normal responses to her. In the most crass sense, Tantric practices seem a series of exercises designed for using the woman's energy and presence without ever relating to her directly, or naturally. The more ascetic disciplines reject women altogether, but Tantra tends to prefer that she be right there in all her glory, giving the yogi the best opportunity to practice his art of self-mastery. Even Gandhi, we know now, thanks to Mary Daly, slept with young beautiful women with whom he apparently did not "have sex," in order to practice the ancient art of brahmacārya (celibacy) in an experimental way.[6] Women in Tantric practices are encouraged to dress (and undress) beautifully and seductively, dance, move, and generally undulate in ways that are provocative for the benefit of our heroic male, who will not actually allow himself to "taste" of her delights and will not "lose his power" in relation to her.[7] When he finally does make "love" with her, he makes sure not to climax but to "retain" his semen, which presumably builds up and accumulates as higher consciousness. Taoist erotic practices seem slightly more progressive, in the sense that the man engages with the woman and encourages her to have many orgasms, knowing that with each orgasmic release she feeds him energy that will actually nourish his "longevity." This is the model for the old sage and the young consort.

Now, I will not argue with the fact that a man who can control himself makes a better lover than one who can't and that premature ejaculation is a social problem we can do better without. But this entire heroic paradigm that asks a man to stand tall and be cool while the woman is doing everything in her power to get his attention has become a pervasive ideal in the West, leading to a serious power struggle between men and women, fought out in the bedroom (and now even in the bedrooms of lesbians together). Women become more sexy and seductive (femme), while men become more unavailable and unattainable (butch). Everybody is performing, and nobody is really there. There can be no sacred sexuality without soul, and there is no soul in the common sexual interaction between the two frozen characters I've just described. Sex is energy, and energy is freed through integration and real contact. The mind and its powers can feed sexuality a little, through fantasy and imagination, but when the mind becomes the total arena for the encounter, there ceases to be an expression of sexuality. When two people have to add new paraphernalia and scripts to their lovemaking every time, because the old thing doesn't work anymore, and when they have to hurt each other or dominate or submit in order to "get off," then we have a serious breakdown on our hands.

The sexual conditioning to which we have been subjected in our culture has been evolving for five thousand years and has been through numerous shifts. Marija Gimbutas's books give us a view into the most ancient strata — that of the Neolithic period of early agriculture and the beginnings of city life. Our early female ancestors in the town of Çatal Hüyük had a good life. They built shrines to the Goddess, where female priestesses facilitated rituals of initiation, with music, dance, and meditation, in rooms adorned with breasts and bulls' heads and horns. Gimbutas has pointed out that the shape of the bull's head is exactly the same anatomically as a woman's uterus and fallopian tubes and that the ancient women clearly knew this (fig. 54).

One pottery vessel from this site contains the figures of a man and woman and a slightly larger female figure standing between them as if facilitating a sacred marriage (fig. 55). This may be one of the earliest Tantric images we have, since in India old women (priestesses of the Snake Goddess) teach the young couple about the sexual mysteries. In Çatal Hüyük the women and children were buried inside the city walls, beneath the houses. Men were buried outside. In one temple model excavated from this site, a group of women sit in a circle with larger female figures circled around them. It looks

▲ *Fig. 54 The bull's head, with its uncanny similarity to the female uterus and fallopian tubes, represented regeneration in the ancient Goddess religion. Scholars usually assume "he" represented her fertilizing "consort" (which may also be true). Marija Gimbutas distinguishes between this deeper meaning at the heart of the Goddess religion and the later Indo-European bull perceived as the Thunder God. To take this distortion all the way through its evolution, we need only look at the mythology of Zeus, represented as a bull, who raped Europa (and all the other female gods and mortals he came into contact with!). Drawing by Susan Ashley.*

like a council of women, whose higher selves are coaching them in their work of self-government or community leadership (see fig. 9). In another ceramic grouping, the women are dancing and playing musical instruments and drums. The dating on Çatal Hüyük has been traditionally put at about 7000 B.C.E., but recent information from Merlin Stone suggests a much earlier radiocarbon date, going back as far as 11,000 B.C.E.[8] This peaceful, egalitarian city existed in essentially the same form until the sixth millennium, when the patriarchal hordes began to overrun the place.

Modern Western women can date our sacred sexual beginnings at least to the communities of Çatal Hüyük and Jericho. We can read about the downfall of the Goddess cultures and the sexuality that they embodied in the horrendous stories of the Old Testament. "Joshua fit the battle of Jericho . . ." is a historic tale told by the victors about the vanquished ancient, sacred women who had kept the rites of the Goddess since time immemorial. As the Old Testament makes vividly clear, the overthrow of the ancient Goddess religion and the "Whore of Babylon" was not easy or quick but went on for many millennia with a vengeance. The patriarchs would no sooner get rid of all the "harlots" of the Old Religion than one of their own men would marry one of them and start up the old worship again. Over and over, the massacres would take place, glorified as the divine justice of a vengeful Jehovah who will have "no other gods before me." The mak-

▲ *Fig. 55   Marija Gimbutas identifies this vase as a shrine model with a hole in the center for libations. The Goddess holds her hands over her pregnant belly between a male and female figurine, which reminds us of the Tantric tradition of sacred sexual rites in honor of the Goddess and also of the earlier Venus of Laussel from the cave in France (see figs. 3 and 4). Contrary to the idea that our ancestors didn't understand reproduction, this is another visual proof of their knowledge and utilization of that generative power. Drawing by Laurelin Remington-Wolf.*

ing of idols or images of deity became one of the central sacrileges of the new Judeo-Christian religions, and the beautiful figures of the Divine Female that had been fashioned since the early Paleolithic era were destroyed, forbidden, and demonized.

During the transition period between the beginnings of this destruction and the completion of it (from about 4000 B.C.E. to about the beginning of Christianity), the sacred women found themselves in the position of being harnessed into service by the new governmental hierarchies. They were allowed to keep their sacred sexual practices in the temples but became distorted and degraded into prostitutes. Once "virgin" (belonging to no man) and married to the Goddess, serving her energies and purpose, now they were officially in the service of the men in the community. In many cases and for many centuries, they still practiced their rites in the name of the Goddess, but now male priests officiated and ruled over

**189**

them. Money was exchanged in the temples for their services, and women were even forced to give themselves at least once in their lives as an offering to the divine. Even the famous story of Inanna[9] tells about this process of change. Her new husband, Dummuzi, builds her a sacred bed from the old hulupa tree that grew in her garden. Dummuzi is a shepherd, replacing her older husband, who was a farmer. (The invading nomads replaced the earlier farming males by killing them and marrying their women.) Dummuzi fells the sacred Tree of Life with his ax, causing the bird, the snake, and Lilith to flee into exile. Lilith's life on the shores of the red sea (menstruation) is described as "unbridled promiscuity," in the service of demons, with demon children as the offspring. Inanna's permission for the act that exiled her earlier sister, Lilith, is the necessary compromise for her retention of the sacred office of temple priestess in the new regime. *Sarah, the Priestess* is Savina Teubal's excellent research on this transition and the difficulties it presented for the sacred women who were attempting to keep their temple offices, while necessarily capitulating to colonization, marriage with the invading males, and exile from their homelands.[10]

Men during the period from biblical Moses to the so-called birth of Christ donned women's robes, wore false breasts, and began officiating in the place of women in the sacred ceremonies. During this time they invented the concept of kingship and instituted dynasties (around 3000 B.C.E. all over the world). Men became kings by sitting on the lap of the Goddess (Ishtar, Isis, etc.) and by lying with the priestess in the *hieros gamos*, or sacred marriage. The male priests replaced the female menstrual blood offerings with sacrificed animals,[11] and in some cases, humans. They even castrated themselves and served as eunuch priests in the service of the Distorted Feminine. Barbara Walker maintains that the Apostle Paul himself, fanatical on the subject of celibacy, was a castrated eunuch priest.[12] Men's relationship to sex in general became deeply tied to their sense of ownership of women and children, and in Egypt the newly invented word that meant "slave" also meant "wife."[13] Men began seeing themselves in the image of the Father God, defining themselves as divine sons of that authority, with unlimited sovereignty over women and children (as parent to child). Sex was gradually taken out of the temple and separated from religion. Prostitution became a secular "profession" into which certain women (often slave women captured in wars) were forced. *The Reign of the Phallus*, by classics professor Eva Keuls, is a graphic testimony of hierarchical life for women in Olympian Greece, where married women lived cloistered, indoors, while their husbands practiced sexual acts in public with young male partners and female *hetairae* hired or owned for that purpose.[14]

When the Greek city-states were invented, Greek vase painting rose to an elevated status (around 500 B.C.E.), and stories of Greek heroes killing Amazons became the main myth portrayed in all the artwork. The Olympian Gods and Goddesses came into being, fragmenting the old creatrix Earth Goddess, Gaia, into sex-role-stereotyped pieces of her ancient self. Aphrodite became the wanton sweetheart, Hera became a hysterical and jealous wife of a philandering sky god, Artemis was relegated to the wilderness (like Lilith before her), and Athene was re-created as her father's daughter. Women of Western cultural descent have had to make do with these remnants of an earlier feminine wholeness that was eradicated almost five thousand years ago. What kind of sexuality can we have, segmented off into prostitution (Aphrodite) or motherhood (Demeter) or frustration (Hera) or separation (Artemis) or cerebral expression (Athene)?

The earliest threads of Christianity appear to be more benign than the later orthodox tradition.[15] The Gnostic gospels show us rites and ceremonies that recall Indian Tantric practices, with their male-female groups and menstrual blood as a sacrament. The Magdalene was a sacred name for the office of the priestess, linking Mary Magdalene and Jesus to these earlier female roots.[16] But by the time Christianity was officially anchored in the Western world, there were no more sacred women. Sexuality was officially banned, except for the purpose of procreation, and only then practiced in distaste. By 400 C.E. the Church Council had formally declared cyclic reality (female, lunar, menstrual reality) a heresy, including the doctrine of reincarnation. Whatever role Mary Magdalene had played in the origins of early Gnostic Christianity had been rescinded and her name blackened by the usual stamp of disapproval: whore, harlot, prostitute. Eve, Adam's second wife and Lilith's replacement, was presented as the archetypal woman, the root of all evil, with an untempered lust for the fruit of knowledge in the Garden. The Apostle Paul's books in the New Testament are the foundational text for contemporary Christianity, and the celibate priesthood walks in Paul's, rather than Jesus', footsteps.[17]

Even so, the old practices continued in all of Europe and the Mediterranean area well into the Middle Ages through the Dianic religion of the peasant people. At that point the virulence of the enforced celibacy erupted as a rather active shadow from the unconscious of the practitioners. The burning of nine million women in Europe by the Catholic priests of the Inquisition cannot be logically separated from the malicious and repressive beginnings a thousand years earlier. The invention of the printing press in the Middle Ages led to the widespread distribution of the world's worst book, the *Malleus Maleficarum,* all over Europe. This book charged women, in the lewd details that sprang from the repressed minds of the Catholic clergy, with all manner of lust and fornication. But most prominently the book declared in no uncertain terms that any woman who was successful at healing was by definition a witch and would be burned. Children were forced to watch their mothers burn at the stake, and women were routinely raped, violated, and tortured until they confessed to anything the Inquisitors accused them of. The Catholic church confiscated all property of the women they murdered and became rich as a result of this plunder. Records tell of whole villages in which all the women were wiped out.[18]

Contemporary Western women healers must contend with our racial and genetic fears not only in regard to healing but also in direct relationship to our sexuality. Women were accused of being "carnal" at the core and of being the source of every evil temptation for men. Our psychic powers and healing practices were linked with evil, sin, and degradation, leading the whole Western world in the centuries that followed to fear women's unconscious power. "Uppity women" everywhere have reason to fear for our lives. Although many of the accusations and descriptions of what the "witches" were doing are clearly fabricated from the minds of the murderers, some of the behaviors and attitudes described in the official records point to shamanic practices of healing and empowerment and to the worship of the Goddess of the Old Religion from the ancient past. Herbal knowledge was very deep before the witch burnings, and midwife-healers were the main practitioners in European villages and towns. In those days women controlled their own fertility. When peasants met in the sacred groves for their earth-based ceremonies in honor of Diana and Nature, they undoubtedly practiced the forbidden arts of magic and shamanism. They covered themselves with hallucinogenic herbal ointments that endowed them with the ability to "fly," that is, to leave their physical bodies like a shaman and travel in their soul-bodies.[19] They certainly must have still practiced the ancient sexual rites, as they had always done, in spite of the new Christian dogmas. It is for these actual "heretical acts" that the witches were burned, as well as for their healing practices, which were quickly appropriated by the new male doctors.

Some of the shamanic practices, although taboo, are apparently still known today in France and Britain and probably other places, where they are practiced in secret by some of the old women.[20] Marija Gimbutas chronicles many customs from Lithuania that demonstrate this unbroken thread from the past, including the use of saunas for birthing right up into the twentieth century.[21] I would imagine this might include sexual mysteries as well as healing rituals. The seasonal festivals celebrated until recently by the peasants in Europe marked the points of power in the old calendar and were originally celebrated, at least in part, through sexual expression. The cross-quarter holidays were feasts of fire, meaning the female sexual fire, the kundalini. It was understood that sexuality kept the community healthy, that the union of the male and female in ecstatic embrace raised energy that made for a fertile agricultural year. Rumors and legends about how our ancestors used to run naked in the fields on Beltane and practice total sexual license during the festivals, such as Bacchanalia, are remnants of what was once Goddess worship. And Beltane is the May Day holiday when the church burned the most "witches," in direct response to the practice of sexual customs that had prevailed.[22] Throughout the entire five-thousand-year history of transition away from the Goddess to God, there has been uninterrupted suppression and hatred of female sexuality, which is said to be the work of the devil.

Five thousand years of denigration and massacre have been enacted against the female, whose crime is that she loves and produces life. The biological base of our fundamental power has become the root of our now-universal oppression. As women have become more liberated since the late 1960s, the rise in rape (four times the rise in other crimes) has kept up with whatever small gains we might have made. Ancient images of women giving birth have been replaced by the specter of a male doctor "delivering" the woman of her child, and C-section has become a norm in birthing practices in this country. We also have the highest young unwed mother count of any country in the world due to our absurd insistence that young people abstain from sexuality, while it is pushed on them from an extremely early age and from every direction. Our refusal to provide them with safe, simple birth control information and materials is equally geared toward the inevitable outcome we are experiencing. The double bind of our sexuality in a male-dominated culture is very complex.

How are we ever going to find our way back to the garden? My ancient cenote is now a pathetic concrete goldfish pond in back of an apartment building. The hot springs of the ancient world are now cold and boundaried by manmade forms. Women today are remembering their early sexual invasions. The father, stepfather, grandfather, brother, uncle — all the males who should be protecting the young girls until they are old enough to leave the nest — are fucking them against their will, even before they have developed the will. These memories went underground, to lay unnoticed for decades alongside of our memories of other lifetimes when we loved in different ways. And now, miraculously, painfully, these memories are coming up. They are becoming available to us, en masse, like an urgent uprushing from within the collective psyche. It's a sexual emergency. Ever since the Dark Mother herself, our outermost planet Pluto, entered into the sign of Scorpio where she belongs, the purging of these memories has been taking place. Pluto remains in Scorpio only fourteen years and then moves on, but the results of the transit will be felt for generations. The deep, ugly, formerly hidden truth about sexuality and power in our culture has hit the popular newspapers and magazines, and modern women are determined to get out from under the devastation of these early childhood experiences.

When I was six years old, my kundalini energy came in full throttle. I was becoming disconnected from my real self, and I imagine that the influx of this high-voltage source energy rescued me from my own potential destruction. (I had jumped from a lawn chair and broken my collar bone, gotten bit by a dog and had rabies shots, and had to have my tonsils removed all in a little over a year.) What kundalini meant in real-life terms was that I became sexual, by myself, with myself. I began to experience sexual energy and orgasm regularly, every day, by crossing my legs and rubbing them together in a certain way. I didn't have a name for this experience or any context to put it in, but I spent hours, as I remember it, happy to be by myself, having this amazing experience. Unfortunately I also did it in school, and I remember very clearly the day in second grade when my teacher came over to my desk and stopped me by putting her hands firmly on my shoulders and letting me know that what I was doing was not OK. The experience submerged after that, becoming more private, something I learned to do without others' knowing it. Always before anything difficult, like exams, even into college, I would use the internal masturbation as a practice to calm and strengthen myself. But in that moment in second grade, I became aware of my social reality, as psychology says seven-year-olds are expected to do. I split myself between private (good thing, do it) and public (bad thing, don't let anyone know). This split was further fueled by my mother's disturbed reaction to my masturbation when she would burst into my bedroom and "catch me." It didn't occur to me that she was out of bounds, coming into my sanctuary without knocking; I was only aware of her emotional withdrawal from me for a time following each exposure and her mean glance in my direction. Clearly my activity was unspeakable, and it must have worried her terribly. Learning later that many American girls who masturbated were subjected to clitoridectomies by the gynecological establishment, I can see why she was upset!

Women with incest and molestation experiences have even stronger issues in this area. The supportive literature that has finally come out is breaking through the incredible isolation experienced by the (at least) one out of three of us who has been violated during her growing-up time.[23] Later, in high school, when my mother initiated me into the esoteric use of tampons instead of pads, I had an experience that added to my own confusion about my sexuality. Being able to wear tampons made me feel mature and accomplished at one of the female mysteries. During this time I was being very careful not to let my boyfriend "go too far" with me in our petting sessions and feeling very confident about what a "good girl" I was. One day out of nowhere my father accused me of being pregnant. I was shattered. On some unconscious level I must have been keeping my hymen intact for him, because I felt utterly betrayed by his wild accusation. It turned out that he had been aware of my menstrual cycle from taking out the trash cans with my used pads in them, and when three months went by without any pads in the garbage, he assumed I was pregnant (meaning he assumed I was having sex, which I was being so careful not to do, just for him!). The illusion of my sacred chaste state went out the window, and I lost (or gave away) my virginity shortly after that.

Given the climate of middle America in the late 1950s and early 1960s, I feel very lucky to have had a pleasant, creative, and somewhat self-directed sexual initiation with a boy who was also having his first experience with me. My long years of sexual experience through my spiritual masturbation helped me make good instinctual choices in this area. Even so, losing my virginity in the front seat of a Ford in the parking lot of the local college wasn't exactly mystical. At least he was my good friend, and I learned to have orgasms with him and to more or less freely express myself. After that, we were lovers, which was so totally private and taboo, I didn't even tell my very best girlfriend about it. So strict was Iowa in 1964, so clearly spelled out were the rules that separated good girls from bad ones, that none of us ever told the others, until she "had to" get married. We were all doing it, and we were all keeping it a secret. When I found out that one of my girlfriends had had an abortion, I all but abandoned her in shock and disapproval. Once in a while a "test" would circulate that had numbers for answers to graphic questions about our sexuality, which we would take in private and then share the numerical outcome with each other. The test purported to delineate good from bad girls, depending on what our total score was. We all cheated to keep the numbers down.

The repressed and submerged feelings and energies that passed between and among us girls makes up part of this picture too. My best girlfriend in high school—the one I didn't tell that I was sleeping with my boyfriend—used to sleep cuddled up with me several nights a week in her little twin bed. We were so close I can't imagine in retrospect how we kept anything from each other. I can only think we had a tacit agreement not to talk about it out loud, since it was part of our private, versus our public, reality. (Synchronistically twenty years later I married my husband, Jonathan, whose birthday is exactly the same as hers. Their astrology charts have only a different ascendant.) My relationships with girls were crucially important, central in my life, from the time I was in kindergarten until I married. When I left my first husband, five years and two babies later, I fell in love with a woman and experienced the flush of lesbian love. It awakened in me a memory I had totally suppressed until that time, of making love with girls during my preadolescence. I used to have my girlfriends stay overnight, and we used to get naked and cuddle, kiss and fondle each other in bed. We pretended to be practicing for when we would be with boys, but it was breasts we were kissing and nuzzling, and that's what stays in my memory. When I have mentioned this to other women over the years, many have told similar stories of being sexual with girls during that in-between period of budding sexuality, just prior to dating.

One of the important differences between our lifestyles and the way our ancestors lived in Çatal Hüyük or ancient India is that a woman didn't live in an isolated unit with a man and her children. The women in these ancient communal societies lived together, practicing their religion together as a fundamental way of life. They cooked, made art, raised children, gathered food, healed the sick, and birthed the next generation together. Men hunted and practiced the arts of commerce, traveling from place to place, returning home to the women and children regularly. There is no evidence to show that women and men got along with one another in any other way but harmoniously, but no one woman was dependent on a single man for her survival. And no one woman was locked in a cage with her male partner, whose frustration might at any moment be the source of harm to her and her children. Our contemporary social form of organization is quite insane and is rapidly breaking down. The death of the nuclear family, although uncomfortable in the present moment, as women become en masse the lower caste in our culture, may ultimately prove to be our freedom. As we are abandoned by the individual men in our lives, hopefully we will begin once more to turn to one another and rely on the group form that women can create together.

There are two poles of experience, two avenues to source energy, the male and the female. In the Old Religion the Goddess had a male counterpart who was not a father but a sexual partner. He was imagined in the image of an earth-based, lunar male energy, named Shiva, Dionysus, Adonis, and finally Jesus. The female had a direct link with the Goddess, and with female source energy. She did not search for truth through the mediation of the male but danced a dance of opposites in relation to him. The garden within is the sacred sanctuary where we reconnect with the Goddess, the deep Feminine, the underground source of female empowerment and expression. We were once deeply rooted in that place, expressing power and sexuality from there without any splitting. That's the unambiguous wholeness we see in the ancient female figurines. We were snake and bird, earth and sky, body and spirit. We could invite the male into that place for an encounter, and he came. And even now, from that sacred enclosure, as a priestess, when I perform the magical rites of the ancient, deep Feminine, I can initiate and heal the male through his simple encounter with me there.

But what if the heroic male is now afraid to enter there, afraid of the clashing rocks, the *vagina dentata*, the gaping maw, the devouring womb of the Feminine? What if (collectively) he has developed society, religion, and psychology to the point where they encourage and reinforce his absence from that place, his refusal to enter there, even when he falls in love and experiences his longing to return there? What if all of civilization is an elaborate attempt to create structures that will withstand the power of the woman over the man at the moment when he falls in love, keeping him in control through the danger period until he has proper ownership of the woman? The heroic epics are full of temptations and resistances of the ancient heroes in their struggles to remain dominant in the face of the overwhelming allure of the (sacred) female. And what is she offering that is so dangerous, that it is made taboo? She simply invites him to enter her garden, her island, her enclosure. There he will experience mystical sexuality through *her* perspective, a female-centered instinctual approach that will by definition transform him. She is overpoweringly at home there, larger than life. It is more than the average male can handle.

When I gave up men for five years, during my shamanic healing period, I thought I would live without them. To my surprise, I missed them. I missed having that brother-friend, some experience of polarity and dialogue that didn't exist in my all-female world. When I'm too long away from women, I miss them too. I wonder about all the focus on sexual preference, when it seems that the heart does not naturally discriminate on the basis of gender. Shamans generally have a spirit lover of the other sex, a relationship that supercedes any on the physical plane. The presence that saved my life at the age of six has been a friendly and powerful lover to me my whole life, and my physical lovers have held another place in my heart and life. When I opened again at the age of twenty-nine, I officially married myself to the Goddess, acknowledging my spirit lover as the central carrier of my fidelity.

It's not easy to relate to either men or women these days. Being true to ourselves while following the compelling lead of the sexual energies that drive us to mate is a spiritual path. We are damaged and repressed beyond repair, like the goldfish pond in my dream, yet we long for completion and fulfillment in our sexual relationships. The true Tantra is a bond made from the deepest level of spiritual memory between two people then brought into a container created for that purpose in this lifetime and held there. If two people can hold the sacred trust with each other in the container of their ongoing relationship, allowing all the pain and disappointment and anger to be present yet not annihilate them, transformation can begin to occur. This is radically different from our romantic fantasies of the perfect relationship, making it difficult to recognize our soul mates when they appear right in front of us. Or we recognize them but can't deal with the ways they will not bend to fit our fantasies over time. Allowing the real person to emerge in your lover while not abandoning yourself in hopes of keeping him or her is a test of faith. Allowing the relationship to lead the way while the two egos burn in the fire of our struggle is the work. The relationship has an organic process of development and individuation, just as each person does. It winds its way somewhere, like a snake, instinctually knowing what is needed and moving toward it, just as the evolving consciousness tends to do.

One form of liberated sexuality available to women as a birthright is represented by Kali in India or the dakini in Tibet. This expression of the sexual energy has little to do with our relationships and dependency needs and everything to do with cosmic energy and its manifestation on earth. In order to come into contact with this archaic stratum of female sexuality, it is necessary to dissolve the ego structure to some degree and become more fluid as a vessel of ancient power. Both Kali and the dakini are becoming spontaneously available to women today. The dakini is an icon of liberated energy, spiritual freedom, and the untamed spiritual nature. She is the Feminine in a much larger sense than any archetypes carried by Western culture for at least the last two thousand years. Like Kali, she is trickster, sexual teacher, power holder, and compassionate bodhisattva, and she awakens in us through the avenue of spontaneous sacred play. Her teachings may not be easy for us, since we are conditioned to need and expect rigid definitions of reality, but the process once begun leads to freedom from those very rigidities that make us so uncomfortable. Both Kali and the Black Dakini carry a knife, sword, or blade of some kind that they swing over their heads for eradicating ego obscurations. Kali even goes so far as to be seen cutting off Shiva's head (ego, identity) so that his energy can get free. She represents the archetypal function of the female in a sacred heterosexual encounter: to provide enough energy that the male can become very still, enter into an ecstatic trance state (i.e., like Shiva, become a "corpse"), and restrain his ejaculation for a time during which the two dance in the spirit realm together. During this period of cosmic dance, healing energies are released for both people as well as their community, and total regeneration is possible. This sexual dance between two people (opposite sexes or same sex) is one of the oldest forms of ritual practiced by human beings on this planet since it predates the expression of sexual ritual connected with procreation. Although I believe the Paleolithic cave-dwellers understood the connection between procreation and heterosexual intercourse, there is no proof that as primates we didn't first celebrate sexuality for its healing power alone.

We don't seem to know much about coming to the altar naked and unashamed, closely personal, without drugs and props, yet so radiantly incarnate with Goddess and/or God that we hardly recognize each other for the blinding light of deity. The Tantras tell us that the two partners need to be connecting on many levels in order to be able to experience such a union. It is not enough for him to be fantasizing about some Playboy bunny, while she is imagining some other equally unlikely scenario, expecting that together they are going to be able to reach an ecstatic state. As the Scriptures point out, when they are involved in these different "pictures" and fantasies, their chakras or energy centers are not connecting. Contemporary Tantra in the West focuses almost exclusively on how-tos and step-by-step technical performances designed somehow to stimulate her G Spot and bring the couple together in the Big O, now known as the Valley Orgasm. Even the current trend toward sharing our fantasies out loud and dressing up for each other isn't the solution. It takes being open and completely present. We must somehow have the nerve to come together and actually face each other, being ourselves and encountering the sacred other, without subterfuge or mask. We must be comfortable with all our sexual feelings, energies, and the forces that push through us during the sexual encounter. That means at times we will be having feelings and images that don't fit into our sex-role stereotype, and we may have experiences that can't be explained from the rational mind.

*Female-
Centered
Sexuality:
Return
to the
Garden*

When I enter this space myself, I feel in the presence of the Divine, and I am awestruck. When my male partner experiences this state in me, he has at times been ambivalent, feeling drawn to its power and sacredness yet threatened by its intensity. We have both worked at allowing the space to exist for us for long enough that we can participate in it. It reminds me of lucid dreaming or being awake in trance. The mind is so shocked by the higher intensity of the place-space that it wants to seize on it and either take control or make it more familiar. We both feel electrically wired and full of grace in this place I call the garden. The kind of telepathic communication that becomes available to people who are truly "in love," in the moment, eye to eye, can be overwhelmingly spiritual. There is a need for staying grounded while channeling high-voltage energies, as during a healing session.

The spiritual heat that rises in this electric setting is able to purify and cleanse the body and can even empty the psyche of negative images so that the two hearts can open. Sometimes in this magical space I have seen and felt the deity enter my partners — the male God into my husband, the Goddess into my female partner — or I have embodied them myself. When I "am" the serpent woman, or Aphrodite, or Kali with a male partner, it is unforgettable and wondrous; and when I have "become" Dionysus with a female partner, it has been awesome. Once sexuality is experienced at this level, there is no going back to what we used to call casual sex or getting laid. Why would I want to waste my energy in an encounter that is essentially no more meaningful than a fix, when I can experience spiritual ecstasy through passionate union with another human being whom I am able to meet with my full self?

# Shaman Mother: Artemis and Her Cubs

THE MAJORITY OF CONTEMPO-
rary women working with the female shamanic principles are
also mothers, and our mothering is a direct offshoot of the
philosophy of life we hold within us. A shamanic philosophy
demands a way of parenting completely different from the
North American norm, and the ability to change the rules of
such a rigid, sex-role-stereotyped form as "mother" is more
than most of us can do by ourselves. If we don't change the
way we relate to our children, we will not be effective in
changing either ourselves or the world.

My daughters were already ten and eight
when I experienced the radical breakthrough I have
described as my shamanic healing crisis. They had been with
me as a harried single mother since they were five and three.
We had developed many unhealthy patterns of behaving
together that formed a clearly dysfunctional system. Bound
to one another through guilty love and dependencies, we
blamed and punished one another for the problems in our
lives. Sometimes when I heard myself yelling at my children,
it seemed as if some terrible mother (much worse than my
own mother, who was not abusive) lived within me and got
activated at times in reaction to the behaviors of my daughters. My stress level and the sense of being out of control led
to scenarios that I felt had been invented by someone other
than myself. Or I would have flashes of my real mother's
voice or hear myself mouthing words that had once come
out of her mouth that had absolutely nothing to do with my

current situation. I even recognized that my own mother must have repeated whatever patterns and beliefs she had learned from her mother, and so on, back through the ages. It was a horrifying vision. Hopeless conditioning, with no end in sight.

One day, in the midst of my intense, concentrated psychic opening and self-healing process, I simply decided I had to completely change the way I related to my daughters. I could not bear the vision I saw of a future of hopelessness and despair, repeated patterns, the female sex role enacted over and over without a break in the rhythm, and I just said no. Even though I didn't have the slightest idea how to do what I needed to do, like everything else that was changing in my life, I knew the parenting function would have to become more authentic and self-generated. I couldn't stand to be a robot, simply doing what my culture expected in this area of central importance in my life. I need to pause here and say how much I loved (and love) my children, how bonded and connected we have been to one another, and what a blessing that connection has been in my life. Like so many women I have known, I longed to be a perfect, loving mother to them: to do it right instead of always being overwhelmed and angry and helpless.

I brought my eldest daughter into the world when I was nineteen and totally unconscious, having exhausted whatever meager possibilities my future seemed to hold. My parents didn't really value college enough to send me where I had chosen and been accepted, so even though my grades were excellent, I was denied the opportunity that I had assumed was ahead of me and had planned for all those years of SAT tests and college entrance exams. When I finally started my freshman year at a large university in my home state, I was disoriented and confused and steadily developing a superficial personality. I was learning to behave as people seemed to expect me to, while underneath my authentic self was contracting into a tiny dormant cell that would wait for liberation when it became more possible. By the end of my freshman year, I had gotten myself hooked up with an ROTC senior who aimed to travel as a career air force officer. He was my ticket out of the state. I got myself pregnant on the couch in his fraternity house meeting room, and three months later we were married. My sorority deactivated me, along with the five other new members that "had to" get married that year.

We moved to an air force base in New Hampshire, where I was given a pamphlet from the base library called *Mrs. Lieutenant*. I centered myself in the activities of my precocious toddler and soon actively lobbied for a second child, who was born less than two years after the first. (I must say, we formed a collective psychic support system that has lasted through all of our growing up years!) Although I was terribly unhappy in my marriage, I knew I was stuck there for a while, but I made a conscious agreement with myself that when a door opened to me, I would go through it. Until that time I made the best of it by being a creative mother, in the most traditional sense, reading Dr. Spock, *Parent Effectiveness Training*, Glenn Doman's *How to Teach Your Baby to Read*, and so on (Robyn could read when she was three). I sewed adorable clothes for my tiny daughters, playing with them like the dolls I had when I was ten, and when they napped, I read the *New York Times* from front to back so that I would know about the world. My best friend from high school, who had been accepted and gone to the college I had originally chosen, kept me distantly informed about what was happening in the world: marijuana, civil rights, and antiwar protests.

I used to have bizarre thoughts about my husband, wishing that he would disappear from my life and I could be free. How often must this be true of women in situations of enforced passivity and unhappiness, our shamanic powers turned toward the dark side in desperation and ignorance. I knew that wishing him dead was a bad idea, so I redirected my thoughts toward wishing that he would be sent to Vietnam; within a year he received orders. (He went there as a support officer who built golf courses for the other officers.) The year without him was completely liberating for me. I learned to earn money on my own, selling cosmetics at parties for women, and I even paid my way on a trip somewhere by myself while my girls stayed with my mother. I became more self-confident and self-reliant than I had ever been before. I also watched TV news and read the papers about what was going on in Vietnam, and when I saw Seymour Hersch talking about the My Lai massacre, I became permanently politicized.

When my husband came home, I was not the woman he had married. In the car on the drive home from the airport, I confronted him about My Lai and we had our first political argument. We would never be the same again. We moved to

Colorado to take a post at the Air Force Academy, and within a little more than a year, I had sought out women's liberation, opened to women sexually and emotionally, and divorced him. When I announced to my daughters that he was moving out of the house, they were sitting at the kitchen counter in our new suburban home, coloring in their color books. Robyn went on coloring without skipping a beat, and said, "Good, now you won't fight anymore." I felt exhilarated and glad to be alive, opening to an adventure of my own life for the first time. But the difficulty of doing it all—single parenting, earning a living, returning to college, being active in the women's movement, and trying to maintain relationships—was overwhelming, and my headaches became almost unbearable. I couldn't acknowledge the power of the tension and stress in my life because I was so authentically happy to be, finally, my own person. It would be five more years before I would open shamanically and let healing into my life.

During the years of my active single motherhood in Colorado, my children were lucky to go to a local community school set up by parents connected with the small liberal arts college there. Their experience there was truly one of community, and my feminist friends were also their teachers and the principal of their school. They went to school on scholarship, and I completed my college courses the same way. In some ways I see I was tremendously privileged—white, middle class, and part of the quota of older mothers returning to college. I feel in retrospect, however, a deep pain in regard to my relationships with my children. So much yelling and screaming. I used to recognize clearly that the fine line between me and a child abuser was no more than some internalized control mechanism that stopped me (fortunately) from enacting the fantasies I had of throwing them across the room. I have so much sympathy for the pain and frustration of single mothers in this country. No one really knows what it's like unless she's in the same spot. And, of course, more and more women are in that spot.

What could be more isolating than to be defeated by having "failed" in the role of wife, to be trapped in cheap, cramped housing by herself with small children who need space to run and play, needing to be both mother and father to them day in and day out, living on food stamps or welfare because a woman hasn't the earning capacity to support all of them? She attempts to get her life together by going to school and working outside the home, requiring child care that isn't adequate and makes her feel guilty, as if she is abandoning these little ones she loves more than her own life. I think of the dolphin babies caught in Japanese tuna nets, so confused they can't escape. The males get away and so can the females — but they don't. They choose to come back. They curl around the babies and sing to them all the way to their deaths in the grinder.[1] Modern women, although less instinctually bonded to our babies due to the unnatural ways of birthing in the hospital setting, still find ourselves in the same kinds of conflict in relation to what is happening to the children. Children want to participate in the culture, and almost everything is terrible for them. The conflict is unbelievable, an enormous rift occurring between your "good self" that loves them and your "bad self" that spanks or abuses them. In my own case, my need to have meaningful activities outside the home was so great by this time that I often felt I was sacrificing my children to the work of the women's movement or whatever urgent project I was involved in at the moment. I used to fight with them much of the day then sit by them while they slept and weep for all of us. I don't know of any love that hurts as much as mother love when you can't live up to what you know is necessary to the growth and well-being of your child.

Western culture leaves the entire responsibility of child rearing to mothers then blames us for everything that goes wrong. In no way are we allowed to do the work of raising our children according to our own principles or ethics. We have "experts" to tell us exactly what needs to be done, in exactly what way, in order to be morally "correct." Women spend the time when our children are young doing everything we can to be "right" and "good." Then we watch helplessly as our children are lured from our realm into the world of the men and their ideals. We sit anxiously by as our children are molested, abused, threatened, invaded, mistreated, brainwashed, and stolen from us, and when it's all over, we are held responsible for whatever ways they rebel or don't generally turn out "OK." Motherhood in a patriarchal society is the ultimate in passive, existential angst. The only spiritual base for most American women is a kind of distant, moral God who hands down edicts and regulations that forbid certain behaviors that we hope our children will have the good sense to avoid. We attempt to protect our growing children from the incredible dangers and temptations that exist all around them, without making them afraid. We want them to be happy and have pleasure, but we don't want them to be sexual or to get in trouble (like we did!). I think this is especially true for mothers with girls. How could they not turn out just like us, as we turned out to be just like our mothers?

In 1976, in the middle of my healing crisis, I decided to do it differently. A clear intention emerged from within me, and I never wavered from it. Like quitting smoking or giving up sugar, it took some practice, but eventually changing my parenting behaviors was even more rewarding than giving up my other addictions. In the same way that people told me and Karen we really couldn't make a tarot deck, many women warned me that I couldn't do what I was setting out to do with my children. "Wait until they're fifteen," one woman challenged when I expressed confidence that we could find a positive way through. But I had a deep spiritual vision of how to do it, and I began to operate from it as if it were the right way. When my voices would start yammering about all the horrific things that might happen, I held my vision like a beam of white light through my children's adolescent years, and we are all happier for it. Sometimes I had to stop myself in midsentence, hearing my voice taking on the ring of my mother or the culture, and I would look at the faces of my daughters and ask them to wait a minute. I would have to laugh or cry and explain to them that I was caught in some old movie that didn't reflect the way I actually felt but that I wasn't really sure how I actually felt because I had never had the opportunity to find out. We would join together, and I would ask them to cancel whatever I had just said or done out of rote behavior, and I would search within myself for the deeper, truer response that wanted to come.

We began to invent together how I should raise them. I let them know I really didn't have the slightest idea how to do it, and the ways that the culture told me how to do it were unappealing to me. I told them how the culture wanted me to control and socialize them to be "good little girls" in their proper sex roles. I told them they were supposed to follow all the societal rules and regulations and grow up to be just like everyone else and not question authority or their government and so on. And I told them that for myself, I didn't believe in those values anymore, having found them to be inauthentic. But I also told them that little girls are in terrible, real danger in our society, and I was afraid to let them simply run wild without any controls. I didn't want them hurt or abused or defiled. I told them I didn't want to stay home with them all the time or join the P.T.A. and be a "good mother" within the context of their public school system. I wanted to write books and study yoga, explore psychic healing, and learn about other realities. I wanted to hang out with lesbians and politicos and other "weirdos" and not act normal. I didn't want to eat or cook meat anymore, even though they wanted to eat hamburgers every day, so I said they would have to start cooking for themselves if they didn't want to eat brown rice and beans; I didn't want to be a short-order cook.

At the tender ages of eight and ten, Robyn and Brooke were cooking their own dinners and taking buses around Berkeley. I told them I didn't want to get a straight job because it would curtail my creative freedom, which was the most important thing in life. That meant we didn't have a car, and we never had any money for anything, and we lived on food stamps. Brooke wanted to be an Olympic gymnast, but I could hardly afford to send her to classes at the Y. We had to make sacrifices that they didn't really have any choice about. I wondered if they would ever forgive me for choosing myself. But I knew on a deeper level that I was modeling how a woman might do that, so that when they grew up, they would have it within the realm of possibility to make such a choice. Steadily I held this vision. Although it was painfully embarrassing for my daughters that I was exclusively a lesbian during this period, when all they wanted was for me to be a normal person, I even considered that I was protecting them—for their own good—through their formative years from the influence and control of the male.

It was wonderful, ten years later, when I was introduced to the asteroid astrology of Demetra George, to learn that the asteroid Diana, protector of young girls, is conjunct my North Node (my destiny), and that the asteroid Ceres, the mother, is conjunct my Mars in Aries.[2] I have been a warrior mother, a protective mama bear, and once awakened to it, I took to it like a calling. I decided that since I didn't feel like the culture had much to offer me in most areas, why should I let anyone judge the way I raised my children? Why not commit to doing it my own way and hold my prayers and my intentions for their lives in such a strong way that no harm would come to any of us? Why not raise them in a way that would honor our natural process and the actual feelings and impulses we all had? But what a test for a woman, to go against the grain of contemporary opinions on child rearing. All of religion and psychology seem dedicated to telling mothers how-to. Even before birth they have their ways of controlling the pregnant mother, making her do it their way. I remember during my most recent pregnancy reading a women's health pamphlet from New York that discussed court injunctions gotten against pregnant women, forcing them against their will to give birth in a hospital rather than at home or to have a C-section rather than a vaginal birth.

So the difficulty in raising children from instinct, in a culture that is much more dangerous for them than wild animals in a more "primitive" setting might be, is that you don't really have any external rules of thumb to follow. Everything must come from within, creating a constant trial-and-error process in which you run the risk of finding out, after all, that you were wrong. I remember a significant event in relation to my elder daughter when she was in her early teens. She was beginning to act a little wild, breaking rules, drinking and smoking, doing things I basically disapproved of (along with the rest of my society). I didn't want to crack down on her in the way that my parents had done with me at that age, because I so clearly remembered the futility of such a measure. Even though I was basically a "nice" girl growing up, still when things tightened up at home in terms of discipline and control, I made it my creative task to break the rules and figure out ways of not getting caught. I knew my daughters had at least the same capacity to lie, sneak, and break the rules that I had had myself, and I couldn't see that force had done my parents any good at all. And the relationships between me and my parents seemed to steadily deteriorate as I matured through adolescence, until I wanted only to get away from home and be on my own. Even at the point I'm describing, when I was raising my young daughters, I was estranged from my parents because I didn't have a normal job, had divorced my husband, and was living with a woman.

I sat down then with a clear and loving intention and wrote my elder daughter a letter. I explained to her, as best I understood it, the law of karma—cause and effect. I said that when she was "under my wing," so to speak, minding my rules as my child, I was still basically able to protect her in the world. But that if she insisted, as she seemed intent on doing, that she was not in agreement with my way of seeing things, and she didn't intend to follow my rules and behave as I advised her to do, that I could feel how that lifted her out from under my wing of protection and into her own field of karmic responsibility. I said that I could love her, but she would have to become protective of herself if she was ready to break from me. I told her I was worried but that I trusted her to make the right choices in the long run and come through the other side of the tunnel of adolescence. I vowed to hold a beam of spiritual light for her in my mind—literally to see her safely to the other side. She told me recently that she has always kept this letter and that she gets it out and reads it about once a year. It was one of the most significant transactions that ever passed between us. We got free together.

One of the main things I had to overcome in relation to my two daughters was the tendency to want to treat them just the same when in fact they are very different. Having raised one, I assumed I knew how to do it already with the other one. This is what the rule books rely on. But then my second child, Brooke, asked me why I didn't let her go in the same way or at the same age I let Robyn go. I remember sitting and telling her, quite truthfully, that she was really a different child, and she wasn't ready (at the same age) to be as independent as Robyn, and that I actually didn't hear her asking me to be out from under my wing, that when she did, she would be. It was profound. It was Brooke who taught me about children's need to be loved through having limits set and behavior circumscribed. After Robyn's incisive lessons to me about her need for freedom and autonomy, I was totally shocked to realize that sometimes Brooke's behaviors demanded a totally different response from me. I had to be completely awake in relation to her so that I didn't assume she was having the same experience as her older sister. When I would respond to her by saying no or stopping her from doing something destructive, she would react with a renewed calm and equilibrium, happy to have been helped in regaining her center in the midst of some internal confusion.

One of the most difficult struggles in general for me as a single mother was the need to set limits of any kind. I wouldn't be surprised if this were true for modern or radical women as a rule. We want to be permissive, to give our children opportunities for growth and self-expression that we

**211**

were denied, and we sometimes forget that part of parenting is helping children to learn the safety of boundaries. It's generally the father in the family system who instigates and makes certain the rules are kept, even if it is the mother who actually keeps them. She keeps them by threatening the ultimate retaliation of the father. So if there is no father in the system, in a sense, there may not be any clear limits. Certainly I wanted to be such a good mother (since I was the only parent for so many years) that I neglected to do the stern things that needed to be done sometimes, which in the long run would have made things more peaceful for all of us. I had to learn, over the years and the hard way, to set some boundaries.

I remember a period when Robyn and Brooke were using their upstairs bedroom window as a doorway for entering and leaving the house without my knowing it. When I found out, I was freaked out because of the visibility in the city neighborhood of such a vulnerable opening into our house, and I feared for our safety. I told the girls absolutely to stop the behavior. One night Robyn and a friend came home, and I heard Robyn say she would go around and come in the bedroom window then open the front door to her friend. I got out of bed and met her as she came in the window. It was the only time I ever saw either of my children face-to-face completely drunk. It was shocking, and I responded instinctually. Obviously I couldn't talk sense to her. I went downstairs, got the hammer, and nailed her window shut. It was one of the strongest measures I ever took in relation to my children, unforgettable in our family history, although Robyn tells me that she later took the nails out. Still, it was meaningful at the time.

During the one period when my daughters' behavior got out of hand and they got picked up for shoplifting, among other things, Karen and I took them into family therapy with a lesbian therapist at the Pacific Center in Berkeley. It turned out they were really upset with me for being with a woman. Brooke once wrote on the side of a box in her room: "Families have a Daddy, a Mommy, and kids!" And it emerged that I was really upset with them for dressing up in female sex-role stereotypes (like Charlie's Angels) in front of the mirror. We thrashed it out in group therapy, making sculptures and doing theater and releasing much of the anger and resentment that had festered in our situation. Shortly

▲ *Fig. 56 This family photo was taken of the author, my two daughters, and my partner Karen Vogel in the late 1970s during the time we were creating the* Motherpeace *Tarot Cards. It was to be part of a photo-art book on alternative families by Helen Nestor, which was not published at that time after all.*

Shaman
Mother:
Artemis and
Her Cubs

after this the girls were invited by their father to live with him for a year and they accepted. What a clear test for my hard-won theories of independence and authentic mothering! Were they leaving me because I was inadequate and weird, just as they suspected? Was I, in fact, a terrible mother, like everyone must think, for letting my children go away for a year? The conflict raged through my dreams and in my journals.

But the reality—the authenticity of it—was that I was tremendously freed and out of the experience of free time and unleashed energy, the *Motherpeace* images emerged. For the first six months, I felt lucky. After all, they weren't abandoned, they were with their dad. When spring came, I dreamed that I had lost them at the ocean, and I was calling and calling and crying. So I began to worry and want them to come home, which they did soon enough. When they came home, they apologized to me for thinking it would be better somewhere else. They thanked me for being the way I was, saying that although we didn't have material wealth, they were aware of my willingness to share whatever I had with them, and they were grateful. We never had another serious period of conflict or disharmony. We had gained a new respect for and new perspective on one another, having somehow withdrawn our negative projections.

One of the clearest things I learned during the year they were not living with me was a lesson about my own debilitating codependence. As soon as I didn't have my real children in my life, with their needs and demands on my time

**213**

and energy, I immediately filled the vacancy with grown-up people who seemed to need to be taken care of like children. It became clear to me that I must have a pretty strong (that is to say neurotic) need to be the mother all the time if I could manifest so many "children" around me with so many unmet needs. I had thought I would experience sustained, spacious free time while they were gone, and instead I always had someone interrupting my process with their needs and emotions and so forth. It was the best possible teaching. To get control of myself I had to barricade myself in a room for two hours first thing every morning and do yoga before I spoke with a single person or in any way began my day. If I got out of bed and started the day without this ritual of focusing, I would be completely lost and at the mercy of whatever forces flowed through my life that particular day. It was as if I had been trained to be completely available to everyone except myself. When my girls came home after that year away, I had stopped projecting on them again that they were draining me or that they were the source of my incessant distraction from whatever was important to me. This was a decade before I learned about Arnold Mindell's concept of the dreambody and how we throw up what's familiar in front of us as part of the dream or movie we're having then react against it as if it were from "out there."[3]

It is tremendously difficult — like a breach of taboo or breaking the law — for a woman to raise her children the way she sees fit. For a mother to relate to her children from her inner authority is absolutely forbidden. Remember the mother who went to jail because she put her daughter in hiding in order to protect her from the sexual abuse of the father. The judge continuously refused to see or hear the mounting evidence that the child was being molested by the father and kept ordering unsupervised visits, while the child became visibly more afflicted by the experience. Finally the mother simply put the child in hiding and went to jail without budging from her protective position. Like Artemis, the mother bear, she functioned as a visible model for contemporary women of the necessity and the possibility of staunch advocacy for our children, even in the face of societal punishment and disapproval. This mother's clear sense of what was right overrode whatever feelings she may have had about breaking the law and refusing to comply with the judge's order.

▲ *Fig. 57 This birthing image was sketched by Jennifer Roberts from the work of Leo Frobenius in Africa and the South Pacific.*

Before that was another case where the mother was passive and didn't advocate for the girl child, whom the abusive adult male eventually murdered. What links both cases together is that it was the woman who was punished socially. Before that, remember the lawyer in New York City who murdered his wife, probably in front of the children, and then (in spite of public outcry) was granted custody of the children by the courts. It is just not possible for a mother to do the "right" thing, so mothers must train ourselves to do what we must. We must somehow develop an inner sense of well-being, a center within ourselves where we judge ourselves less harshly than the external culture and allow ourselves to act from our impulses. A mother must learn to act from her instincts, otherwise she will be torn apart with conflict and guilt. Once having chosen to act instinctively, it feels so good — so grounded — the reward is immediate, and the behavior begins to generalize. We feel our courage, our natural bravery, our internally developed sense of real ethics taking over.

Ancient cultures were matriarchal — matri (mother) arche (beginning), beginning with the mother (see fig. 57). Mother-centered or matristic cultures were those societies that formed around the mother-child bond and rippled out from there. Feminist physical anthropologists have theorized that the leap from ape to human consciousness was accomplished not through "man the hunter and his powerful weapons" but through the mother-child bonding and the sharing of food and language that came through it.[4] The mother's brother was the original male role model or authority figure, and some feminists have hypothesized that this blood bond made the man a good parent, since it kept him from wanting to harm the mother (his sister) or her offspring. They were, after all, related by blood. By contrast, patriarchal marriage—male ownership of women and children as property, for status and value—brings with it a certain amount of disorientation and alienation between the man and the woman, who is not his sister but a stranger, over whom he has power and authority by virtue of his gender.

It is truly uncomfortable for women to break free of our sex roles. In some more "primitive" cultures, such as New Guinea, for example, women are specifically threatened with gang rape if they act independently, leave the gates of the village, or in any way break the rules that the men set.[5] But it's the same in our culture, if slightly more covert. The Old Testament is full of stories that have been repeated ad nauseum by feminists trying to make the point that the laws were created in very clear ways to shape and define women's behavior "under God."[6] Women were stoned to death in ancient times for doing almost anything autonomous, especially if it related to the free expression of their sexuality.[7] We have arrived at the present state of conditioned reality—and all the beliefs we carry about how things are—through that history. We come from that beginning; we are made of that stuff. How we rear our children is one of the central cogs in the presently functioning patriarchal machine, so when we begin to do our mothering in our own ways, we are revolutionaries. It brings up a certain amount of fear in most contemporary women. It is not possible to talk about shamanic mothering without raising the specter of patriarchal violence. A woman must have her will firmly set on this path, and hopefully some sisterhood or support, in order to accomplish the task.

It has become more rather than less difficult to give birth at home in the last decade. Hospitals have co-opted the home-birth movement, creating "birthing rooms" and "alternative birthing centers" to seem as if they are carrying out the philosophies and ideals of that movement. In fact the opposite has happened. Women are becoming more and more dependent on traditional medicine and the ever-present technology. Fetal monitors plugged into the unborn baby's skull have replaced the old form of observation, which included the mother's and the midwife's sensations and intuitions. Midwives knew how to turn babies in the womb, so that a breech presentation wasn't the end of the world; but contemporary medical school curriculum doesn't include any such thing. Medical doctors know about equipment and drugs, and one quarter of the women in California now give birth by Cesarean section. Less than 1 percent of us give birth at home anymore — fewer than when the birthing movement began. In a certain serious way, we who have worked toward natural birthing must simply admit defeat on this issue. It is women themselves now who chant the miserable litanies of the doctors, about safety, responsibility to the child, gratitude for technological assistance, and so on.

Five years ago I decided to have another baby. The thought of being anywhere near a hospital made my hair stand on end. I am certainly an extremist, but I felt so threatened by hospital intrusion that I would have sworn I was in mortal danger if you put me near one. My husband and I moved to rural Arizona, to a lovely little adobe house in the desert near beautiful Oak Creek, where the blue herons live. It was idyllic. The day we moved I found out I was pregnant, and it made our purpose in moving totally clear. I wanted to be anonymous — to be left alone to birth in my own way, exactly how I wanted to. Partly I was on a personal quest to make up for my earlier births in hospitals, before I knew better. I felt so violated and victimized by those birth experiences, robbed of the pleasure of breast-feeding and bonding so important to the mother-infant process of development. Drugged for no reason, bossed around, treated without respect, shaved, humiliated, the sacredness of the experience completely taken from it. I grieved for those births and had shared that with my daughters. I vowed this birth would be different.

I found a midwife, who was unlicensed. She was afraid this might be a liability to me and suggested I shop around. I laughed, happy to have found exactly what I needed. She asked what that was, and I said, "As little medical intervention as possible!" We contracted that I would not go to the hospital, no matter what, and my husband promised he wouldn't let anyone transport me to the hospital. So our little drama was in place. I walked every day in the desert to strengthen myself for the birth, drank raspberry-leaf tea, and ate fresh greens from our garden. One day I got a particular yen for fish — a real hunger, like only a pregnant woman can get. So I went out and bought a fishing license, a pole, and some worms. I went down to the creek and caught myself a huge catfish for dinner. I asked the Mother of the Fishes to give me only as much as we needed — this baby and me — and the fish practically jumped up on the bank. I even killed it myself, feeling that I needed to do the whole thing if I was going to do it at all. I felt more instinctual than I have ever experienced before or since. (Oddly enough, I was never able to repeat the experience. I never felt in perfect harmony with it again, and the fish never bit again.)

Once during that pregnancy there was a huge, impressive lightning storm while I was out walking up on the cliffs overlooking the river. Lightning in the desert is always awe inspiring, but this time it seemed especially so. The lightning forked and streaked clear across the wide expanse of desert sky. I was totally opened by it and gave myself and the baby to the Earth Mother right then and there. I promised her that we belonged to her completely, no matter what happened, and I put us in her hands. After that I had no concerns for our safety. I felt honestly that I would go out and squat under the willow tree, giving birth and biting the cord myself if I had to, so connected to the earth did I feel. It was a wonderful, unconflicted feeling, unobstructed by any negativity, doubts, or fears that would get in the way of a healthy, happy birth. I simply began to pretend that there wasn't a medical establishment, that there weren't any other choices for me to think about, other than my own little adobe house and this little baby who was coming into our life there. I often imagined, as I walked on the land, all the pregnant women who had walked there before me. I felt native, like I belonged.

Only once did I have to encounter the medical establishment for real. My midwife asked me to get lab work done in town at the office of the one obstetrician. I called and made sure I could do that without any interference and they said yes. I had blood drawn and the tests run without any problem. But when I went to the window to pay, the receptionist changed her tune and looked concerned and grave. She told me the doctor wanted to speak with me. Since I had been so clear with them that I didn't want prenatal care at that office, and that I had a midwife, I felt offended and said brusquely,

"I don't want to speak to the doctor." She looked shocked, and turned and looked in the other room where he sat out of my sight, and said, "Well, he just wants to talk with you about the risks of a pregnancy at your age" (I was thirty-six at the time). My knees were knocking by this time, and I was having fantasies of running out of the office and getting my husband to come in and advocate for me. I was getting hysterical. "I know that's what he wants to talk about, that's why I don't want to talk to him." She was totally blown away by my insolence toward the Almighty Doctor, and I just paid and left without any further intervention. I worried for a while that they would bother me, but they never did.

My midwife always dreamed whatever complications were going to come up for her clients, and toward the end of my pregnancy she dreamed that I would give birth very early but that it would be OK. Yet she saw in the dream that something was wrong, we were sad or something, and she didn't know what it meant. On March 14, 1985, our little Aaron Eagle was born naturally, in a relaxed six-hour labor, with friends and family gathered around us. He came three and a half weeks early, as predicted, my uterus having prolapsed a week before the birth, causing me to have to take to my bed and wait. Aaron was like an elf, so light and strange, we joked that he'd come from under a plant. He was a little blue when he came out but quickly got his breathing and seemed very quiet and reflective, like a little Pisces boy with a Neptune-moon conjunction might be. We predicted he would be psychic, and we loved him intensely. Twenty-four hours after he was born, while I was holding him in my arms, we put on some music we had played often while I was pregnant, and Aaron began gently moving in exact time to the beat of the music. Amazing!

In the next few days, however, he seemed unable to begin nursing in earnest. At first we thought he would catch on after my milk came in. But he didn't. The milk came, and he still didn't suck, and he began to fade. We tried many things, but finally I just used my will to reach over the veil into the other world and bring him back. I said to him in perfectly clear telepathic language, "You stay here. We want you." And he began to thrive. Jonathan went out and bought a breast pump and an eye dropper, and we started feeding him like a little bird until he got the hang of swallowing and sucking. I would sit up in the night, trying to get him to nurse, failing as often as I succeeded. One night I was feeling discouraged and beaten down by the whole process, wondering what I was doing wrong that this little being couldn't seem to learn to nurse properly, when suddenly I remembered the La Leche League, and I thought to myself that there must be thousands of mothers all over the country, awake in the night, nursing their babies. I took heart from them, telling myself that if they could do it, so could I. It was a moving, profoundly unifying experience.

When Aaron was six days old, we made an appointment to take him to the doctor, just to see if there was something Western medicine knew that we didn't. It was Spring Equinox. I had sat up all that night, rocking Aaron in the rocker in our living room, having a profound experience of loving him, of feeling the deepest patience I've ever felt. I heard a voice form within me, calm, soothing, saying over and over, "Be gentle with this one." As the dawn appeared, there was suddenly a huge commotion at the window behind me. I turned to see one of our cats catching a bird. It seemed a very strange, and not very auspicious, omen on this sacred morning. I felt uneasy. We took Aaron to the obstetrician-pediatrician (the same one whose office I had gone to earlier), and as the nurse handled him roughly, for the first time in his short life Aaron cried. The doctor came in the room, briefly examined him, and announced without ceremony, "I'm not sure, but I think he has Down's syndrome."

It was as if everything receded into a foggy distance for me. "What do you mean?" I asked, but I was stalling, keeping the words and what they meant at bay. "Down's syndrome. Mongolism. I can't tell for sure, he doesn't have all the symptoms, but I think so." He pointed to Aaron's eyes, mentioned something about his "raised palate," while sticking his finger in Aaron's mouth. "You can have him tested," he said, and walked out of the room. All I could hear was the voice inside of me saying, "Don't do anything, just be a crystal. Be a crystal. Let it pass through you." The brusqueness of the doctor's voice, the punitive attitude of the staff. If they had said, "We told you so," it wouldn't have rung louder. All I could think of was getting out of the room, out of the building. When we got outside, I began to cry and cry, releasing the tension, and Jonathan began to curse about doctors and how we would never, ever go to one again. As we drove home we began to have our own process in regard to what we had been told and to *wonder* what it would mean for us. We had been sure our child would be special — but what was this? Now, suddenly, all his little idiosyncrasies began to make some coherent sense in this new framework. His little Asian-almond eyes (we pretended it was a connection to Jonathan's past life in China), his little pointy ears (we knew he was an elf), his slowness to respond (we thought he was placid), and his unusual sensitivity to music (we thought he was a genius).

Aaron Eagle is a precious child, the child of my heart, sent to me — I believe — as a sign of my prior accomplishments as a mother. Having raised my girls so well in the eyes and paths of the Goddess, I am given this challenging task as my reward, an opportunity to stay awake and take nothing for granted. If my protective urges were called into action before, imagine how alive they are now! If my creativity as a young mother was dynamic, imagine how my middle-aged wisdom functions with this one. If ever I felt needed, now is the time. If ever I felt like an anchor, a lightning rod, staying centered in the face of confusion or disorientation, now my work is cut out for me. If ever I felt commitment, it was untested compared with the depth of its force in my life at this time. All those years of practicing my mothering so that it would be authentic and come from the heart of my instincts must have been in some sense a preparation for my work with Aaron. From his conception I have been like an animal with him, and I interact that way with him now more of the time than not. Our physical connection is terribly important, our pawing and roaring and nuzzling and rolling around and tickling and laughing. Aaron has many fine qualities, and he relates with many people in many different ways, but it is this physical, animal bond — Artemis/Diana and her cub — that works the best for us.

I am so glad for the trust I have in my way of being with my children, built over time, through trial and error. I am so grateful for the grace of motherhood in my life and my being able to experience it on this deep, archetypal, instinctual level. I feel that my experience of raising my children and how wonderful they are, how truly proud I am of them, gives me a sense of self-esteem that is no small thing, totally unrelated to my work identity or my identity as a person in the outer world. My being with Aaron now, at this late stage in life, with him five years old and still in diapers — so labor

▲ *Fig. 58    This second family photo, taken ten years
after the earlier one (fig. 56), shows the author's
extended family: Motherpeace partner Karen Vogel,
Vicki, daughters Robyn and Brooke, husband Jonathan,
son Aaron Eagle, and Jonathan's mother, Marga, the
matriarch of the family. Except for my daughters, who
live away from home, we all share a house together in
Berkeley. Helen Nestor's book on alternative families
has been updated and is being published by NewSage
Press, tentatively entitled* Family Portraits: A Changing View of the American Family. *Photo by Helen
Nestor.*

intensive and demanding, such a long, drawn-out infancy — is
wholly grounding for me. It anchors me in physical, nurturing reality in a way I don't know what else could have. He
functions for me as the perfect "excuse" for taking care of
myself (my inner child), because he is right there in my life,
and he needs taking care of. I make him a priority, and I keep
a clear separation between my work and my home life, keeping our time together sacred and special, something set aside
as we do with ritual or ceremony.

I have moved at least another step in my process of
healing from codependence. Since I have this real child with
real needs who really needs me, I am less inclined to be
manipulated by others who might masquerade as children on
the movie screen of my projective mind and seduce me into

taking care of them. I am simply too busy for this, taking care of this child who came from my body. I even feel it has changed my relationship with my husband (along with my husband's changes, which are also related to Aaron's presence in our life). I no longer need to be married to a boy, because I have a real boy I am raising. Similarly Jonathan doesn't need to be a boy, since he has this real boy to demonstrate being a man for. It's all very complex and simple at the same time, miraculous and ordinary all at once.

The impact on my life of having given birth to this child out of my own body, in my own way, in the context of my loving family at home, has changed me forever. Perhaps being in the desert for that year, living on the land, helped with this too. But I am not the same person that I was. Since my natural pregnancy and birth, I am less afraid, more empowered. I believe I underwent an initiation of the most ancient variety, birth as a shamanic experience, the central act of female shamanism — the quintessential act that offers a woman a completed experience of facing and moving through her fears to the other side. It isn't that birth is the only way for a woman to experience this initiation — many women climb mountains or face other kinds of physical endurance tests and also come through it reborn into their power. But biologically birth is a doorway, a given for most women on the planet. It is a fundamental opportunity to become empowered. Most of us giving birth today do not have the full experience, which is co-opted and distorted beyond recognition, changed from an active process into something that is done to us, as if we don't know how to do it ourselves. Reclaiming the right to birth in our own instinctual way is a shamanic act of courage that has unfortunately become as remote to us as our ability to fly through the night in the form of an owl or heal the sick with the power of the drum. It wouldn't hurt if we began to think of our birthing and child rearing as central parts of our shamanic work — activities to be mastered through practice and discipline over a period of years.

# Female Shamanism and the Patriarchal Possessing Entity

THE SITUATION IN WHICH WE FIND ourselves at the present moment on this planet is a dire one indeed, requiring a radical reassessment of what we have been led to believe. All over the world people are dying of starvation or killing one another over disagreements about land ownership. Our soil is almost ruined, our forests cut down, the oceans, rivers, and air polluted to the point of dying. Our money is spent on building bombs while social services wane; crime has never been so prevalent, with prisons overcrowded and still filling, and drug traffic is replacing all the natural commerce between people and nations. In our own "free country" women are coming out of the closet and telling about their unbelievable, pervasive suffering: early incest (one out of three women), rape (one reported rape for every six minutes in 1988), battering and murder by boyfriends or husbands ("Nine out of every ten women murder victims were murdered by men, and three of every ten of these murders were committed by husbands or boyfriends."[1]), unwanted pregnancy and abortion, sexual harassment at work, in therapy, in spiritual centers, sexual abuse in the dentist's office, the doctor's office, on the street, and in the movies. Nowhere is there real safety for women and children, whose main enemy would appear, on the surface at least, to be the male of the species! And at this point there is also no place on the earth that is free from the pollutions and contaminations of a mind-set that would poison and kill everything that lives. Feminists have named this mind-set Patriarchy,

225

and Patriarchy—it turns out—is only about five thousand years old. In the larger overview of things, that is a blessedly short period of time. We needn't assume that Patriarchy defines human existence or that our current way of life is the human condition.

A substantial part of the problem is rooted in the mistaken version of history we have been taught and in our blind faith in the concepts of forward motion, linear development, and progress. Our Western education insists that civilization began five thousand years ago in the West, with the rise of cities, class stratification, kingship and lineages, and male dominance. Scholars posit a linear view of human evolution, imagining a gradual development out of primitive "cave-man" mentality into our present-day focus on technology and science. History and archaeology describe life in prehistoric (pre-patriarchal) times as hardship and a struggle for survival, a contest against Nature waged by a humanity that was unformed and lacked self-actualization. When we read this material, how can we help but feel lucky to be alive today, with all the modern conveniences at our disposal? How could we not place our faith in science to come up with the appropriate solutions to our problems?

Scholars also mistakenly equate human sacrifice with the primitive religions of the most ancient (archaic) past, when in fact it didn't begin to be prevalent until the patriarchal culture developed. Then they posit that we have risen out of this early stage of "barbarism" to our current high development, ignoring the sacrificial attitude of modern civilizations toward their "citizens" as little more than consumers or cannon fodder. Concurrently with this framework runs the assumption that "development" in other cultures (Asia, Africa) was naturally more primitive, happened later than our own, and was less evolved.

Yet nothing could be further from the truth. It is becoming more obvious every day that something is wrong with this picture. As archaeology digs into the ancient past and comes up with more precise dating and documentation, we learn that the early cultures were remarkably developed artistically and scientifically and yet managed to evolve and survive without warfare. Although they seem to have existed without class stratification and slavery, they managed to build large cities and live in them peacefully together. They made the most beautiful and self-realized art the world has ever known, and in some places (the Indus Valley or Knossos, Crete, for example) they had flush toilets, bathtubs, and other conveniences we consider to be the necessities of life. These ancient, highly civilized societies existed without rape, without kingship, without male domination, without war against nature. If we were truly objective in our observations, we would have to conclude that they were superior to or more advanced than our own culture. What they had in common was the worship of a central female deity, a Creator Goddess or Great Mother, and women functioning to facilitate the sacred practices and rites. The existence of these cultures poses a threat to established scholarship, which assumes "progress" to be taking place throughout the development of the world as we know it and male domination to be the natural or preferred state of things. This concept of progress cripples intellectual exploration because it makes it impossible for us to see clearly what we are observing, as if we were wearing dirty lenses.

The literature about these ancient Goddess cultures is abundant, beginning with early intuitive pioneers like Helen Diner *(Mothers and Amazons)*, Esther Harding *(Women's Mysteries)*, and Elizabeth Gould Davis *(The First Sex)*. Later, during the second wave of the feminist movement in North America, came Merlin Stone *(When God Was a Woman)*, Anne Kent Rush *(Moon, Moon)*, Starhawk *(The Spiral Dance)*, Charlene Spretnak *(Lost Goddesses of Early Greece)*, and Marija Gimbutas *(Gods and Goddesses of Old Europe)*. Finally, in the last decade, a wellspring of oracular writers and artists has come forth, beginning with Monica Sjöö and Barbara Mor *(The Great Cosmic Mother)*, Riane Eisler *(The Chalice and the Blade)*, Buffie Johnson *(Lady of the Beasts)*, Judith Gleason *(Oya: In Praise of the Goddess)*, Marija Gimbutas *(The Language of the Goddess)*, and Elinor Gadon *(The Once and Future Goddess)*. My own *Motherpeace Tarot Cards* and *Motherpeace: A Way to the Goddess* fit into this genre as well.

Although these works vary a great deal, they all agree on the essential nature of the early cultures, which were female centered or matristic in social organization. At the center of their religious imagination lived a female deity, with priestesses governing the rituals. They practiced magic, a free and highly creative artistic expression, and lived with an absence of war, rape, murder, and the general forms of violence to which we have become numbly accustomed in

**227**

modern times. Without class stratification, centralized government, taxation, technology, warfare, or slavery, these early Goddess-loving people were able to invent everything we consider relevant today (except plastic and toxic chemicals) and live together in harmony with the earth. They were horticulturally advanced and able to provide enough food for themselves, wherever they lived, by appropriately tilling the land and relating to Nature as a living, communicative reality with a will and purpose of its own. Among their many advanced achievements were pottery, weaving, writing, complex calendrical and mathematical systems, astronomy and astrology, painting, basket making, domestication of animals, cultivation of grains and seeds, masonry, and sacred architecture. Scholars tend to act as if these ideas are mere fantasies of the feminist movement, but the evidence is there to support every one of these claims.

The most serious documentation of this reality comes to us from the archaeologist Marija Gimbutas, whose recent work, *The Language of the Goddess*, sets the story straight in the land she calls Old Europe, including the Mediterranean area and the Balkan countries. Using her own excavations, as well as others', Gimbutas discusses the artifactual materials from early Neolithic civilizations in Yugoslavia, Bulgaria, Turkey, and Greece from more than simply the limited point of view of a physical scientist. In addition to being an archaeologist, Gimbutas is a linguist (she has twenty-five languages at her disposal) and a folklore and mythology specialist, which allows her to understand ancient materials from varied places in the context of the living people still inhabiting the places and practicing some of the same rites as their ancestors. All early cultures worshiped the Mother, and they all produced female-centered art that can be helpfully read through using Gimbutas's ideas and thoughts. The bird and snake Goddess that she named early in the 1970s can be found everywhere in the ancient world, always preceding the later sky-god religions and war cultures. Even the so-called Quetzelcoatl (the feathered serpent) of ancient Mexico was first a bird and snake Goddess, later replaced by her male offspring when the Toltecs entered the land. The new framework Gimbutas creates, the core of which is the parthenogenic (self-fertilizing, creating from herself) Goddess as the central and most persistent image of these early egalitarian, nonviolent cultures, threatens establishment scholars. Fellow archaeologists, as well as reviewers, have reacted in a strongly negative way to the content of her presentation, calling her a dreamer and referring to her elaborate documentation as fantasy. These are often the same people who admired and respected her work in the past, when she was producing books on more conventional aspects of archaeology.

In my own research into ancient cultures from other parts of the world, Gimbutas's views hold up very well and are supported by similar evidence in those places. I feel very grateful to her dogged quest for the truth in these matters, since the conventional wisdom of the discipline refuses to allow for such a divergent view. When applied to prehistory in China or India or Mexico, Gimbutas's theories are very helpful in clearing up confusion around artifactual evidence that points to female-centered worship in early matristic cultures and civilizations of that place. Scholars of every area of the world consistently exhibit a blind spot to the fact that a significant change took place—always obvious in the physical evidence—that would indicate a patriarchal overthrow of an earlier Goddess or matriarchal culture. Without this view, history looks very confusing, and nothing in the evidence makes much sense. Gimbutas has presented a theoretical base that, when allowed to inform scholarship, brings coherence to the history-prehistory drama.

All over the globe about five thousand years ago these early peaceful civilizations were dramatically overthrown and replaced with dynasties, kings, slavery, centralized government, war, male dominance, female oppression, and the development of modern structures like marriage and organized religion. What is never clarified in the history books and rarely discussed in archaeological interpretations is the fact that universally what was overthrown was female centered and better; and what replaced it was male dominated and worse. It doesn't take a moral giant to see that peace is preferable to war and harmony with nature is preferable to our current massive destruction. What had grown up before the transition was matriarchal (or matristic), with women as clan leaders and tribal mothers—the governing center of society. Children naturally belonged to their mothers, from whose bodies they came, and descent was reckoned logically through the mother. What came after the transition was patriarchal (or patristic) in the sense that men decided they needed to know which children belonged to them, even though the children did not grow in their bodies and could not be easily kept track of. So men, by force, took women as their property in order to keep track of the women, their sexual behavior, and their offspring. In this way the concept of private ownership came into being, and the oppression of women began. This transition has been extremely well documented in the past twenty years, so I will not repeat what those authors I have already mentioned have so painstakingly revealed.

What would a society be like that reckoned descent through the mother and assumed that she and her mother and her daughters were free human beings with a purpose to fulfill in life? What would our experience have been in a culture that respected the female and her biological processes of bleeding and birthing, even to the point of making them sacred? What would life have been like for men who considered themselves sons of this sacred mother who gave them life? What was going on for a people who without any major technology were able to invent everything they needed to live life fully and in harmony with Nature? From all the observable records left to us by these ancient ancestors, it appears that they had enough food, comfortable and attractive shelters, deeply artistic abilities and the leisure to pursue them, a scientific understanding of the movements of the planets and stars that surpasses our own, and a spiritual sense of being part of something larger. We can see remnants of this consciousness in contemporary Native American culture. Sally Roesch-Wagner shows that "Indian men gave white men a vision of how 'civilized' nations treated women" and that men of the nineteenth century in this country knew of the superior position of women in the Iroquois tribe. A native chief mentioned in a written history "the absence of rape among Iroquois men" and that "sexual violation of women was virtually unknown among all Indian men," admiring that "whole nations, consisting of millions, should have been so trained, religiously or domestically, that [nothing] should have tempted them from the strictest honor and the most delicate kindness." This regard for women extended outside the tribes to include alien women as well; Indians did not inflict sexual abuse on captive white women. Iroquois women owned property, reckoned by matrilineal descent, and "were the great power among the clan, as everywhere else."[2] Only the women could decide (or veto) whether the men should go to war!

The men understood opposition to female wishes in this area to be a "bad omen."

So what happened? If the Matriarchate was so great, why didn't it last? Was there an internal seed of destruction in this ancient way of life that led to its demise all over the world? This is always the question put to feminist researchers—the ominous, unanswerable accusation that blames the victim for her own rape. It would somehow please us to think that these early cultures had something inherently wrong with them, which caused their destruction, and upon which we have improved. It hurts to think we ourselves are living in wrong ways and that we may have devolved since earlier times. How humiliating. Such a realization requires personal and collective responsibility that seems out of our reach. I think it becomes very important at this point to get a bigger point of view than simply the personal or the historical. Most of the serious scholars who have looked at the evidence and seen the transition focused necessarily on only one place and time, for example, the end of the Sumerian culture or the end of the Indus Valley culture or the rise of the dynasties in Egypt, and so forth. In these individual situations, there was always an "invader" who came from the north, usually on horses and always with weapons, and wiped out the existing peaceful culture that worshiped Nature and loved the Goddess. Often the invaders are glorified in the histories ("heroic epics"), but when they are held responsible, they seem like anomalies that appeared from out of nowhere. No wonder people are driven to posit extraterrestrial landings to explain the mystery.

But when we pull back from the individual sites and see that the pattern happened in many places at approximately the same time, the mystery increases. How did this invader develop? What made him so violent? How did he develop the concept of a sky god with weapons and a government of male dominance? From where on earth (this is the question) did this form of life come? What made him swoop down on peaceful civilizations and burn their houses to the ground, rape the women, massacre the men, destroying the temples and religious icons and replacing them with his own or harnessing the existing images for his own distorted use?

Radical scientist James DeMeo speaks about the creation of deserts as a root cause of global patriarchal culture. At the present time, people of the earth are cutting down so many trees at such a fast pace that many observers have warned against impending droughts and a change in the temperature of the earth itself, which would catapult us into another Ice Age. Rainforest erasure is occurring at the alarming rate of an acre per second, an incomprehensible statistic to my mind. DeMeo agrees with feminist scholars, saying, "There's no clear and unambiguous evidence for the existence of warfare, sadism, traumatization of babies, subordination of women, nor any of the trappings of patrism *anywhere in the world* prior to around 4,000 B.C. *None!*" He goes on to say that patriarchy first appeared in those areas of the planet that were undergoing weather changes, and land that had been lush and fertile was becoming barren desert. He links all the worst traits of modern cultures around the world to this desertification, from the invasions of Marija Gimbutas's Kurgans into Old Europe down to the present. As Saharasia dried up, he says, there was "the development of the social complex that builds temples devoted to male gods — or subordinates female goddesses to a male god. And they start sacrificing people; they begin to ritually murder women." The Sahara desert is currently spreading south at the rate of five to twenty-five miles every year, causing an "increase in social violence between the various tribal cultures, with guerilla warfare focusing on water rights and ownership of fertile land."[3] Peter Tompkins and Christopher Bird, authors of *Secrets of the Soil,* offer further insights into DeMeo's research.[4] They show clearly how certain approaches to the soil cause it to stop yielding and turn to hard, barren ground, and how other approaches (with compost and love) cause even terribly damaged soil to regenerate almost immediately and become fertile again. Could the invasions of patristic nomads into fertile valleys and their callous, life-hating methods of domination have caused the deserts to form rather than the other way around and to continue to the present point where the whole earth is rapidly becoming a desert?

It is absolutely incredible that this phenomenon of patriarchy appeared in so many places at the same time, ruining the existing cultures and creating mayhem, and that its characteristics are so similar. Traditional scholarship stubbornly sticks to the belief that people in the different cultures weren't in physical contact with each other from continent to continent in those days (approximately 3500 B.C.E.), let alone that they could have been sharing an experience. In contrast to this view, traditional tribal peoples like the Cherokee on this continent or the Tibetans in the East or the Dogon in Africa attribute the beginnings of civilization to Atlantis, a large continent that was the mother culture of all the later civilizations. Even when faced with evidence of ships that were able to travel across the ocean and diffusion of artifacts and cultural ideas that are identical, modern scholars hold firm to the concept that humans in different places coincidentally thought up exactly the same things. Jungians rationalize the whole thing by explanation of the collective unconscious and everyone having approximately the same idea at the same time due to our unconscious connections. But this is abstract, and what happened was very concrete. Real live men turned brutal and wiped out real live women-centered cultures. And they did it in many places at once and with amazing brutality. In every case it took many, many centuries — millennia — for the job to get done. But it always looks the same. They always wrote their own story about what happened, creating the mythological base for the next few thousand years. Merlin Stone and Riane Eisler have quoted endless passages from the Old Testament of the Bible, telling and retelling the stories of massacres of the Goddess-worshiping people and the burning of their temples in an effort to eradicate their religion.[5]

In China they have recently dug up an ancient city, dated to around 7500 B.C.E. This is very early and roughly corresponds to the highly developed cities of Jericho and Çatal Hüyük in the Middle East, where the most scholarly attention has been focused. In this ancient Chinese city the Chinese characters were already in use and can be read today. There was a temple, with an altar, where grains were sacrificed to the deity, and on the outside of this temple it says, plain as day, *Female Spirit Temple*. The seeds and grains found at the altar, when planted, still grow into little tomatoes and so on, and the texts tell about the practices of the ancient shaman-priestesses.[6] (A serious problem today is that most modern hybrid seeds couldn't grow after even a few years, let alone millennia. Scholars who care about seeds fear that a terrible famine could be the outcome of our loss of natural, wild seeds.) Until now the only in-depth information available on ancient matriarchal China was Joseph Needham's *Science and Civilization in China* (several volumes), which discussed the ancient female shamans called *Wu,* who wore feathers and danced to make rain. (This would have been around the time of the Bronze Age in China, or about 2500 B.C.E.) By 200 B.C.E. the *Wu* had been kicked out of the courts and officially replaced by male shamans at the order of the emperor. This corresponds ("coincidentally") to the origins of Taoism and Confucianism in China.[7]

In China we have the remarkable advantage of a system of writing that has remained intact for apparently at least nine thousand years, so the history can be researched with a certain amount of documentation. In the Middle East and other places where these early cultures grew up and flourished, we have not been so lucky, since the ancient languages that predate the invaders cannot, for the most part, be translated. They are different from the language used after their demise, so the story is harder to get. But in Çatal Hüyük, as I mentioned earlier, there are hundreds of female figurines found all over the ruins, Goddesses painted on the walls, breasts and bulls' heads that perfectly resemble the female uterus, and temple models showing us that women baked bread in the temples. Women and children are buried within the walls of the city; men outside. The untranslated language exists only on the clay pots, in the weaving, and on the female figures.

In all these places now we see only male dominance and a system of philosophy positing that this is what Nature intended, what has always been, and what will always be. Yet the evidence shows us something entirely other than this, and it is this other vision that feminist scholarship has been set on uncovering for the past twenty years. Why bother? you might ask. What difference does it make, since we are now completely immersed in the other way of life? To know that the way we live today is not necessarily an expression of human nature or positive evolution frees our minds from their bindings. When I see these ancient places and figurines, I am moved beyond description. Something in me awakens and remembers. I know, all the way to my core, that there is another way to live. Most important, I know that something else is possible, we are not doomed to this one form. I create from this knowledge. I want to make a new world from the experience of remembering something more humane and just than the world I live in today. I want to be a part of the healing of the earth and the creation of a world in which all children are wanted and valued equally, where food is abundant and scarcity unknown. I want communion with Nature and the universe. I want to know myself at my sacred center and to know and touch others in that space. I want to know what it means to be a woman, to be a man, in a world that values both for their uniqueness and their gifts and oppresses neither. And I believe that the knowledge of how to do this lives within me and you, if only we will contact it before it is too late.

Twenty years ago feminists began as a group to uncover the ancient matriarchal past. Yet even fairly recently the *New York Times* was still able to find a female professor of history who would ridicule rather than review Riane Eisler's *The Chalice and the Blade*, making her position sound like a fantasy rather than documented fact.[8] Even Marija Gimbutas's new book, *The Language of the Goddess*, received similar treatment from the *Women's Review of Books*.[9] But now, since the science of archaeology is more or less proving that ancient cultures worshiped a Great Mother, had women as priestesses, and so forth, traditional scholarship has invented a new model for interpreting this. This model suggests that ancient matriarchal culture was a homogeneous "group mind," analogous to children playing within the protective confines of the Great Mother. This the model defines as the Feminine. Then, naturally and inevitably, humans began to hunger for individuation and differentiation from this amorphous mass, and this was the development of civilization (Patriarchy). Naturally, if we posit that Patriarchy is a manifestation of the Masculine having its own turn at creating civilization, we are forced to find ways of describing it as good, or at least inevitable and fair. But if I were a man, I would cringe at this definition. I would never want to identify the culture we presently live in with the Masculine. How ugly and gross to equate masculinity with murder and rape, pillage, greed, and a mindless ransacking of the planet. I'd like to think there is some other manifestation of the Masculine waiting to be revealed to us, just as there is another form of the Feminine coming into being at the present hour.

What does show in the evidence from five thousand years ago is a change in values from earth-based culture to something more abstract and at the same time, as James DeMeo asserts, sadistic. There was a radical separation of the individual from "his" place within the group—within the species, within all life, within the universe. We got off track and gave up our connection to the earth and to the Mother in favor of an allegiance to an abstract concept of Father. The Father Creator was mean but all-powerful, and his rules had to be followed or else. The invention of war and rape, the institutions of fatherhood, marriage, and slavery, and the organization of religion with men in the position of God all came at once. Contemporary scholars tend to perceive and discuss this change as a universal form of "differentiation." But that is not the appropriate language to use for describing the characteristics we see in the two cultures. Differentiation literally means "to make different" and "to recognize the difference" between one thing and another. It implies knowing that you are a unique individual, different from others like yourself, and distinct from your environment. Early people, even in being able to create a tool for working on something or to make art as an externalized expression of a relationship to something, already show differentiation. They clearly experienced themselves as organisms, individuals — they have "individuated" in the Jungian sense of the word. They knew who they were better than contemporary Western people do. And they no doubt used more of their brains than we do, given the current estimate that we use only 10 percent of what is available to us. We in the West have a strong, abstract concept of individualism, but we tend actually to practice cultism and conformism to a high degree. Just the fact that people in our culture watch, on the average, nine to ten hours of television per day is astonishing in this regard. As esoteric teacher Alice Bailey points out, what we call thinking is nothing but regurgitated programming in our brain-consciousness.[10] Early humans didn't see themselves as separated from nature and other beings. There is no sense of hierarchy or caste operating in the early epochs, no sign of slavery or inequality. The changeover that marks the beginnings of Western culture, five thousand years ago, was a lethal separation from nature and the body in favor of the domination of the ego over everything.

The shamanic metaphor is useful here. When a person becomes ill in a shamanic tribal setting, a shaman is called in to deal with the "invading illness." Illness is seen as a form of being out of balance, of soul loss, and the invasion from the outside of an "evil spirit" or "possessing entity." The person who is ill needs to generate enough will or force to throw off the invading force and return to a state of balance and harmony, and the shaman helps with this process. Sometimes the shaman facilitates this through hands-on healing and the transmission of a powerful force or energy that drives the "demon" out; other times the healer simply catalyzes the healing force within the sick person's body and psyche. In either case there is a nonjudgmental recognition of some invasion from outside that has caused the soul to become weak or unavailable. If the soul cannot be redeemed and the invading force expelled, sooner or later the body will inevitably die.[11]

If we apply this shamanic metaphor to the earth as a body, we could say that five thousand years ago something in the way of an invading entity came onto or into this planet and made it very sick, caused it to become highly out of balance. Mary Daly posited something like this in *Gyn/Ecology,* suggesting that Patriarchy was a world religion of sado-rituals that functioned as a "possessing entity." The "patriarchal possessing entity" in Daly's view can be thrown off by women because we have nothing to lose and everything to gain by getting rid of its tenacious hold on our lives.[12] The idea of a possessing entity big enough to invade the planet seems either unrealistic in our scientific framework, like science fiction, or superstitious, like the so-called primitive mind. If we can give up our ideas about superstition and our allegiance to the evolutionary model of progress, we may see that we are in a state of possession, and the soul of the world *(anima mundi)* is at stake. A person doesn't have to believe in extraterrestrials to see things this way, although the two views are not incompatible.[13] All it takes is an agreement that something happened all over the planet — it was not local — and that it was not positive, not "progress." The transition looks, at the very least, like a serious detour in our "evolution." It also looks like if we don't do something right away about this dis-ease from which our planet suffers, this body will die very soon.

Some new-age philosophies posit that what is happening to us now is not only evolutionary but involves at this very moment an "evolutionary leap" in our consciousness and in the awakening consciousness of our planet. There is a general trend toward the unsupportable idea that Gaia is awakening to herself for the first time. Given the archaeological evidence, I can't help but see this as either ignorance of the material or a denial of our actual past in favor of an appropriation of the events of the moment into a new paradigm. The danger of this particular mind-set is that instead of seriously confronting our difficulties in the moment (killing the ocean, the air, the forests, the earth itself, and becoming extinct), we are urged to imagine that we are on an evolutionary track where "everything is perfect." This can lead to heartless conclusions and astonishing inaction. For instance, some esoteric teachers or "channels" have suggested that big leaps require a huge, somehow necessary sacrifice of most of the people, animals, trees, and so on all over the earth in order that a chosen few might be rescued or "harvested." Those who are chosen are here on earth for the last time, never to incarnate again, because by virtue of some special characteristic, they do not need to return to matter, even though the rest of us do. (Although it is very unlikely that there will be any matter to which to return if things proceed in this direction at this rate for much longer.) This isn't very different from the Christian fundamentalist version of Armageddon, in which God in his anger and outrage over people's wickedness will destroy all but the 144,000 of his faithful. These various approaches have a kind of "I-told-you-so" attitude toward the planet's pain and suffering. In a similar vein, I remember reading when I was a very young mother a seemingly intelligent, serious book called *Famine 1975*, in which the author suggested (among other things) that since India had such serious overpopulation problems, we should stop giving them aid and let them die en masse as a necessary and unavoidable sacrifice for the benefit of saving the rest of the people on the planet. I wondered how the people who lived in India would feel about such a cold-blooded theory.

The whole idea of being special and being "harvested" is an interesting blend of Christian and Hindu ideas applied to current trends in thinking. Such a punitive attitude toward life on earth is understandable under the present circumstances. After all, we have suffered more than two thousand years of those organized religions that equate spirit with good and matter with bad; men with spirit and women with matter. It isn't easy to bond with the earth and the body (and women) when the "Great Religions" are telling us that these are the very sources of evil and filth and karma. If however, what is happening to us in the world today is serious and not evolutionary, as Native Americans such as the Hopi would certainly agree, what do we do? What is the correct response to a shamanic illness of such global proportions? Should we settle in for the inevitable death and rebirth? Mayan and Hopi calendars seem to indicate that this five thousand years is coming to an end. Like any terminal or incurable illness, a certain surrender is required before anything new can happen. But then the remarkable phenomenon of healing takes place for what doctors have called the exceptional few who have spontaneous remissions. For no *apparent* reason, some people with cancer don't die; they recover their powers and vitality and go on to lead healthy lives. The power that allows some people with incurable illness to survive can help the earth heal herself at this time as well. The forms may die, but the living spirit can reincarnate again.

When we remember the Goddess and the old earth-based religion, we come back into contact with cycles and the eternal return that lets us face death without fear. It wasn't until 400 C.E. that the Christian church declared that there were no cycles, no reincarnation. Until that time, everyone knew the obvious, that there certainly is life after death, and it is not only in the eternal realm. One of the joyous reclaimings that accompanies our re-membering is that we get over the insidious fear of the Death Goddess and realize she is only the other face of the Mother. In surrender to her, we leave the problem in her hands; in allowing ourselves to be used in the healing of the planet, we become part of her solution. It has only been since World War II that we were educated to believe that the soil is dead and requires chemical pesticides and fertilizers to make it work. When we come again to understand recycling of our lives through lifetimes, we can perhaps more easily comprehend the recycling of the micro-organisms that make life possible for all of us through their death and rebirth in the soil and how the trees are necessary for us to be able to breathe. The organic farmers know, through their own miraculous experiences, that regeneration of even the worst soil is possible and that when that soil is replenished, people, plants, and animals who live on it become healthy. Even radiation and chemical pollution are removed and health reigns naturally. The bio-dynamic farming movement is one of the few groups that actually evidences the faith and has the methods we need to restore things quickly enough to counteract the devastation that has already taken place. Yet even these hardy souls fear that the deforestation is proceeding at too quick a pace for organic methods to save us. We need a miracle.

239

In India they say the Great Goddess Durga is a Warrior Goddess present always in the eternal but who manifests in the physical when the demons get out of hand. Today's resurgence of interest in shamanism and a return of the Goddess is our version of Durga making her presence felt. Goddess as Shaman is manifesting to rid the planet of the evil forces, and the obvious way she can take form is through women — her embodied priestesses — and all people behaving in a "feminine" way. Women as a group are re-membering. It seems that because we have nothing to lose and everything to regain, we are able to open to these memories and access this available information as it arises from the center of our psyches. As we do this, if we are willing to stand our ground and refuse to have it co-opted or compromised by established values and paradigms, sooner or later men will also hunger for these changes, joining us in the creation of a world from this memory.

But for a woman in our time to hold her ground is a most difficult task. People seem to want to distort her knowledge into something familiar and manageable; they clamor to fit it into existing frameworks. For a woman to hold to her instincts, her gut feelings, and her inner voice is an enormous task. The goal is to make ourselves strong enough to be leaders, healers, and teachers in this time. We must create a strong enough central axis that each of us can stand her ground in the face of all opposition, visible or invisible, that might attempt to stop the expulsion of the possessing entity who has taken over the world. A process of embodiment is taking place wherein women (and men) without any particular education for it become willing vessels of the vision. The women who perform this function I call Shakti women, Shakti meaning "to be able" and referring to the power of the feminine force of creative, instinctual becoming. We are giving form and expression to the return of the Goddess through a global recovery movement that is the modern-day equivalent of a shamanic healing crisis.

# Afterword

DURING PRODUCTION OF *SHAKTI Woman*, the United States, led by George Bush, waged a quick and merciless war on Iraq and Saddam Hussein, leaving in its aftermath untold destruction to people and the global environment. Those of us who have dedicated our lives to the goal of a peaceful planet were devastated by this act performed in our name. When the bombing began on the January Dark Moon in 1991, I (like so many others) was unable to sleep at night and felt the need to join others in the streets to protest and make known my will. One night during the following weeks, as I patted my little boy to sleep, I had a terrifying vision of some poor mother in Iraq, also patting her child to sleep while bombs dropped all around them, and I felt joined to her in anguish. Her only "crime" was being born there, as mine was to be born here. And since I pay taxes here, my hands are bloody, and I am inadvertently implicated in the death of her precious child. I can hardly bear this karmic burden.

At the present moment I know of no way to directly affect my will on the decision-making process of this country. The media work as tools and mouthpieces of the governing body, and people around me seem hypnotized by the excitement of nonstop television programming. As I put my hands on a client in one of my healing circles during the war, I had a clear vision of my responsibility in the moment. A body with cancer is terminally ill because the cancer cells have gone crazy. They split and increase in an aberrant, autonomous way, without regard for the interest of the organism of which they are a part. Eventually, through their sheer numbers and the speed of their blind growth, they take over and so weaken the immune system that the body dies. *The way I relate to cancer as a healer is not to fight or "kill" the cancer cells, but rather to focus attention on the healthy cells.* If the cells can be awakened and enlivened, so that they begin to vibrate at a higher level, the cancer has been known to miraculously and spontaneously leave the body for no apparent reason.

Surely this global body is suffering from terminal cancer—George Bush and Saddam Hussein acting as the crazy cancer cells, taking up more and more space and overpowering the organic process of life on Earth. But I am a healthy cell in this poor, sick body, and I'll wager that you are, too. It seems to me that our responsibility as healthy cells, on a daily basis, is simply to raise our vibration and join together for health. I saw us doing this when thousands of us hit the streets together, chanting and singing for peace. I see it in my healing circles, when we join together to drum and sing, awakening the sleeping cells in the body and jump-starting the weakened immune system. One night in a performance with singer Barbara Higbie and drummer Barbara Borden, I led an audience in joining their energies together with this image in mind: I am a healthy cell, I am a healer, I want to live in peace. Together we chanted, holding hands and letting the drumbeat enter into our bodies on a cellular level, reminding us of the heartbeat of Mother Earth, beating, beating for life.

We need to keep up the ceremonies, sisters and brothers. Even if our death is imminent, we need to join together and go out singing. I pray that the force for peace is stronger than it looks at the present moment and that the movement toward healing on this planet will ultimately prevail. Blessed Be.

# Notes

## Introduction

1. Riane Eisler, *The Chalice and the Blade: Our History, Our Future* (San Francisco: Harper & Row, 1987).

2. Mary Daly, *Gyn/Ecology: The Metaethics of Radical Feminism* (Boston: Beacon Press, 1978).

## Chapter 1: The Female Blood Roots of Shamanism

1. Sonia Montecino and Ana Conejeros, *Mujeres Mapuches: el saber tradicional en la curación de enfermedades comunes* (Santiago, Chile: Centro de Estudios de la mujer, n.d.).

2. Susan Eger (a.k.a. Susana Valadez), "Huichol Women's Art," in *Art of the Huichol Indians* (San Francisco: M. H. de Young Museum, 1979).

3. Geoffrey Ashe, *Ancient Wisdom* (Tumbridge-Wells, England: Abacus Books, 1979).

4. Menstrual Health Foundation, *Scarlet Moon: A Journal of the Feminine*, P.O. Box 3248, Santa Rosa, CA 95402.

5. Monica Sjöö and Barbara Mor, *The Ancient Religion of the Great Cosmic Mother of All* (Trondheim, Norway: Rainbow Press, 1981), 187.

6. Lawrence Durdin-Robertson, *The Cult of the Goddess* (Enniscorthy, Eire: Cesara Publications, 1974).

7. Stephan Beyer, *The Cult of Tara: Magic and Ritual in Tibet* (Berkeley: Univ. of California Press, 1978).

8. Peter Tompkins and Christopher Bird, *Secrets of the Soil* (New York: Harper & Row, 1989).

9. Raphael Girard, *The Esotericism of the Popul Vuh* (Pasadena, CA: Theosophical Univ. Press, 1979).

10. Durdin-Robertson, *The Cult of the Goddess*.

11. Alexander Marshack, *The Roots of Civilization: The Cognitive Beginnings of Man's First Art, Symbol, and Notation* (New York: McGraw-Hill, 1972).

12. Marija Gimbutas, *The Language of the Goddess* (San Francisco: Harper & Row, 1989).

13. Barbara Tedlock, *Time and the Highland Maya* (Albuquerque: Univ. of New Mexico Press, 1982).

14. Philip Rawson, *Tantra: The Indian Cult of Ecstasy* (New York: Bounty Books, 1974).

15. Dhyahni Ywahoo, *Voices of Our Ancestors* (Boston: Shambhala, 1987).

16. Robert K. Temple, *The Sirius Mystery* (New York: St. Martin's Press, 1976).

17. Bruce Lincoln, *Emerging from the Chrysalis: Studies in Rituals of Women's Initiation* (Cambridge: Harvard Univ. Press, 1981).

18. Barbara Walker, *The Woman's Encyclopedia of Myths and Secrets* (San Francisco: Harper & Row, 1983).

19. Durdin-Robertson, *The Cult of the Goddess*.

20. Evan Hadingham, *Secrets of the Ice Age* (New York: Walker, 1979).

21. Sjöö and Mor, *The Ancient Religion of the Great Cosmic Mother of All*, 196.

22. Ibid., 185.

23. Merlin Stone, *When God Was a Woman* (New York: Harcourt Brace Jovanovich, 1978).

24. Sally Roesch Wagner, "The Iroquois Confederacy: A Native American Model for Non-sexist Men," *Changing Men*, Spring-Summer 1988, 32.

25. Frédérique Marglin, *Wives of the God-King: The Rituals of the Devadasis of Puri* (New York: Oxford Univ. Press, 1985).

26. Ibid., 18.

27. Ibid., 203.

28. Ibid., 60.

29. Ibid., 203.

30. Ibid., 234.

31. James Preston, *Cult of the Goddess: Social and Religious Change in a Hindu Temple* (Delhi: Vikas Publishing House, 1980).

32. Pauline Kolenda, "Pox and the Terror of Childlessness: Images and Ideas of the Smallpox Goddess in a North Indian Village," in *Mother Worship*, ed. James Preston (North Carolina: University Press, 1982), 243.

33. Walker, *The Woman's Encyclopedia of Myths and Secrets*, 636.

34. Marglin, *Wives of the God-King*, 243.

35. Walker, *The Woman's Encyclopedia of Myths and Secrets*, 636.

36. Durdin-Robertson, *The Cult of the Goddess*.

37. Sjöö and Mor, *The Ancient Religion of the Great Cosmic Mother of all*, 27.

38. Penelope Shuttle and Peter Redgrove, *The Wise Wound: Menstruation and Everywoman* (London: Victor Gollancz, 1978).

39. Walker, *The Woman's Encyclopedia of Myths and Secrets*, 643.

40. Ibid., 638.

41. Ibid., 635.

42. Daly, *Gyn/Ecology*, 237.

43. Polly Young-Eisendrath and Florence Wiedemann, *Female Authority: Empowering Women Through Psychotherapy* (New York: Guilford Press, 1987).

44. Sylvia Perera, *Descent to the Goddess: A Way of Initiation for Women* (Toronto: Inner City Books, 1981), 26.

45. Ibid., 24.

46. Ibid., 13.

47. Ibid., 51.

48. Ibid., 55.

49. Ibid., 36.

50. Ann and Barry Ulanov, *The Witch and the Clown: Two Archetypes of Human Sexuality* (Wilmette, IL: Chiron Publications, 1987), 7.

51. Daly, *Gyn/Ecology*, 15.

52. Ulanov, *The Witch and the Clown*, 12.

53. Ibid., 76.

54. Ibid., 77.

55. Daly, *Gyn/Ecology*, 277.

## Chapter 2: Cellular Shamanism

1. Nancy Makepeace Tanner, *On Becoming Human* (Cambridge: Cambridge Univ. Press, 1981).

2. Ron Williams, personal communication with author, 8 June 1990.

3. I should add that this break with Women's Health was not permanent but a necessary period of reorientation for me as a healer. I am currently

working to unite and synthesize the work of the Women's Health Movement with shamanic healing, in the healing circles I lead, and in conferences I am planning with other interested women, some from the Menstrual Health Foundation in Santa Rosa, California. I hope to initiate and co-sponsor (with Isis International, a women's health organization in Santiago, Chile) an inter-American women's health and shamanic healing conference/cultural event to take place in Central America, bringing together healers and activists from as far north as Canada and as far south as Chile. Our intent is to bridge the gap between healing and health, and to unite the false splits that have been wedged between women of different races and cultures, through events where women celebrate an end to war and a reinstatement of the sacred blood mysteries.

4. Robert Temple, *The Sirius Mystery.* (Rochester, VT: Inner Traditions, 1987).

5. Michael Dames, *The Avebury Cycle* (London: Thames & Hudson, 1976).

6. Temple, *The Sirius Mystery.*

7. Janet Gyatso "Down with the Demoness: Reflections on a Feminine Ground in Tibet" from *Feminine Ground: Essays on Women and Tibet,* 51. ed. Janet Willis (Ithaca: Snow Lion Press, 1987).

8. Namkhai Norbu, *The Crystal and the Way of Light* (New York: Routledge & Kegan Paul, 1986), 47.

9. Mircea Eliade, *Shamanism: Archaic Techniques of Ecstasy,* trans. Willard R. Trask (Princeton, N.J.: Princeton Univ. Press for the Bollingen Foundation, 1964).

10. John Robbins, *Diet for a New America* (Walpole, NH: Stillpoint Publishing, 1987).

11. Bruce L. Cathie, "Acoustic Levitations of Stones," *Anti-Gravity and the World Grid,* ed. David Hatcher Childress (Stlelle, IL: Adventures Unlimited Press, 1986).

12. Peggy Dylan is available for leading the sacred firewalk and can be reached through Sundoor Spiritual Adventures, PO Box 669, Twain Harte, CA 95383; phone (209) 928-4800. Or you can read the book she and her former husband, Tolly Burkan, wrote about the process of overcoming fear and limiting beliefs, *Guiding Yourself into a Spiritual Reality* (Reunion Press, Inc., 1983).

13. Tedlock, *Time and the Highland Maya.*

14. Barbara Wilt, "Is There an Enemy?" *Snake Power: A Journal of Contemporary Female Shamanism* 1, 1 (1989), 43.

## Chapter 3: Synchronicity

1. Margaret Pavel, personal communication with author, spring 1990.

2. Tompkins and Bird, *Secrets of the Soil.*

3. Ibid.

4. Judy Chicago, *The Birth Project* (Garden City, NY: Doubleday, 1985).

5. Monica Sjöö, personal communication with author, spring 1990.

6. Many capitalist companies exploit and distort women's natural biology in favor of the use of their products. However, Nestle's has been targeted as particularly lethal in its successful campaign to get African babies off the breast and onto the bottle. This has been the cause of untold suffering, as the mothers can't afford the formula and therefore dilute it with water. Since the water is bad, the babies die, either from malnutrition or from the more direct toxicity of the water. Nestle's products have been boycotted for

this reason, and for a while they appeared to respond to this boycott. But recently the problem has once again come to the attention of feminist and other observers, and we are urged to continue boycotting all Nestle's products.

**7.** To order *Motherpeace Tarot Cards* (and other good things) write to the Gaia Bookstore, 1400 Shattuck Avenue, Berkeley, CA 94709. For three dollars, they will send you a delightful catalog of Goddess goodies.

**8.** Peter Redgrove, *The Black Goddess and the Unseen Real* (New York: Grove Press, 1987).

**9.** Nigel Pennick, *Geomancy: The Ancient Science of Living in Harmony with the Earth* (Sebastapol, CA: CRCS Publications, 1989).

**10.** Anne Kent Rush, *Moon Moon* (New York: Random House; and Berkeley: Moon Books, 1976).

**11.** Norbu, *The Crystal and the Way of Light.*

**12.** For good texts with suggestions on holiday rituals, see Zsuzsanna Emese Budapest, *The Holy Book of Women's Mysteries, Volumes I & II* (Los Angeles: Susan B. Anthony Coven Number One, 1979, 1980); Starhawk, *The Spiral Dance: A Rebirth of the Ancient Religion of the Great Goddess* (San Francisco: Harper & Row, 1979, 1989); Diane Stein, *The Women's Spirituality Book* (St. Paul, Minnesota: Llewellyn Publications, 1987).

**13.** Wagner, "The Iroquois Confederacy."

## Chapter 4: Astrology

**1.** Tedlock, *Time and the Highland Maya.*

**2.** Gary Urton, *At the Crossroads of the Earth and the Sky: An Andean Cosmology* (Austin, TX: University Press, 1981), 37.

**3.** Urton, ibid., 179.

**4.** Urton, ibid., 79.

**5.** Urton, ibid., 199.

**6.** Urton, ibid., 198.

**7.** Palden Jenkins, *Living in Time: Learning to Experience Astrology in Your Life* (Bath: Gateway Books, 1987).

**8.** Daly, *Gyn/Ecology.*

**9.** *Ever'woman's Calendar,* Morning Glory Collective, P.O. Box 1631, Tallahassee, FL 32301.

**10.** There are a number of good lunar and astrological calendars on the market these days. The classic *Lunar Calendar* is put out each year by Luna Press, Box 511, Kenmore Station, Boston, MA 02215. More recently is *Take Back the Night* from Full Womoon Productions, P.O. Box 1205, Santa Cruz, CA 95061. Both of these present the lunar phases visually as a replacement to the traditional square Julian calendar we're used to seeing. *The We'Moon Calendar* is a datebook format with Goddess art and an ephemeris in the back. You can order it from Mother Tongue Ink, 37010 S.E. Snuffin Road, Estacada, OR 97023. Llewellyn's puts out astrological calendars of all kinds and sizes. Order from Llewellyn Publications, P.O. Box 64383-460, St. Paul, MN 55164. My favorite astrological calendars are from Celestial Arts, especially their tiny *Pocket Astrologer* for easy carrying; order from Quicksilver Productions, P.O. Box 340, Ashland, OR 97520. This tiny calendar tells you every move the planets make from sign to sign every day, all the aspects each day, and includes an ephemeris in the back. I never go anywhere without one.

**11.** Stone, *When God Was a Woman.*

12. Marglin, *Wives of the God-King.*

13. Elinor Gadon, *The Once and Future Goddess: A Symbol for Our Time* (San Francisco: Harper & Row, 1989).

14. Vicki Noble and Jonathan Tenney, *The Motherpeace Tarot Playbook* (Berkeley: Wingbow Press, 1988).

15. You can order computer charts for three dollars from Astro Computing Services, Dept. AEN390, P.O. Box 16430, San Diego, CA 92116-0430, or call 1-800-888-9983.

16. Demetra George and Douglas Bloch, *Astrology for Yourself: A Workbook for Personal Transformation* (Berkeley: Wingbow Press, 1987).

17. See note 14 above.

18. Neil Michelsen, *The American Ephemeris for the Twentieth Century* (San Diego: ACS Publications, 1988).

19. Melanie Reinhart, *Chiron and the Healing Journey: An Astrological and Psychological Perspective* (London: Arcana, 1989).

20. Besides natal charts, you can get all kinds of composites, transits, progressions, and so forth from Astro Computing Services (see note 15 above).

21. Demetra George, *Asteroid Goddess* (San Diego: ACS Publications, 1986).

22. *Snake Power* 1, no. 1, 18.

### Chapter 5: The Dreamer

1. For further study of this concept see Patricia Garfield, *Pathway to Ecstasy: The Way of the Dream Mandala* (New York: Prentice-Hall, 1979).

2. For more work with this practice, see Strephon Kaplan Williams, *Jungian Senoi Dreamwork Manual* (Berkeley: Journey Press, 1980).

3. Arnold Mindell, *Dreambody* (Santa Monica: Sigo, 1982).

### Chapter 6: Trance Journey and Spirit Flight

1. Alice Bailey, *Esoteric Healing* (New York: Lucis, 1984).

2. Vicki Noble, "The Matriarchal Backbone of Huichol Shamanic Culture," in *Mirrors of the Gods: Proceedings of a Symposium on the Huichol Indians,* ed. Susan Bernstein (San Diego: Museum of Man, 1989).

3. Gordon Wasson, *Soma: Divine Mushroom of Immortality* (New York: Harcourt Brace Jovanovich, 1973).

4. Joan Halifax, *Shaman Voices: A Survey of Visionary Narratives* (New York: E. P. Dutton, 1979).

5. John Grim, *The Shaman: Patterns of Siberian and Ojibway Healing* (Norman: Univ. of Oklahoma Press, 1983).

6. Carmen Blacker, *Catalpa Bow: A Study of Shamanistic Practices in Japan* (London: Allen & Unwin, 1975).

7. Michael Harner, *The Way of the Shaman: A Guide to Power and Healing* (New York: Bantam, 1980).

### Chapter 7: Shamanic Art

1. Laurette Séjourné, *Burning Water: Thought and Religion in Ancient Mexico* (Berkeley: Shambhala Publications, 1976).

2. Marija Gimbutas, *The Gods and Goddesses of Old Europe* (London: Thames & Hudson 1982), and Gimbutas, *The Language of the Goddess.*

3. Sigfried Giedion, *The Eternal Present: The Beginnings of Art: A Contribution on Constancy and Change* (New York: Bollingen Foundation, distributed by Pantheon Books, 1962).

**4.** Vicki Noble, "Marija Gimbutas: Reclaiming the Great Goddess," *Snake Power: A Journal of Contemporary Female Shamanism* 1, 1, 6 (1989).

**5.** For further study see Elinor Gadon, *The Once and Future Goddess: A Symbol for Our Time* (San Francisco: Harper & Row, 1989); Lucy Lippard, *Overlay: Contemporary Art and the Art of Prehistory* (New York: Pantheon Books, 1983); and Gloria Orenstein, *The Reflowering of the Goddess* (New York: Pergamon Press, 1990).

**6.** William H. Bates, *Better Eyesight Without Glasses* (New York: Holt, Rinehart & Winston, 1940).

**7.** Madhu Khanna, *Yantra: The Tantric Symbol of Cosmic Unity* (London: Thames & Hudson, 1979).

**8.** *Heresies: A Feminist Publication on Art and Politics,* no. 5, "The Great Goddess," Spring 1978.

**9.** The whole issue of collecting feathers or bird parts takes on a bizarre aspect when we consider the Migratory Bird Act, initiated by environmentalists in order to protect wildlife against poachers and those capitalists who murder animals for profit. Unfortunately the act applies literally to possession of any and all parts of migratory birds and makes a person who stops on the highway to pick up a dead owl liable to a five-thousand-dollar fine. Native Americans have gone to court and gotten around this law, since their traditional religious practices make it necessary to use eagle feathers and so on. But Anglos who get caught with protected animal parts will have to answer to our own laws! So far, the law doesn't recognize that we also might have a sacred relationship to nature.

**10.** Rupert Sheldrake, *The Presence of the Past: Morphic Resonance and the Habits of Nature.* (New York: Times Books, 1988).

**11.** Lawrence Durdin-Robertson, *The Goddesses of Chaldea, Syria, and Egypt* (Enniscorthy, Eire: Cesara Publications, 1978).

**12.** Elizabeth Gould Davis, *The First Sex* (New York: G. P. Putnam's Sons, 1971).

**13.** Vicki Noble, *Motherpeace: A Way to the Goddess Through Myth, Art and Tarot* (San Francisco: Harper & Row, 1983).

**14.** Richard Luxton with Pablo Balam, *The Mystery of the Mayan Hieroglyphs: The Vision of an Ancient Tradition* (San Francisco: Harper & Row, 1981).

**15.** Erich Neumann, *The Great Mother: An Analysis of the Archetype,* trans. Ralph Manheim (Princeton, NJ: Princeton Univ. Press for the Bollingen Foundation, 1972).

### Chapter 8: Female-Centered Sexuality

**1.** Eloise Salholz with Eleanor Clift, Karen Springen, and Patrice Johnson, "Women Under Assault," *Newsweek,* 16 July 1990, 23.

**2.** Jane Caputi and Diana E. H. Russell, " 'Femicide': Speaking the Unspeakable" from *Ms.: The World of Women,* vol. 1, no. 2, September–October 1990, 34.

**3.** Robin Morgan, *The Demon Lover: On the Sexuality of Terrorism* (New York: W. W. Norton, 1989).

**4.** Daly, *Gyn/Ecology.*

**5.** Kate Millet, *Sexual Politics* (Garden City, NY: Doubleday, 1970).

**6.** Mary Daly, *Pure Lust: Elemental Feminist Philosophy* (Boston: Beacon Press, 1984).

**7.** Kenneth Grant, *Cults of the Shadow* (New York: Samuel Weiser, 1975).

**8.** Merlin Stone, "A Letter from Merlin" (newsletter), Summer 1990. To order write: P.O. Box 266, 201 Varick Street, New York, NY 10014.

**9.** Diane Wolkstein and Samuel Kramer, *Inanna: Queen of Heaven and Earth* (San Francisco: Harper & Row, 1983).

**10.** Savina Teubal, *Sarah the Priestess: The First Matriarch of the Genesis* (Athens, OH: Swallow Press, 1984).

**11.** Carol J. Adams, *The Sexual Politics of Meat: A Feminist Vegetarian Critical Theory* (New York: Continuum Publications, distributed by Harper & Row, 1990).

**12.** Walker, *The Woman's Encyclopedia of Myths and Secrets*.

**13.** W. B. Emery, *Archaic Egypt* (Hammondsworth, England: Penguin Books, 1963).

**14.** Eva Keuls, *The Reign of the Phallus: Sexual Politics in Ancient Athens.* (San Francisco: Harper & Row, 1985).

**15.** Elaine Pagels, *The Gnostic Gospels* (New York: Random House, 1979).

**16.** Walker, *The Woman's Encyclopedia of Myths and Secrets*.

**17.** Ibid.

**18.** As feminist research becomes more sophisticated and accepted as "real scholarship," more and more women are exposing these horrendous facts from the European Middle Ages. The first resource was a still-informative pamphlet by Barbara Ehrenreich and Deirdre English called *Witches, Midwives and Nurses*, which set gynecology in its proper context: over the dead bodies of our female ancestors. Since then, three excellent texts have come out, all of which agree on the basic story of a female holocaust that lasted four centuries in Europe during the so-called Age of Enlightenment: Mary Daly, *Gyn/Ecology*; Andrea Dworkin, *Woman Hating* (New York: E. P. Dutton, 1974); Jeanne Achterberg, *Woman as Healer* (Boston: Shambhala Publications, 1990).

**19.** Hans Peter Deurr, *Dreamtime: Concerning the Boundary Between Wilderness and Civilization* (Oxford: Basic Blackwell, 1985).

**20.** Pamela Berger, Annie Leibovici, and George Reinhart, producers, *The Sorceress*, Mystic Fire Video, 1988.

**21.** Gimbutas, *The Language of the Goddess*.

**22.** Lippard, *Overlay*.

**23.** Since the eruptive planet Pluto began its fourteen-year transit through its own sign of Scorpio, women have been remembering their incest experiences and coming together to share the horrors of this pervasive social problem. Some of the best books of the new genre of writing on incest and childhood sexual abuse are Ellen Bass and Laura Davis, *The Courage to Heal* (New York: Harper & Row, 1988); Ellen Bass and Loise Thornton, eds., *I Never Told Anyone* (New York: Harper & Row, 1983).

### Chapter 9: Shaman Mother

**1.** John Robbins, "Your Food Choices Can Change the World," *New Times* 6, 2 (July 1990).

**2.** George, *Asteroid Goddesses*.

**3.** Mindell, *Dreambody*.

**4.** Tanner, *On Becoming Human*.

**5.** Marilyn Strathern, *Women in Between* (New York: Seminar Press, 1972), 186, 187, 188; or Yolanda Murphy and Robert F. Murphy, *Women of the Forest* (New York: Columbia University Press, 1974), 88. Both of these books describe gang rape as a form of acknowledged social control in patriarchal tribal cultures, the first in Papua, New Guinea, and the second the Mundurucu tribe of Brazil.

6. Eisler, *The Chalice and the Blade: Our History, Our Future.*

7. "It's War: Our Bodies, Our Business," *Ms* magazine, 17th anniversary issue, 1990.

## Chapter 10: Female Shamanism and the Patriarchal Possessing Entity

1. Tamar Raphael, "Feminist Analysis: The Assassinations in Montreal," *The Feminist Majority Report* 2, 3 (February 1990), 7.

2. Wagner, "The Iroquois Confederacy."

3. James DeMeo, "The Origins and Diffusion of Armoring (Patrism) in Saharasia, c. 4000 BCE: Evidence for a Climate-Linked, Global Geographical Pattern in Human Behavior," *Pulse of the Planet*, no. 3, Fall 1990.

4. Tompkins and Bird, *Secrets of the Soil.*

5. Eisler, *The Chalice and the Blade.* Stone, *When God Was a Woman.*

6. Lily Siou, personal communication with author, January 1988.

7. Joseph Needham, *Science and Civilization in China,* vol. 2 (Cambridge: Cambridge Univ. Press, 1969).

8. *New York Times Book Review* 92, 4 October 1987.

9. *Woman's Review of Books* 7, 9 (June 1990). This reviewer seems especially threatened by the material, announcing that Marija Gimbutas is "just plain wrong!"

10. Bailey, *Esoteric Healing.*

11. Grim, *The Shaman.*

12. Daly, *Gyn/Ecology.*

13. When I wrote this statement I had not read *The Gods of Eden: A New Look at Human History* by William Bramley. In a well-researched and carefully documented thesis, Bramley contends that the planet earth has indeed been colonized by UFOs, and that war, famine, plague, and other unfortunate characteristics of modern society, which I call patriarchy, are part of the intentional design of the colonizers, whom he calls "Custodians." Their "Custodial Religions" (referring to all the patriarchal religions) have oppressed humanity since at least the time of the ancient culture of Sumer, first through kingship and religious hierarchy and, in more recent history, through secret societies up to and including the Masons. See William Bramley, *The Gods of Eden* (San Jose, CA: Dahlin Family Press, 1989).

# Index

*Index*